RED-HOT AND RIGHTEOUS

The Urban Religion of
The Salvation Army

DIANE WINSTON

Harvard University Press
Cambridge, Massachusetts
London, England
1999

Library of Congress Cataloging-in-Publication Data
Winston, Diane H.
Red-hot and righteous: the urban religion of the Salvation Army/Diane Winston.
p. cm.
Includes bibliographical references and index.
ISBN 0-674-86706-8 (alk. paper)
1. Salvation Army—New York (State)—New York—History.
I. Title.
BX9718.N7w56 1999
287.9′6′097471—dc21
98-47842

For my parents,
Dan and Suzanne Winston
"Strong at the Finish"

CONTENTS

Abbreviations

AWC   *The American War Cry,* published by The Salvation Army's
        National Headquarters from 1881 to 1921. After 1921 it be-
        came *The War Cry,* Eastern Edition; all citations after 1921
        are from the Eastern Edition.

MOMA   Museum of Modern Art, New York

NYT   *New York Times*

SAA   Salvation Army Archives, Alexandria, Va.

RED-HOT AND RIGHTEOUS

INTRODUCTION

THERE WAS no mistaking the drum-thumping missionaries parading on-stage at the Broadway opening of *Guys and Dolls*. To the audience attending the 1950 premiere, the uniformed soul-savers were as much a part of city life as the gamblers and showgirls who provided the action in the musical adaptation of Damon Runyon's stories and sketches. In both book and play, the prim and proper band was dubbed the "Save-A-Soul Mission." But the opening night crowd, like Runyon's many readers, knew them as ringers for The Salvation Army.

For many years scholars believed that the modern American city—diverse, cosmopolitan, and commercial—was inhospitable to religion. But the history of The Salvation Army, an evangelical mission to the unchurched, belies that contention. Like Runyon's gangsters and their molls, the Army was both a symptom of and a catalyst for a new, evolving urban culture driven by commerce and fueled by consumption. Intimately familiar with life on the streets, Salvationists developed missionizing strategies that reflected and legitimated the increasingly commercialized culture of those streets—and, in the process, became a part of it.

Upon arriving in New York in 1880, The Salvation Army staked a claim to city life as no religious group had done before. Municipal laws discouraged outdoor preaching, and except for an occasional processional or ritual ceremony, Protestants, Catholics, and Jews rarely took to the streets. Not so The Salvation Army. A living metaphor bent on territorial conquest, its members regularly occupied city thoroughfares. Commanded by Holiness theology to transform the secular world into the Kingdom of God, Salvationists marched up the avenues and down the boulevards—even raiding brothels, saloons, and dance halls—in pursuit of lost souls. Their "Cathedral of the Open Air," a figurative canopy spread over the city, turned all of New York into sanctified ground.

Later, as the Army's mission expanded to include humanitarian aid, New Yorkers encountered its network of social services throughout the city's neighborhoods. Salvationists sent out ice carts in summer, coal wagons in winter, and salvage crews all year round. They established soup kitchens, rescue homes, employment bureaus, hospitals, shelters, and thrift shops. Along with the annual Macy's Thanksgiving Day Parade, the Army's annual kettle drive marked the onset of the Christmas holiday season, and each spring colorful posters heralded its fundraising appeal.

Salvationists could be heard around the city, too. In the early days their brass instruments, jingling tambourines, and resonant bass drums clamored over the din of horse-drawn carriages and noisy peddlers. Their testimonies, shouted from streetcorners, captured the curious, while their renditions of popular tunes—"Swanee River" or "Tramp, Tramp, Tramp" rewritten as hymns—roused critics to decry such blasphemous stratagems. Over the years the music acquired more sophistication and the testimonies toned down, but the open-air outreach continued. When *Guys and Dolls* opened, Salvationists still played lunch-hour concerts on Wall Street and pounded the bass drum along the Great White Way. In winter the tinkle of their bells was an unmistakable call to help the poor—just as their radio and television broadcasts reminded listeners of their need for donations.

When they drafted The Salvation Army to provide the essential element in their dramatization of Runyon's good girl/bad boy plot, the playwrights of *Guys and Dolls* could assume the Army was an integral part of the urban landscape, even though most Americans had no idea what it really was or what it did. Impressions sufficed: Salvationists were religious do-gooders—saintly, if a bit old-fashioned. The Save-A-Soul mission in the play reflected this widely held opinion: large-hearted and well-intentioned, its members were (mostly) ineffectual against the mobsters' machinations. Even if they saved a soul or two by the play's end, such quaint zealots seemed unprepared to compete, much less succeed, in the modern world.

This was the popular view of the Army circa 1950. But it was not an especially accurate one. The Salvation Army was doing quite well; it raised significant sums of money and was on its way to becoming a highly respected provider of social services. By the mid-1990s it proved to be the nation's top-grossing charity. In 1996 it raised one billion dollars, far outpacing the second-place American Red Cross. A ragtag band of street-corner evangelicals had become one of the nation's most successful charitable fundraisers with a strong symbolic claim not only on America's purse strings but also on its psyche.

The City of New York provides a comprehensive field for exploring that claim. During the apogee of the Army's public visibility, 1880 to 1950, New York was the nation's cultural and commercial hub. Chicago had a larger Army presence, but New York was home to the movement's national headquarters as well as being the country's symbolic center. Knit into the warp and woof of New York life were the hallmarks of the era—debates over philanthropy and gender relations, the development of leisure activities and mass marketing. Thus to trace the history of The Salvation Army in New York is to follow one religion's institutional trajectory in an increasingly pluralist society and its concurrent evolution into a modern, urban faith.

While other religious traditions survived, even thrived, in New York, they were not urban religions. In the city but not of the city, they served discrete memberships by offering a respite from the outside world. Sunday (or Saturday) was a spiritual time distinct from the rest of the week just as the sanctuary was a place apart, designated for private worship. Catholics might get out for the annual *festa,* Jews for *tashlich,* but only The Salvation Army pounded the pavements each day of the week. Even in smaller cities and towns, the Army existed only insofar as it had a public presence. Unlike other faiths, the Army did not have a natural constituency; during its formative years, no one was born a Salvationist. People converted or contributed because they saw the Army in action. That required the Army to go where people worked and lived—and to reach out in ways the public could understand.

Placing The Salvation Army in the context of urbanization and commercialization provides a new perspective on the interplay between religion and culture. Historians have looked at the Army as a religious movement seeking to provide social and spiritual relief to the casualties of industrial capitalism. Most have evaluated the Army as more or less successful depending on their interpretive stance—their view of the Army as an agent of social control, evangelical outreach, or metropolitan mission. But using commercial culture as an interpretative lens places the

Army in the thick of urban life, illuminating a religious movement actively engaged with the city's life, its streets, and its people.

The Army's desire to "secularize religion" or to "religionize secular things" meant hallowing space, activities, objects, and even relationships.[1] Most basically, Salvationists sought to saturate the secular with the sacred. To accomplish this they adapted two key facets of the commercial culture—performed entertainment and material objects—for spiritual purposes. Suffusing secular forms with religious content, Salvationists staged vaudeville shows and epic pageants that subverted the very culture that gave rise to these entertainments. Likewise, by investing ordinary objects with religious meaning, they attempted to transform consumption into consecration.

Army parades were a both aural and visual metaphor of the saturation campaign. Flamboyant incursions into hostile territory, the parades appropriated a secular style in the hope of literally bringing spectators to their knees. Marching through commercial and residential areas, rich and poor neighborhoods, Salvationists blurred boundaries that urban Baedekers had studiously drawn, proclaiming all space as God's own. Not content to transgress geographic borders, Salvationists defied symbolic boundaries, too. The spectacle of a religious parade with brass bands and uniformed women struck many New Yorkers as a violation of Christian norms.

The Army's use of clothes was significant. At a time when city dwellers were intrigued by masquerade as a means to re-create or reposition the self, Salvationists made strategic use of costumes and disguises. When working in neighborhoods filled with Catholics and Jews, they traded their uniforms for garb that hid their identity. While such tactics were intended to serve a higher goal—the saving of souls—they also reinforced the modern, secular notion of the self as a succession of roles. In fact, joining the Army entailed adopting a role: performing military discipline and dedication. Constructed as a complete way of being-in-the-world, the role regulated the clothes Salvationists wore, the language they spoke, and the organizational pattern that governed their lives. Indeed the performance of soldiery, the commitment to conquer, even made it possible for members to assume new personas for the sake of duty. Salvationists became minstrels or musicians, lassies or slum sisters because these identities furthered their spiritual warfare. In this way Salvationist pragmatism encouraged a protean, performative dimension of evangelical selfhood which was intriguingly at odds with the Army's stated goal of unifying external and internal appearances.

The Army viewed performance as a crucial tool for bringing individuals into a new relationship with God. Publicly testifying to one's conversion was one kind of performance and assuming the role of a Salvationist soldier was another. Acting out this military identity remained a constant performance even as Army outreach strategies—the use of popular entertainment to spread its religious message—changed over time. Between 1880 and 1950 the Army "performed" parades, lectures, vaudeville, slide shows, pageants, films, radio, and television for audiences it hoped to win over—initially as converts, later as contributors. Its message began to change, too. As the city resisted sacralization, often co-opting the Army's identity and purpose, Salvationists reoriented their focus. By 1917 sacralizing the everyday no longer had a primarily spatial dimension; rather, it referred to one's activities. Its meaning was most graphically embodied by the Sallies, Salvationist women who served American troops fighting in France during World War I.

The Sallies expressed their commitment to salvation by serving coffee and doughnuts, a secular communion of a nonsectarian character. The Army's war work, spanning divisions of religion and class, secured its place in the modern city by giving Americans new ways to interpret its activities. Praising the Army in a letter home, one soldier wrote, "The Salvation Army do not theorize or advertise themselves or try to bother a soldier or officer, but just get right down to brass tacks and serve."[2] Such service, devoid of proselytizing, made supporters of those who were not predisposed to an evangelical Christian message. By permitting this audience to separate Salvationists' actions from their intentions, the Army multiplied the possible readings of its activities and enabled the organization to serve as a canvas onto which men and women could project their own needs, hopes, and beliefs. What began as a movement to sanctify the culture became a manifestation of it—a product whose wide appeal could be measured in dollars and cents.

In this and other ways, commercial culture plays a significant part in The Salvation Army's American experience. The Army tailored itself to fit the times, an era when market relations were governed by competition, expansion, and profit. Initially the Army was "selling" salvation, but in order to survive—to pay officers, open corps, provide services—it had to "sell" itself, too. Devising performances for those with money to spend, Army leaders did not stress the subversive quality of a religious movement preparing for the imminent arrival of the Kingdom of God. Rather, they highlighted the ways in which the Army contributed to the well-being of a broken and blighted society.

In New York in the 1880s that society was undergoing rapid change. The small Salvationist party that arrived from England encountered a bustling commercial hub with a population larger, more diverse, and more cosmopolitan than anywhere else in the United States. New York was the site of great social and cultural change as technological advances propelled the city into the twentieth century. Trolleys and horse-drawn carriages still crowded the streets, but elevated trains suggested new possibilities for conquering distance through speed. Telephone and telegraph wires as well as electric lights were changing the look of the streets while also transforming communications and creating new opportunities for business. These new inventions intensified a phenomenon that pundits were fond of describing—the city's breathless pace.

New Yorkers were in a hurry, and many commentators believed their speed was spurred by the quest for money. Buying and selling were highly developed urban arts whether practiced among the dens of Wall Street, the pushcarts of the Lower East Side, or the sumptuous shopping emporiums of the Ladies' Mile. There was a keen sense, shared by many clergy, entrepreneurs, and political leaders, that money was given by God to be enjoyed by those blessed enough to have received it. But having it wasn't enough. By the 1880s New Yorkers eagerly embraced new ways to spend their dollars, and the entertainments, attractions, and commodities in which they indulged formed the basis of an expanding commercial culture.

This culture thrived on the bold use of spectacle and display. It enabled city dwellers to see and hear the excitement that money could buy and to contrast it with a dark, drab existence bereft of acquisitions and entertainments. The depiction of metropolitan life as closed sets of stark distinctions was familiar to nineteenth-century New Yorkers. Writers described Manhattan as a city of contradictions, employing a palette of "light and shadow," "darkness and daylight" to paint its extremes. A vast gulf separated poverty from wealth, virtue from wickedness, worthiness from indolence. To embody these themes, authors evoked familiar figures—robber barons and mission workers, streetwalkers and society matrons—as the dramatic personae in the novels, metropolitan guidebooks, and newspaper accounts that explained an increasingly complex city to itself and the outside world.

Despite the pervasive use of polarities, an accurate portrait of New York City's 1.2 million residents revealed much that was in between. A large working class, almost two-thirds of the population, created a kaleidoscope of religious and ethnic diversity. Workers ranged from young, single shop girls transplanted from rural America to middle-aged family men newly arrived from Europe. These men and women differed not only in their circumstances but also in the ways they defined themselves as "consumers" of city life. Some, eager to expand their children's horizons, saved money to move to better neighborhoods. Others succumbed to the more immediate lure of spending. Young singles, in particular, traded paychecks for the latest in fashion or entertainment. Still other workers survived at the edge of poverty, sweating long hours for small wages that barely enabled them to subsist in the Lower East Side's warren of dilapidated tenements.

At the same time, the city's middle class was growing, buoyed by expanded opportunities in retail, manufacturing, and the service professions. The impact of the middle class on city life was felt even beyond its increased economic power and political clout. As David Scobey has argued, the city became a register of both "national character" and "bourgeois cultural values" where "how the built environment was represented—as a marketplace, a scene of domestic life, a theater of public sociability—offers historians a displaced commentary on the career of middle-class values in the volatile, urbanizing world of Gilded Age America." William R. Taylor develops a related argument in his pursuit of Gotham, an "ideational village embedded in New York." For Taylor, Gotham signifies "the city as a cultural marketplace, as the site of the lively exchange between the city's commercial life and the media it developed."[3]

But the production of this commercial culture extended beyond both the geographic boundaries of Taylor's midtown "ideational village" and the "lively exchanges" between the city's commercial life and the media. In this new look at The Salvation Army I heed Scobey's call to augment Taylor's work by treating religion as a significant social force in the new cultural history occurring at "the crossroads of urbanism, commerce and culture."[4] The Salvation Army, whose postmillennial Holiness theology held that all aspects of everyday life could be sacralized, had the same kind of expansive, totalizing spirit as the commercial culture of advanced industrial capitalism. Both sought to imbue public discourse with a vision of individual transformation that had important consequences for urban, social, and moral space. While the Army offered an internal experience of salvation, the commercial culture promised fulfillment through external experiences of self.

Liberally adopting idioms from business and entertainment to communicate the Army's religious message, Salvationists served as pioneer religious modernizers, building on Dwight Moody's revivals and foreshadowing Aimee Semple McPherson's dramatic extravaganzas. Meanwhile their pragmatic focus on saving souls took Salvationists from streetcorner evangelizing to establishing slum ministries and, within a decade, to setting up a citywide network of social services. As eager as they were for converts, Army officers understood that the hungry, homeless, ill, and unemployed needed material relief before their spiritual pangs could be addressed.

The Army's early experiences in New York, preaching in the vernacular—the language and experience of everyday life—and providing social services, were fundamental to its later success. During World War I the Sallies, sent to "mother" American troops, never proselytized; they expressed their faith through action. Their stalwart service won over soldiers and war correspondents whose dispatches vividly described the women's tender ministrations. In the wake of media coverage of the war, the stock image of Salvationists—blue-suited Bible-thumpers who collected for the poor—was quickly revised. Comely lassies appeared on magazine covers, Broadway stages, and movie screens. Testimonies to the Army's social services—and its inclusive religious vision—flooded the media.

Salvationists offered a religious vision rooted in a vernacular faith and expressed in the coalescence of the Army's Holiness theology and the culture's regnant consumerist ideology. Salvationist doctrine instructed followers in an activist religion expressed in everyday life, positing a second baptism which empowered believers to serve God by saving souls and redeeming a fallen world. Redeeming the world, according to the Army's founder, William Booth, meant facing its challenges (poverty, unemployment, alcoholism, and prostitution) and turning its secular idioms (advertisements, music, and theater) into spiritual texts.

The pragmatism inherent in Army theology mirrored the bottom-line orientation of corporate capitalism. Activist and willing to do whatever worked, the sect's theology and the era's ideology had strong affinities. The Army was part of the discursive world of nineteenth-century evangelical Protestantism: family was central, the Bible was literal, and society was ordered and hierarchical. Yet even as Salvationists cleaved to these principles and asked others to do the same, they acted on a more pluralist and modern understanding. They were tolerant of others' faiths, inclusive in their delivery of services, and circumspect in sharing their witness. Aware of the need to distinguish private faith from public religion, the Army modeled a new form of Christianity which, as the century pro-

gressed, became increasingly distant from its militant evangelical roots—
and more at home in the modern world.

Examining the history of The Salvation Army reveals significant shifts
in the ways Americans understand themselves, their society, and their
ideas about faith. At the same time, the Army offers a fascinating study of
religious transformation. When Salvationists came to New York in 1880
they were free to make their own way in a country of which they knew
little and where they were little known. Moreover, they were relatively
independent of their English commanders and the particular limitations
imposed by proximity to the British class structure and the established
Church of England. Open to new possibilities, Salvationists devised novel
strategies to occupy the territory.

Seeing New York with fresh eyes, they pioneered a new way of doing
religion. Rather than depend on buildings, hierarchies, or congregations,
Salvationists built from the ground up. The city was their space and its
citizenry was their congregation. Supporters did not have to follow Army
doctrine, they simply had to affirm its practices. Donors contributed for
various reasons. Some threw money in the kettle because they wanted to
help the poor. Others hoped to propagate Christianity. Still others considered it a ritual of the season. For these and other reasons, The Salvation
Army became a charity of universal appeal. And its success in attracting
public support disproportionate to its actual membership marks its evolution as an urban religion, a faith transformed through its interaction with
the surrounding culture and able to speak across religious, economic, and
social lines.

I AM NOT a Salvationist and I began with no brief for or against the
movement. However, my research has given me a deep appreciation for
the selfless work Salvationists have done and continue to do. Their compassion and dedication are truly compelling. In telling their story, I mean
no disrespect by chronicling the changes that have shaped their movement. Rather, I hope to demonstrate how religion finds new meaning and
agency through its interaction with specific places and times.

1

THE CATHEDRAL OF
THE OPEN AIR

1880–1886

GRAY SKIES and winter winds greeted passengers disembarking at Castle Garden, the immigrant reception center at the southernmost tip of Manhattan, on March 10, 1880. Among those leaving the ocean liner *Australia,* which had sailed from London almost four weeks earlier, were seven somberly dressed young women and their blue-uniformed male leader. These eight, the official landing party of The Salvation Army, had expected a ten-day voyage to the New World. But when a disabled engine slowed the crossing the missionaries took advantage of the delay to proselytize. Undaunted by rolling seas or clouds of tobacco smoke, they led services punctuated by rollicking hymns and dramatic exhortations. But the passengers and the crew disdained their efforts. Whistles and jeers rebutted their pleas for repentance, and the ship's unofficial newspaper mocked their religious fervor.[1]

Commissioner George Scott Railton, the group's leader, and the seven Hallelujah lassies, as Salvationist women were called, were accustomed to ridicule. At home in England, the Army's novel methods, including loud parades, female preachers, and hymns set to popular tunes, were attacked not only in the press but also in the streets. Yet persecution only strengthened their resolve. Marching down the *Australia*'s gangplank followed by the seven women, Railton waved a colorful silk standard. "Blood and Fire," the blue-bordered, red Salvationist banner, had a bright yellow sun in the foreground and a small American flag in one corner. A blazing

A New York illustrator captured the Army's first dockside service in 1880. Note the details on Blood and Fire (local corps insignia and the American flag) and the distinctive style of the Salvationist uniforms. Corbis-Bettman

testament to the group's theology, the banner's colors—blue for purity, red for the blood of Jesus, yellow for the fire of the Holy Spirit—were emblems of the Holiness movement. Invoking Christopher Columbus's legendary arrival some four centuries earlier, Railton and the lassies knelt on the cold, damp ground, planted their flag, and claimed America for God.[2]

When a United States Customs official asked the identity of this odd

Later representations of the Army's arrival in America romanticized both the landing and the landing party. The lassies here look more attractive and feminine than those in drawings from the period, and their clothing and bonnets are more flattering. This depiction of the party alone is probably not accurate, since Castle Garden was a bustling spot. AWC, Mar. 10, 1904, 1, SAA

band, Railton responded by holding an impromptu service. He asked listeners whether they were bound for hell or heaven; preached on the text John 3:16, "For God so loved the world that he gave his only begotten Son," and joined the lassies in hymns set to the familiar tunes of "Swanee River" and "My Old Kentucky Home."[3] This unexpected display sparked the curiosity of reporters who frequented Castle Garden looking for colorful copy. Railton did not disappoint. At thirty-one, he was a small, wiry man with a thick beard, a balding pate, and a storehouse of restless energy. Making himself available for interviews, Railton told the press that his party represented an "army of men and women mostly belonging to the working class" who had been saved from "lives of immorality and ruffianism." They worshiped like the early Methodists, but instead of employing regular preachers they encouraged new converts "to speak from their own experience." Averring that this "was not a society of unruly religionists defying or rushing into conflict with order, law and society," Railton explained that it was "an army for missionary purposes."[4]

From its first steps on American soil to its subsequent parades, open-air services, and visits to dance halls, saloons, and brothels, The Salvation Army sought out the unchurched, "heathen" masses on their own ground—the city's streets and its commercial attractions. Hoping to compete with secular amusements, the Army used popular music, lively pageantry, and dramatic testimonies to express themes of love, service, and salvation. But the Army's underlying aim was more than just saving individual sinners. Fired by a postmillennial fervor that was itself a legacy of American revivalism, Salvationist leaders planned to spiritualize the world and, in the process, sacralize secular space. The crusade to hallow the city—its buildings, public squares, and streets—was part of the Army's attempt to establish the Kingdom of God. As an 1896 editorial in the *War Cry*, the Salvationist newspaper, explained:

> The genius of the Army has been from the first that it has secularized religion, or rather that it has religionized secular things . . . On the one hand it has brought religion out of the clouds into everyday life, and has taught the world that we may and ought to be as religious about our eatings and drinkings and dressing as we are about our prayings. On the other hand it has taught that there is no religion in a place or in an attitude. A house or a store or factory can be just as holy a place as a church; hence we have commonly preferred to engage a secular place for our meetings . . . our greatest triumphs have been witnessed in theatres, music halls, rinks, breweries, saloons, stores and similar places.[5]

In its early years in New York many of the Army's greatest triumphs occurred, as its landing illustrated, in the open air. Believing they could "purify the moral atmosphere," Salvationists occupied the streets: first they marched and then they preached, invoking what they called "the cathedral of the open air."[6] The open-airs were part of a campaign to

In the middle of the "cathedral of the open air," represented here in Greenwich Village's Abingdon Square, Salvationists form a circle for prayer and testimony. The typography on the masthead continues the outdoor theme with words spelled out in stars. AWC, Oct. 7, 1893, 1, SAA

spiritualize social, moral, and urban space in preparation for the King-dom of God. The image of the cathedral signified a sacred space large enough to encompass the entire city and also, by evoking the holy sites of medieval Christendom, signaled the belief that God was the hub of all life, the center of all meaning, and the base for human activity. Yet while Europe's sacred spaces were material archetypes of a theological model, Salvationists in the New World made do with a figurative version.

In the first half of the nineteenth century America's postmillennial per-fectionists likewise had attempted to spread a sacred canopy over the nation, but their zeal had waned. Triumphalist dreams had fallen on the blood-soaked fields of Gettysburg and Antietam, while new currents in biblical scholarship, natural science, and the social sciences challenged the centrality of religious truths. Resigned to a shrinking portion of the social and political discourse, some Gilded Era religious leaders contented themselves with ambitious building programs and stratagems for enlarg-ing their congregations while others sought new methods to reach the poor.

The commercial culture of advanced industrial capitalism swept into the breach with its own normative set of meanings, symbols, and signs. Although there is little scholarly consensus on when and where commer-cial culture first arose, there is growing agreement that a new commercial aesthetic, made possible by the rise of mass production, reshaped culture and society in the last quarter of the nineteenth century. William Leach has argued that department stores, for example, "democratiz[ed] desire" by facilitating the growth of "a secular business and market-oriented culture, with the exchange and circulation of money and goods at the foundation of its aesthetic life and of its moral sensibility." Animating this culture was a set of beliefs antithetical to republican political philosophy, traditional Christian values, and the economic axioms of an earlier pro-ducer-oriented era. The new beliefs hallowed acquisition as the key to happiness, the new as superior to the old, and money as the measure of all value. They predicated a society in which democracy did not mean equal opportunities for owning land or for wielding political power but rather for desiring and obtaining commodities and goods.[7]

This new culture seduced citizens with enticements of abundance. De-partment stores caught the eye with tantalizing displays of color and light. Commercial amusements whispered of possibilities for adventure, excitement, and romance. A profusion of advertisements in newspapers and magazines, on billboards and signs, promised that serenity and con-tentment were just a product away. Although Salvationists rarely mounted direct challenges to the new philosophy of consumerism, they disparaged the pastimes it spawned. They decried Coney Island, theater-going, baseball, and the racetrack as worldly amusements which turned attention away from God and salvation. Their publications featured stories of young women who happily exchanged their shallow round of shopping, teas, and balls for the fulfillment that accompanied donning the uniform. But rather than engage in heated polemics or unpleasant confrontation, the Army vied with the commercial culture by contesting public space, saturating it with religious meaning, and by draping the city in a sacred canopy, "an open-air cathedral." Whether parading in the streets, singing in saloons, or appearing on the city's stages, the Army used the venues and forms of the contemporary culture to promote an alternate, even subversive, message.

In 1885 Rev. Josiah Strong, an early proponent of the Social Gospel movement, expressed the concerns of his generation and the conclusions of many who followed when he wrote, "The city has become a serious threat to our civilization, because in it . . . each of the dangers we have discussed (Romanism, socialism, wealth, intemperance, immigration—except Mormonism) is enhanced, and all are focalized." The subsequent narrative of Protestantism's course in the city, whether told by secular or denominational historians, related the religious decline resulting from the very threats Strong enumerated. Yet in 1885 Strong may have overlooked the real danger the city posed to "civilization": the city as the initiating site for a consumer discourse that displaced the Protestant, republican, producer-oriented ethos. Strong admitted as much in his later writings, noting in 1911, "If, now, it is true of modern civilization that materialism is its supreme peril, preeminently true is it of American civilization; and if material growth finds its comparative in the New World, the modern city furnishes its superlative."[8]

The Salvation Army took seriously the threats posed by Catholicism, socialism, wealth, intemperance, and immigration at the same time as it challenged the animating spirit behind the new commercial culture. Through religious performances intended to suffuse the city with an alternative discourse—the primacy of the sacred and spiritual in everyday life—Salvationists made themselves at home in New York in ways that other religious groups, focused on more traditional activities, did not. For example, many Christians in the late nineteenth century observed their religion privately in churches and within their own homes. For them religion was a refuge from the world, not a way into it, and the realms of the sacred and the secular functioned separately. Others did participate in socially engaged expressions of faith. But their outreach efforts, conducted in missions and churches, presupposed that the needy would seek them out, in contrast to The Salvation Army's daily encounters on the city streets.

The Army's novel activities captured attention at a time when a growing number of religious and philanthropic initiatives competed for support. YMCAs, city missions, institutional churches, and settlement houses all tried to save the masses while also addressing poverty and displacement. But the Army's religious performances, social programs, and astute publicity were singularly successful at occupying city spaces and capturing popular imagination. One measure of its success was the number of converts won: Army statistics claimed 40,000 Salvationists by 1895.[9] Another measure was its place in contemporary culture. During its first decade in New York, the Army was covered extensively by local newspapers and magazines. Popular entertainers routinely satirized its peculiar performances.

The Army accepted public ribbing because its founder, William Booth, taught that all publicity was good publicity. The goal, he wrote, was "TO ATTRACT ATTENTION. If the people are in danger of the damnation of Hell, and asleep in the danger, awaken them." Steeped in this straightforward dictum, Salvationists used the tools of popular culture and advanced industrial capitalism to facilitate religious renewal. Railton had no sooner disembarked from the *Australia* than he began courting the media. In later years Army leaders shared his techniques in the *War Cry*. Corps leaders were instructed to keep the local city editor informed about corps activities (but never bore him) and not to take offense at anything in print. While respectable Christians were appalled by the Army's willingness to make a public spectacle of itself, Salvationists understood that that was exactly the point. As early as 1882 New York audiences delighted in a Harrigan and Hart theatrical which portrayed a mock Army banging cymbals, beating drums, and singing, "We'll give you a point and we'll give it a square, The guy in the middle's a millionaire." Ten years later Salvationists had the last laugh when their Continental Congress drew more spectators than the Harrigan and Hart performance ever had. By then the Army had evolved from "a mere episode of street life to be introduced in order to make a foil for the excellent fooling of a Tony Hart or a Billy Gray into a recognized factor in religious effort."[10]

Yet in its early years the Army's strength was its ability to be a part of street life; its success was predicated on attracting crowds who confused it with a circus, a variety show, or minstrelsy.[11] Pioneer posters promised an exhibition of "men who were as wild as LIONS as savage as TIGERS and as stubborn as old JUMBO" but had been "captured by Army troops and tamed." The Army adopted the stacked headlines, multiple typefaces, and bold exclamations associated with posters for popular entertainments. The "Converted Minstrel," one of the Army's most popular traveling evangelists, was a banjo player whose belt read "Eternity." The *War Cry* regularly ran contests asking readers to turn familiar tunes, such as "Marching through Georgia" and "Silver Threads among the Gold," into Salvationist hymns. Using the celebratory aspects of popular culture to enliven its message, the Army successfully competed with the commercial aesthetic by offering adherents a religious experience that was fun: "Sister A. Hartelius sees no reason why the devil's children should have the monopoly of dancing and singing on the way to hell, while we who are on the way to heaven are expected to be silent and still. Sister M. Hartelius once enjoyed going to entertainments, but now she has no occasion to go outside of herself for she has continual entertainment in her heart."[12]

A Red-Hot Religion

Railton and his party of seven were not the first Salvationists to lay siege to America, but they were the first landing party officially sanctioned by the Army's founder, William Booth. Booth's supporters had begun work in the United States when James Jermy, a cabinetmaker and early Booth protégé, emigrated from London in 1872. In August of that year Jermy opened an outpost of The Christian Mission, the name of Booth's evangelical outreach prior to 1878, in Cleveland, Ohio. Jermy, who eventually set up two missions, worked among the city's poor and African-American communities. But his mission faltered when he returned to England in 1875.[13]

Four years later the Shirley family brought The Salvation Army to Philadelphia. In 1879 Amos Shirley had left his home in Coventry to work as the foreman of a silk mill in Philadelphia. His teenage daughter Eliza was serving as a lieutenant under General William Booth when Amos sent for her and her mother. Loath to abandon her Army duties, Eliza asked Booth for permission to start the Army in the United States. Unprepared to lend her preliminary support, the General promised that if she launched a mission along Army lines and if it succeeded, he would consider taking it over.

With that equivocal offer in hand, Eliza enlisted her mother's aid to begin outreach work in Philadelphia. The two women rented a run-down chair factory, whitewashed the walls, and blanketed the floor with sawdust. After hanging kerosene lamps from the ceiling and building a platform, they posted signs announcing "two Hallelujah females" who sang and preached for Jesus. These initial efforts yielded little until one Saturday evening when the Shirleys began a street meeting near a tar-barrel fire. With blazing flames providing a dramatic backdrop, Eliza and her parents led several hundred spectators to an indoor service. Soon the family was saving souls and savoring headlines. When William Booth read the press clippings and received the Shirleys' own reports, he decided to send Railton, his closest aide, to oversee the Army's progress in America.[14]

In late 1879, when William Booth was preparing to "open fire" on the United States, he was the head of a rapidly expanding evangelical movement.[15] But that had not always been the case. For almost fifteen years Booth had struggled in near obscurity as the leader of a small mission in London's poverty-ridden East End. His work with the poor had its roots in Booth's own childhood. Born in 1829, he grew up in Nottingham, a city in northern England's "Wesleyan heartland," a revival-prone area similar to the "Burned-Over District" in upstate New York. Nottingham's economy was depressed, and Booth's working-class parents (his father, Samuel, was a builder) were unable to better their station. In fact, Samuel Booth's unsuccessful speculations reduced the family to the brink of poverty. In 1842 financial desperation drove him to apprentice his son to a pawnbroker. Working in the slums, the younger Booth became intrigued by the Chartists' program of political and social reform. But when his father died and his mother was forced to work in a small shop, William felt lost and frustrated. Searching for answers, he began attending classes at a Wesleyan chapel and was converted before his fifteenth birthday.

Catherine Mumford, the woman who would become Booth's wife and the "mother" of The Salvation Army, was also born in 1829.[16] She grew up in Derbyshire, some thirty-five miles west of Nottingham. Catherine's family, members of the artisan class, were slightly better off than William's. Her father was a Methodist lay minister and a carriage builder. Her mother, a deeply pious woman, grounded Catherine's education in the Bible. Despite his preaching and support for temperance, John Mumford began tippling during Catherine's teenage years and eventually became estranged from the family. The experience convinced Catherine of the evils of alcohol, the depth of human sinfulness, and the absolute need for God.

By the time a friend introduced Catherine and William in 1852, both were committed to the Methodist Reform movement, a revivalist branch of Wesleyanism. In the years since his conversion, William Booth had become a street preacher. He learned his vocation from American revivalists who taught "scientific" methods of soul-winning to English evangelicals between 1846 and 1866.[17] The Americans, whose religious roots were in British and Irish Methodism, now offered an aggressive alternative to the stultifying hierarchy of the homegrown varieties. Their teaching also included a component of social reform which held that converted Christians had a responsibility to work for the Millennium.

Three American revivalists, James Caughey, Charles Finney, and Phoebe Palmer, were especially influential on the Booths. William Booth first heard Caughey, an Irish immigrant to the United States, during an 1846 revival in Nottingham. Caughey combined astute public relations with a passionate pulpit style. "His strength lay in the telling anecdote and in blunt denunciation and frank exposure," Richard Carwardine has written. "Caughey spent most of his time trying to frighten his audience into the Kingdom of God." Many characteristics of Caughey's revivals— dramatic exhortations, personal witness, use of the penitent bench, and advance publicity—became hallmarks of the Booths' work, too.[18]

Charles G. Finney further convinced the Booths of the need to employ dramatic steps for soul-winning. Finney was best known as the popularizer of revivalism's "new measures," techniques that encouraged worshipers to seek salvation actively. A Presbyterian lawyer-turned-revivalist, Finney helped spread Arminianism, the belief that individuals can facilitate their own salvation. His book *Lectures on Revivals of Religion* (1837), which stressed the mechanics of conversion, served as a textbook for the Booths. When they started a training school for new recruits, they assigned the book as required reading.[19]

The third American whose work shaped the Booths' ministry was Phoebe Palmer, a New York lay evangelist. In his classic study of urban revivalism Timothy Smith places Palmer at the center of the Holiness revival that galvanized the mid-nineteenth-century religious reform movement.[20] Ironically, Booth's army returned Palmer's Holiness teaching to New York with a revitalized message of service and sanctification in the century's closing decades.

Palmer's understanding of sanctification provided the Booths with a vocabulary to describe the inner changes that accompanied conversion. Her teaching, a modified version of John Wesley's doctrine of holiness, called for a second baptism which signified an active commitment to God. This baptism, also called sanctification, could occur as a process or as an instantaneous experience. Once it occurred, a Christian was fully committed to God, and God replaced inner sin with spiritual love. That love empowered believers to help others experience the same transformation. It enabled Salvationists, even those who were uneducated or came from humble backgrounds, to testify publicly about their conversion and to embrace the selfless tasks that made up the lives of slum officers, corps leaders, and rescue workers.

For Catherine Booth, Phoebe Palmer was living witness to women's potential. Booth felt strongly about women's abilities even before Palmer visited England. She believed that if women were given the proper educational opportunities they could be the intellectual equals of men. Moreover, she saw no reason why women should not be allowed to speak from the pulpit. Before 1860 women preachers in England, while not unusual, were most often itinerant folk evangelists from sectarian movements. These women also tended to be from the lower classes. They were largely uneducated, and their preaching style resembled ranting. After 1859 the situation changed because American revivalists stirred middle-class English women to undertake public religious work. Palmer, an exemplar of this trend, believed that women should be allowed to address audiences in quiet, conversational tones from the nave rather than preaching from the pulpit. Nevertheless, several clergymen criticized her "unfeminine behavior" during a visit to England in 1859.[21]

One screed written by the Rev. Arthur Augustus Rees, an Independent minister who cited scriptural prohibitions against female preaching, so outraged Catherine Booth that she wrote a pamphlet defending Palmer. In "Female Teaching; or, the Rev. A. A. Rees versus Mrs. Palmer being A Reply," Booth argued that biblical passages cited to silence women actually were intended only to restrict disorderly speech and to prevent the undermining of male authority. She concluded that women had spiritual authority and were entitled to preach:

We think it a matter worthy of the consideration of the church, whether God really intended woman to bury her talents and her influence as she does now? And whether the circumscribed sphere of women's religious labours may not have something to do with the comparative non-success of the gospel in these latter days. We fear that it has, and the Lord of the vineyard will require some more satisfactory excuses for our timidity and backwardness in his service than the one-sided interpretation of detached portions of Holy Writ and the ipse dixit of such men as the Rev. A. A. Rees.[22]

Several scholars have suggested that Palmer represented a link between Holiness theology and female ministry which influenced Catherine Booth and, by extension, shaped The Salvation Army. Pamela Walker and Olive Anderson have argued that Holiness teaching was especially appealing to women because it validated the emotional aspects of religion and justified female preaching by emphasizing the unfettered prompting of the Holy Spirit. George Scott Railton, too, was a strong proponent of women's right to preach. According to Bernard Watson, Railton, even more than Catherine Booth, encouraged William Booth to place women in leadership positions over men. Railton told the Army Mother when he returned from the United States, "Those English may stick to their men as hard as they like, but I am certain it is the women who are going to burst up the world, especially the American women."[23]

The beliefs and praxis of The Salvation Army drew on several religious traditions, including Methodism, Wesleyan revivalism, the Society of Friends, and the Holiness movement. From Methodism came a belief in structure culminating in William Booth's adoption of a military hierarchy which, ironically, the Army's Protestant critics disparagingly compared to the governance of the Roman Catholic Church. From the Wesleyan and the Holiness movements the Booths took the doctrine of sanctification and its corollary, the tenet that the second blessing set the believer apart from worldly pursuits. Accordingly, Salvationists advocated a simple style of life, abstaining from alcohol, tobacco, fancy clothes, personal adornment, rich foods, and worldly entertainments. Quakers—some of whom joined while others expressed sympathy for the Army—were also influential. They, too, advocated simple living and concurred with William Booth's support for lay ministry. Booth's decision of 1883 to forgo the sacraments as external manifestations of an inner reality paralleled Quaker belief, as did the Salvationists' use of the metaphor "inner light" to describe their spiritual experiences.[24]

From American revivalists Booth adopted the postmillennial hope for an imminent Kingdom of God, which was initially expressed in his desire to perfect or sacralize society and later inspired his ambitious social schemes.[25] Many of Booth's ideas on Holiness, such as the connection between sanctification and empowerment for service, were influenced by his early exposure to American revivalism. Booth's beliefs were further nurtured by Hannah and Robert Pearsall Smith, two American leaders of the popular British-based Keswick Movement. But the British bias against American evangelists caused Booth and other Army leaders to downplay their influence in Salvationist circles.[26]

Although nineteenth-century critics frequently charged that the Army lacked a coherent theology, Salvationists had a reasoned theological foundation which grew out of the Booths' own religious odyssey through British and American reform and revivalist movements. Many of the basic tenets of The Christian Mission's 1865 statement of faith were taken from the creedal formulations of the Evangelical Alliance and the Methodist New Connexion.[27] Over the next thirteen years the Booths refashioned that creed until they settled on eleven doctrines which, reflecting the Army's adherence to specifically Wesleyan and Holiness precepts, was truly distinctive from its earlier formulations.

These eleven doctrines, set forth in 1878, stake out a conservative, evangelical position at a time when many Protestants were questioning their faith in light of new findings in science and biblical scholarship. The Booths knew about but had little use for proponents of Darwinism or higher criticism; doubt was not part of their vocabulary. William Booth wrote in 1879, "We are a salvation people—this is our specialty—getting saved and keeping saved and then getting somebody else saved." The Army's eleven doctrines reflect this "old-time religion" approach, affirming in the face of growing cultural skepticism the divine inspiration of scripture, the dual nature of Jesus, and the reality of hell.[28]

Booth's belief in a real and fiery hell drove him to save souls. But he also realized that a gloomy, theoretical religion would save no one. The unchurched needed a "happy" religion whose spark and sizzle were more akin to commercial entertainment than a staid Sunday service. Thus the Army prized "red-hot" preachers over erudite theologians and taught that its "practical religion" should make a difference in everyday life. New converts were quickly put to work saving others, and Booth's Christian Mission started "Food for the Millions," a chain of London soup kitchens serving inexpensive meals. In order to leaven the fear of hellfire with the celebratory nature of salvation, the General sprinkled his sermons with humorous anecdotes and encouraged his officers to do the same. At a 1903 appearance in New York City, Booth told an Academy of Music audience, "People come to the quarters of the army and see our brothers and sisters dancing: they are shocked. 'Is this religion?' they ask. Certainly, why should the devil have all the dancing?"[29]

Those in the Army's ranks adopted monikers such as "Happy Eliza," "Smiling Lydia," and "Laughing Kate." Their joy was infectious, as Sallie Turnage discovered when the Army came to Kingston, North Carolina. In a letter to the *War Cry*, Turnage said she and everyone else in town had been prejudiced against the uniformed revivalists. But their parading piqued her curiosity and she attended a service: "At first it reminded me of a minstrel or comic show; but it was not long after seeing them sing and pray and talk before I was completely captivated. I never saw such a happy set of people before and I soon became convinced that they were a very different set of Christians."[30]

William Booth understood that to capture the unchurched, no less than practicing Christians, the Army first had to attract their attention. During the Army's first decade in the United States the *War Cry* printed numerous stories of converted sinners testifying that Salvationist meetings were better than Barnum's circus or the variety shows. Respectable citizens who liked their religion staid and circumscribed found the Army's "sensationalism" to be a dangerous, if not heretical, lack of propriety. "The invader danced, pranced, sang, tooted and drummed their way up Broadway, attracting more attention than a circus parade and about an equal amount of religious feeling," observed one writer. "To one accustomed to the decorum and reverence of Christian worship in the older sects, nothing could be a more shocking travesty of things sacred than an old time Salvation army meeting." Such Christians deplored William Booth's credo "ATTRACT ATTENTION" and the disorder that followed in its wake.[31]

In England Booth's attention-getting tactics had provoked the ire of Skeleton Armies—gangs of working-class men whose persecution of Salvationists fell within the tradition of "rough music." Located mostly in rural towns and villages, the Skeletons were supported by brewers and publicans who resented the Army's anti-liquor stance. Skeletons taunted and beat up Salvationists while local constables looked the other way. In the United States, where the tradition of rough music was less familiar, The Salvation Army itself took on aspects of a charivari with its loud music and comic antics (putting the devil on trial or preaching in front of a casket). Some spectators may have intuited the subversive quality of the Army's performances: both roughs and local officials often physically assaulted Salvationists for disturbing the peace, while ministers, editorialists, and pundits stoned the group with words.

Attracting the Kingdom of the Devil

From its first steps on American soil, the Army's mix of luck, intuition, and street-smart savvy enabled it to march into the thick of New York's cultural life. Disembarking at Castle Garden, Railton and the lassies surprised onlookers by singing hymns set to popular melodies. They continued to cause consternation when they tacked up posters, resembling P. T. Barnum's advertisements, for their appearance at Harry Hill's concert saloon. Railton's choice of a saloon for the Army's first service guaranteed the kind of press attention that would not have accompanied an appearance at a church or a storefront mission. Unlike the many downtown dives whose dark interiors granted their clientele anonymity, the well-lit Harry Hill's was a tourist trap, a spot where cabbies deposited out-of-town customers who wanted a taste of New York's notorious nightlife.

A series of smoky, beer-sodden rooms, Harry Hill's provided patrons with free entertainment. At one end of the saloon was a stage which featured musicians, boxing matches, puppet shows, and short plays. It was there, on a cold, damp Sunday night, that the Army held its first official American service. Railton led the proceedings, which alternated between hymn-singing and exhortations. Kneeling in prayer with the Hallelujah lassies, Railton surprised spectators with his swaying torso, flailing arms, and frequent cries of "Amen" and "Hallelujah!"

The saloon was packed with spectators. Because of a spelling error, the Army's posters had announced the group would "attract the Kingdom of the Devil at Harry Hill's Variety Theatre." Though they had meant to "attack" rather than "attract," the Salvationists accomplished neither. Members of the audience were cool to their performance. Some were annoyed that Railton forbade liquor sales during the service. Others were put off when he asked them not to smoke. After more than two hours and no penitents, the Army left the stage and was replaced, to general relief, by a panorama of Uncle Tom's Cabin.[32]

At a prayer breakfast the next morning, Railton's more orthodox sponsors voiced displeasure with the group's choice of venue. But one supporter, impressed by their spunk, offered them his own hall. This site, the Hudson River Mission Hall at Ninth Avenue and 29th Street, became the Army's regular meeting place for the next few weeks. But as their movements that first Monday revealed, the English crusaders did not confine their missionizing to one spot. After the early-morning prayer meeting on Fulton Street, Railton and his band headed north to the Baxter Street Mission, a converted brothel in the city's Five Points slums where Phoebe

The April 13, 1880, edition of *Harper's Weekly* showed Salvationists working the crowd at an urban mission. The congregation is racially diverse, the setting dilapidated. SAA

Palmer had proselytized thirty years before. The walls in the meeting room were cracked and peeling; Bible verses hung askew. Most striking, however, was the diversity of the congregation. Seated along the straight-backed wooden benches were many African Americans. While it was not unheard-of to find black worshipers at slum mission meetings, the Army made their participation a priority. Railton explicitly intended to work with American blacks: "We have the honor today to be the only white people to whose company, to whose platforms, to whose operations, colored people have had the same welcome as others . . . If they will not join themselves with other races, we will go farther still, and there will be found officers ready to leave off association with their own race in order to rescue those of another."[33]

Railton's commitment may have been manifest in the welcome given to all worshipers. But the New York press corps reflected the more conventional attitude that conflated race with social status. A reporter from the *New York Herald*, describing the Baxter Street meeting, grouped African Americans with "whores" and "bums": "A more motley, vice-smitten, pestilence-breeding, congregation could seldom be found in a house of worship. There were Negroes, dancing girls, prostitutes, and station house tramps sandwiched between well-dressed visitors who had sauntered in out of curiosity . . . The floors were as clean as a deck of a man-of-war, but in a few minutes they were frescoed with tobacco juice, the stench became overpowering, and a yellow-fever pest-house could not have been less attractive."[34]

From Baxter Street the group went west for a noonday prayer meeting of businessmen on a lower Manhattan streetcorner. Then, uptown at the day's end, the Salvationists held an outdoor service on the steps of the Hudson River Hall at 29th Street. Their enthusiastic praying and singing attracted the notice of residents and drew many inside. At the indoor service, "crowded to overflowing," some listeners seemed to have come out of curiosity, but many others displayed a "sincere interest" in the Army's message.[35]

Earlier that day Railton had applied to Mayor Edward Cooper for a permit allowing The Salvation Army to preach outdoors and hold religious services in the streets. Stringent city laws had restricted street preaching since an 1810 incident when two evangelists, Johny Edwards and Dorothy Ripley, held an outdoor revival that ended in mob violence. Rather than control spectators, city authorities decided to ban open-air services, passing a law that prohibited "disorderly assemblies of persons in the City of New York." When Ripley sought to test the stricture, she was dragged off to jail. Aware that their concern for order came close to abrogating constitutionally guaranteed religious freedom, municipal leaders mediated their stance and allowed licensed clergymen to preach publicly after receiving legal permission. This compromise safeguarded religious tolerance while allowing officials to rebuff zealots they deemed incendiary.[36]

Salvationists were just the kind of zealots whom city leaders wished to rebuff. Their reputation preceded them; according to British newspapers, when they were not tussling with ruffians they were scuffling with the law. Yet the Army's determined pursuit of free speech and assembly proved a significant accomplishment in its adopted homeland. According to John Wertheimer: "The group that used courtroom appeals to challenge open-air ordinances most persistently during these years [1880–1900] was a controversial organization whose radical response to the social problems of the Gilded Age aroused suspicion and even hatred: the Salvation Army." Since New York authorities feared street riots, they told Railton that each member of the group would have to apply for a permit each time they planned to hold an outdoor meeting. Also asked if he was an ordained clergyman, the prerequisite for obtaining a license, Railton admitted he was not. The Mayor explained that under the existing law Railton could not receive a permit but that he was welcome to petition the Common Council to modify the ordinance.[37]

The next day Railton announced that if the law was not changed The Salvation Army would move its National Headquarters to Philadelphia. The ultimatum was an empty threat. City officials did not care whether or where Railton took his army, but his brazen tactics kept Salvationists in the news. In the meantime the band of eight continued its rounds of missionizing. Among its stops was Siloam Mission, a "dingy, but neatly furnished apartment" on the corner of Water and Dover Streets in Lower East Side slums. Leading an "overflowing" afternoon meeting with "merchants and clerks" from the nearby business district and "well-dressed ladies and young girls from up-town churches and missions," Railton focused on a few "hardened sinners." Subsequent articles spoofed the meeting. Railton was described in greasy terms. His smile was "oleaginous" and his comments "interlard[ed]" the proceedings. The women's Cockney accents were ridiculed in quotations which demonstrated an unfamiliarity with both aspirates and the Queen's English. Nevertheless, the audience's enthusiasm was evident from its frequent applause and zealous prayers for repentance. The meeting ended after more than two hours when Jerry McAuley, a local mission worker, began singing a familiar hymn.[38]

McAuley's name was known to newspaper and magazine readers of the day. The city's journalists regularly recounted the story of his conversion from a drunken, thieving river-rat to a respectable man of God. In 1872 McAuley and his wife opened a mission on Water Street, where they welcomed sailors and criminals alongside neighborhood residents. The McAuleys ran their meetings on the same lines as did the Army. There were hymns, exhortations, Bible readings, and personal testimonies which speakers were encouraged to keep brief. As McAuley advised, "When you start to tell, don't you forget an' run over your minute. Cut out the middle an' give us both ends."[39]

McAuley's presence at the Army meeting was not surprising. Since his own mission was nearby, he was likely to know that the Salvationists were holding services on Water Street. But the mention of his presence in newspaper accounts is noteworthy because it was one of the few documented references of Army interaction with other mission workers. Salvationists rarely mentioned social or religious efforts other than their own. Ignoring the competition, they touted their own efforts as the only outreach to the masses. Yet New York had a long history of religious missions that integrated spiritual aid with material relief, and many more sprang up during the Army's early decades in the city. What is striking about The Salvation Army in this era is not the uniqueness of its endeavors but the barrage of publicity that accompanied them.

Newspapers wrote about religion when stories offered a new or idiosyncratic take on the subject. Accordingly, the Army's antics made for headlines. But other groups received coverage, too, when they engaged in unusual activities. In the fall of 1880 the *New York Tribune* ran a story on John Kennion, an Episcopal priest who offered "hot coffee and plain preaching" to the city's poor. One warm Sunday afternoon Kennion was found addressing a large crowd downtown by the East River. Kennion encouraged listeners to "be somebody" while sailors ambled by, children begged for handouts, and small boys fought over marbles. When his sermon ended, he passed out hot coffee and fresh bread. "'I tell you this is the kind of a religion that a man can take stock in,' said a man who had his cup of coffee and a bit of bread. 'There is nothing of the priest in this who charges us for a seat in church and pokes us back in a dark corner where our rags won't make the rich people hold their noses and keep us as far away from us as they can. There is no collection take up here and we ain't told that we'll go to hell if we don't pay to be kept out.'"[40]

Such sentiments were shared by members of the lower classes who had seen a slew of Protestant churches follow their well-heeled members from lower Manhattan to the Upper East Side. Moreover, many churches charged pew rents and discouraged the poor from attending their services. But the coffee-drinker's speech did not sit well with the *Tribune*'s editors. Several days later an editorial excoriated him for contributing to an atmosphere "in which religion is made out hypocrisy, property is counted as a crime, and in the end it widens the chasm between the classes." Since the money to pay for Kennion's good works came from the rich, the editorial writer reasoned, the correct response to such benevolence was not insolence but gratitude.[41]

The *Tribune* article and subsequent editorial exemplified the tensions surrounding public discussions on religion and poverty in the 1880s. Just beneath the surface of religiously inspired charity, the flow of class-based anger, suspicion, and resentment ran in both directions. New Yorkers had reached this impasse a century after the first religious efforts to address the needs of poor in their city. In the late 1780s and 1790s Quakers and Presbyterians fulfilled their religious obligations by providing aid to widows, children, and imprisoned debtors. A generation later a very different kind of outreach began. Reform-oriented evangelicals, suffused with the heady promise of postmillennial perfectionism—the notion that Christians could and should prepare the world for God's Kingdom—set out to save both individuals and society. Groups like the New York City Tract Society (1827), the New York Female Moral Reform Society (1834), and the New York Protestant Episcopal Mission Society (1831) tried to meet the challenge by recruiting laypeople to bring the gospel message to lost souls. Evangelicals visited the poor, opened Sunday schools, distributed tracts, and lectured on temperance until the depression of 1837, when declining funds and rising need overwhelmed their capacities.

When evangelically minded churchgoers regrouped in the 1840s and 1850s, the world around them had changed dramatically. More poor people had flocked to the city, and an increasing number were foreign immigrants and working women. Earlier benevolent endeavors appeared naive, succeeding neither in converting sinners nor in redeeming the world. These failures spurred a growing impatience with the poor. Some Christians suspected that the indigent had only themselves and their alleged propensity for indolence and intemperance to blame. Rather than starting Sunday schools or passing out tracts, a new approach to social welfare favored systematic interventions. Groups like the New York Association for Improving the Poor (1843), the Five Points House of Industry (1854), and the Children's Aid Society (1853) provided opportunities for the poor to learn skills, receive an education, and move away from the slums.

By the time the Panic of 1873 shut down the New York Stock Exchange and plunged the city's economy into chaos, antagonism toward the poor was widespread. Crime, labor agitation, and homelessness undercut social stability. Charity organizations wondered if they were helping the poor or creating paupers, a class of people content to live on a dole. Responding to a growing backlash against indiscriminate relief, a number of church-related and private charity groups reorganized themselves with the idea of coordinating their efforts, investigating their clients, and ending the poor's dependency on handouts. The Bureau of Charity (1873) was among the largest of these new endeavors and the Charity Organization Society (1882) among the best known. Their goal was to make New York City less attractive to the needy by cutting back on outdoor relief and general giving.

Nevertheless, some missions and social-minded ministers still provided unadulterated charity. From 1865 to 1880 Stephen Tyng, the rector of Holy Trinity Episcopal Church, set up aid organizations and encouraged parishioners to help however they could. The Howard Mission for Little Wanderers (1861) created model tenement houses and a hospital for sick children. Jerry McAuley's Water Street Mission (1872) offered temporary relief, and the New York Colored Mission (1865) provided a school, a nursery, an employment bureau, temporary housing, and inexpensive meals. Lutheran, Methodist, Jewish, and Roman Catholic groups looked after newcomers of their own faith, offering a range of services from employment bureaus to shelters to hospitals. A newly reconstituted New York Protestant Episcopal Mission (1865) ran seven institutions, including a rescue home, a shelter, and an asylum for infants. John Kennion, supported by several wealthy businessmen, held meetings throughout the city, offering hot coffee and plain preaching as a "practical demonstration of the glorious gospel."[42]

In New York in 1880 there were a number of people like Kennion and McAuley who believed that the church had to reach the poor where and as they were. In the coming years others would join them. Charles Nelson Crittenden would begin the Florence All-night Mission, a home for abandoned women. W. S. Rainsford would galvanize a fusty Episcopal parish with his vision of "an institutional church." A. B. Simpson would organize the Gospel Tabernacle to salve the body and save the soul. And among the foremost of these efforts was The Salvation Army. Marching through the streets, its soldiers sought converts, ministered to casualties, and spread the message of the Second Coming.

Our Century on Wheels

When Mayor Cooper refused Railton's petition, the Army moved its National Headquarters to Philadelphia. Railton soon headed west, setting up Army outposts as far off as St. Louis before being recalled to England in 1882. His successor, Major Thomas E. Moore, kept new corps in touch with one another and with the parent body in England through the columns of a weekly newspaper, the *War Cry*. Far from the attractive publication it would become, the newspaper's earliest incarnation was a roughly edited, crudely designed four-page broadsheet. The weekly report from the New York 1 Corps depicted a struggling outpost. (Corps were the Army equivalent of churches. The name of a corps signaled the city where it was located and the number of corps already existing there.)

After the initial wave of secular press coverage, the Army had become just another mission to the poor and no more newsworthy than any other. Housed at "Fort Salvation," a building on the corner of Christopher and Bedford Streets in Greenwich Village, the group was headed by Capt. Emma Westbrook and her second-in-command, "Smiling Charlie." Railton's flair and public relations savvy were sorely missed. While an outdoor service on the city's downtown piers might draw several hundred listeners, some Sunday night meetings attracted only a handful. Worse, some of the regulars could not be trusted to resist the devil's bidding.[43]

During one afternoon service a "holiness sister," who had attended Army meetings for over a year, began preaching on the necessity of asking God for French kid shoes. Attempting to intervene, Westbrook was shouted down. She finally quieted the woman, but the effort reduced Westbrook to tears. Stepping in, Smiling Charlie began a prayer meeting, but a gentleman jumped on the platform and began soliciting donations. He, too, was asked to desist. As Smiling Charlie later reported in the *War Cry:* "We had every kind of sympathy, but Capt. W. went up stairs, for a good cry, I guess, but shook it off and helped about in getting supper, and after we had got done giving the 'doubtful convert' (very doubtful) and some others their supper, he walked off with my overcoat! Hallelujah!"[44]

That spring Major Moore moved the Army's Headquarters from Philadelphia to an empty theater in Brooklyn and launched the New York 2 Corps with an open-air meeting on the steps of Brooklyn's City Hall. The third-largest metropolitan area in the nation and home to well-known ministers such as Henry Ward Beecher of Plymouth Church and T. DeWitt Talmadge of Tabernacle Church, Brooklyn was known as the "City of Churches." The Army thrived in its new location, reporting that within several months it won 1,200 converts and began four new corps. By the autumn Moore brought the *War Cry* to Brooklyn, too.[45] The newspaper was branching out from its focus on the corps to commenting on the Army's place in society at large. Even in these early articles, Salvationist writers stressed the Army's interest in bringing religion to bear on all aspects of society and in responding to the tenor of the times:

Of course the world says it is shocking this familiarity with sacred things this pushing in religion everywhere. Oh yes! It is shocking. It is time people were shocked before the last great shock comes.

Our century is on wheels. People are running to and fro, and knowledge is increased. But, alas! which ever way the multitudes run, they are always trying to get away from God.[46]

Moore soon announced the Army's successful nationwide advance. The number of corps had grown from 5 to 28, officers from 11 to 64, and *War Cry* subscriptions from 3,000 to 20,000. An auxiliary group for Army "friends" willing to publicly defend and financially support the work was thriving. For $5 annually, members received a special badge, a subscription to the *War Cry,* and a free pass to all Salvation Army events. The Army had also recaptured public interest. Its odd ways compelled attention, challenging the tacit symbiosis between civility and Christianity. Religious and secular journals published extensive pieces examining the controversial new movement. A running debate questioned whether the Army's ends justified its means. After much equivocation, most religious writers said it did. Still, persistent criticism of the Army's sensationalism, absolutism, and irreverence testified to contemporary discomfort with Salvationist strategies.[47]

The discomfort arose from the Salvationists' seeming disregard for gentility, the hallmark of respectable Protestant Christianity. Describing mid-nineteenth-century American society, Karen Halttunen has charted the growing differentiation between courtesy and Christianity, observing that "social formalism" became necessary in the modern world to "ease the social intercourse of the urban middle classes."[48] The Army's flamboyant behavior not only disrupted that social intercourse but also challenged the place of genteel Protestant Christianity as the foundation of middle-class norms. Critics asked whether Salvationists were correct to concentrate on Christianizing rather than civilizing the masses. While the Army supported middle-class values, including work, family, and sobriety, its behavior undercut bourgeois notions of gender and propriety. Yet in cities like New York and London, where the masses embodied fears of disease, crime, and indolence, the Army's initiatives could not be entirely discounted by citizens whose own churches chose to distance themselves from the poor.

Underlying the criticism of the Army's "sensationalism" was its similarity to (secular) commodity culture. When one commentator decried the Army's reliance on "the modern passion for being gazed at and talked about," the unspoken comparison was between the Army and the object of modern advertising. The Protestant establishment was still uncomfortable with the new techniques of consumer capitalism and its apotheosis of artifice. Secular publications, too, were discomfited by a religious group that so easily embraced the tools of the marketplace. *The Nation* noted disdainfully that William Booth's attention-getting techniques "would do credit to an accomplished advertising agent."[49]

Even sympathetic observers wondered why Salvationists indulged in such unnecessary excess. The author Agnes Maule Machar applauded the Army's use of the very qualities that led young men astray, such as their "fondness for social pleasure." But she deplored services that resembled a "variety show." Worst of all were the unhealthy passions aroused during Salvationist meetings. Machar, like several of her contemporaries, worried that the Army had a negative effect on young women. According to newspaper reports, many young females were seduced by Army officers. Others were compromised by allegations that they lived in mixed-sex barracks and had hysterical fits during services. As Machar noted, "It is seriously open to question whether the nightly excitement and publicity of crowded meetings is at all a wholesome atmosphere for young girls, especially those on the platform."[50]

But many young people saw the Army as a movement to enlighten the world's dark corners. Drawn primarily from small towns and Protestant backgrounds, new recruits were thrilled by the opportunity for excitement, autonomy, and service. Women, in particular, were attracted by the independence that the Army offered. Obedience to a top-down hierarchy was balanced by the freedom to travel, live independently, and serve as spiritual leaders. If families were alienated or citizens offended, most recruits deemed it an understandable price to pay. Not that all Army leaders wanted to shock the bourgeoisie. From the movement's earliest days, efforts were made to win their support. While William Booth organized rollicking open-airs in London's destitute East End, his wife, Catherine, sought backing from the West End's wealthy citizens by explaining the Army's significance to their lives. Addressing a group of Christian businessmen in 1883, she asked, "What if these neglected multitudes should rise up and assert themselves, what will become of your houses and land then?" Seen in this light, the Army's seemingly subversive actions acted as a safety valve, releasing just enough steam to keep the victims of industrial capitalism complaisant.[51]

By 1884 the Army's American advances were impeded by a transatlantic dispute between General Booth and Major Moore. The rift, which culminated in Moore's secession from the Army and his establishment of a rival force, began when he proposed incorporating the Army under the laws of the State of New York. Moore believed there were legal reasons for incorporation, but Booth argued that it would limit the authority of International Headquarters. When Moore pressed forward, the General relieved him of his commission. But the Major had the support of his officers and subsequently registered all Army insignia under New York laws. Although Moore's insubordination was, on the surface, the result of the disagreement over incorporation, issues of national loyalty also came into play. American Salvationists felt slighted by Booth's decision not to attend their fourth anniversary celebration. The American Army had grown to 500 officers, 100 corps, and 5,000 converts, and the majority of new recruits knew little and cared less about the movement's British origins.[52]

The Cathedral of the Open Air

When Major Frank Smith took over General Booth's American army in 1884, Moore controlled 80 percent of its forces and all of the Army's real and intellectual property. Yet Smith never doubted the righteousness and, thus, the ultimate success of his cause. A man of angles and extremes, Smith sported a pince-nez, a Van Dyke beard, and a firm conviction that he was always in the right. He had worked in the art furnishing trade before joining the Army in 1879 and was commander of the London corps when William Booth asked him to go to the United States. A strong leader and a loyal follower, Smith was deeply engaged with the political and social issues of his day. On the voyage from London to New York he read Henry George's bestseller, *Progress and Poverty* (1879), in which George argued that the benefits of industrial capitalism had not reached the lower classes. George rooted his analysis in religious principles and called on Christians to be mindful of the justice and morality attendant on economic decisions. Smith was impressed. After settling in New York he sought out George and became a disciple. George, for his part, saw beyond contemporary ridicule of the Army, calling its soldiers "the warriors of heaven." Smith, mixing George's social philosophy with Booth's Salvationism, advocated an activist, "cheerful" religion which "laughs at policemen" and "sets everybody free." A committed Socialist, Smith helped shape the social proposals explicated in William Booth's *In Darkest England and the Way Out*.[53]

Smith set up the Army's National Headquarters in a small office in lower Manhattan. Within three weeks he was publishing his own *War Cry*, and he soon assembled a force rivaling Moore's Brooklyn-based secessionists. But other problems arose. In *The Salvation War in America for 1885*, Smith described attacks against the Army in some two dozen cities, noting that "it has become a common thing to have young women not only arrested and imprisoned but brutally ill-treated by mobs of

Major Frank Smith in his own version of Salvation Army headgear. SAA

rough young men on the streets, almost under the eyes of the policemen." While young roughs clubbed lassies for "drum-banging" in public, elites attacked the same behavior in print. Unlike earlier journal articles that exonerated Army excesses in the name of evangelicalism, daily newspapers increasingly castigated the movement's shortcomings without citing its strengths. When a *New York Times* editorial of 1885 asked whether the Army was "an ally of virtue or vice," the answer was obvious. Its officers stood accused of offenses ranging from embezzling funds to seducing young women to ridiculing institutional religion: "The Salvation Army appears to be organized for the purpose of applying the methods of the variety show to Christianity. It undertakes to minister to the same craving for vulgar modes of excitement . . . the Salvation Army holds that a man need not be civilized in order to be Christianized."[54]

The offense that most roiled the mob and riled the elite was the Army's sensationalism. Here were Christians who flouted traditional pieties to gain attention, and, as their movement spread, critics again questioned whether such antics were a legitimate means to an end. Christianizing the masses was not as important to the *Times* editorialists as it had been to the *Lutheran Quarterly* or the *Andover Review.* Secular elites were more concerned with civilizing, that is controlling, the masses. The flamboyant improprieties of the Salvationists subverted civil order and mocked genteel decorum, the bulwarks of Victorian society. Secular editorialists disparagingly noted that an early edition of William Booth's *Doctrines of Discipline,* a handbook for Army officers, offered detailed suggestions for attracting public notice. Booth told soldiers to make colorful posters with striking copy and arresting graphics. Moreover, the posters were to be displayed prominently—carried on umbrellas, perched on hats, worn like sandwich boards, or carried on a "monster box" which was "pushed by a man" or "drawn by a donkey." "Invent for yourselves," Booth counseled, and his followers did—to the consternation of New York's staid citizenry.[55]

In New York, Army inventions most often took the form of noisy open-air services and parades. Each corps was expected to hold several open-airs per week. Officers and soldiers paraded through neighborhoods playing loud music on brass instruments. When a crowd gathered, Salvationists would sing, pray, and offer their own testimony before asking sinners to kneel at the bass drum and seek repentance. Salvationists then invited converts to their meeting hall—a local storefront or an auditorium in an Army garrison, lodging, or slum post—for a full service. Frank Smith emphasized the importance of open-air services as a means "to get religion back on the streets" away from "the corrupting influence of the commercial classes"[56] But the open-airs served a social function as well, providing public rituals at a time when privatized notions of faith predominated. Religious groups rarely took to the sidewalks. Catholics held processionals on special feast days, and Jews went outdoors for specific ritual celebrations such as *tashlich* (during the New Year) and *Sukkot.* But for the most part, Christians and Jews in late-nineteenth-century New York observed their religion at a distance from the public gaze.

The open-airs also served as corporate expressions of Salvationist faith. Early Salvationist services were enthusiastic gatherings which resembled the frenzied fervor of a revival service or a camp meeting. Secular newspapers reported "whooping" and "shouting" while the *War Cry* referred to the "Pentecostal waves" and "showers of fire" that accompanied a Salvationist Holiness meeting.[57] Just as indoor services provided opportunities for individual conversion and communion with the Holy Spirit, the open-airs were a collective religious affirmation. As such, they were symbolic activities inscribing the Army's physical presence on the body politic.

In order to take part in the nascent debate on morality, poverty, and the role of religion in civic life, Salvationists had to occupy the "battlefield," specifically, the city streets and the public press. Their most effective weapon was the extended military metaphor by which the small evangelical group originally known as The Christian Mission had already transformed itself into a Salvation Army. The meanings embedded in Army dress, language, and ethos communicated a compelling message to pundits and spectators alike. On the one hand, the Army represented obedience, discipline, and uniformity. William Booth had modeled his troops on the fighting forces of the British empire, and the gravity of the crusade was underscored by the pious dedication of his marching squadrons.[58] On the other hand, the Army was subversive, sensational, and dangerous. It ignored propriety and defied convention. Its women preached on street-corners and its brass bands played popular ditties. Its converts testified publicly about private matters and its accoutrements—circus-type posters, theatrical handbills, a newspaper that looked like the penny press—all seemed to mock Christian respectability.

The contrasting images compelled public attention. New York elites criticized the "Jesuitical" discipline of Booth's adherents and lambasted their "vulgarizing religion," but they could not ignore it.[59] The Army's flamboyant displays and aggressive evangelism quickly were becoming part of the public culture. New Yorkers saw the Army down at Burling Slip pier and up by the midtown Manhattan Academy of Music. In addition to open-air services, the Army could marshal hundreds on special occasions. These large-scale parades occurred when the Army held a "War Congress," its annual interstate gathering, and when religious luminaries, such as William Booth, came to town.

Parades were a familiar sight on city streets in the nineteenth century. Before the Civil War, marches were held to mark civic accomplishments, celebrate holidays, and honor local militia units, trade associations, reform groups, and political parties. In the latter part of the century, parades continued to commemorate civic, military, and work-related achievements. Outdoor gatherings were popular entertainment for the masses. New York's first Labor Day parade in September 1882 attracted

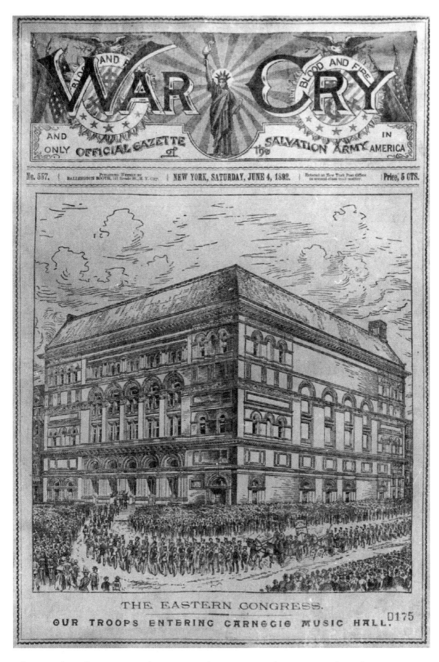

THE EASTERN CONGRESS.
OUR TROOPS ENTERING CARNEGIE MUSIC HALL.

The novelty of Army parades attracted curious, and sometimes hostile, spectators. This *War Cry* cover may have exaggerated the size of the crowd. AWC, June 4, 1892, 1, SAA

several thousand workers, including a squad of flag-waving Socialists, in a march from City Hall to Fifth Avenue. Large crowds also paraded for the 1885 funeral of Ulysses S. Grant, the 1889 centennial of George Washington's inauguration, and the quadricentennial of Columbus's voyage in 1892.[60]

Although parades were commonplace, they were usually not mounted by churches. Even the Easter parade, occasioned by a religious holiday, celebrated consumer culture rather than spiritual values. Parading in the new season's finery was a socially acceptable expression of Christian behavior; marching with Salvationist banners, bands, and uniforms was not. In the commercial culture of advanced industrial capitalism, the contest for public space favored spectacles whose message coincided with market values. Thus the Army's parades, celebrating the sacrality of everyday life and the Kingdom of God, were potentially disruptive; they advocated an alternate meaning system whose message may not have always been explicit but whose challenge was writ clear in the visual text of the parade: Salvationist marches simulated military processions. Mounted leaders, flying banners, and disciplined battalions filled city streets with the sights and sounds of a conquering army. Not surprisingly, spectators stopped to watch this uncharacteristically aggressive display of the Christian faith.

During the 1885 War Congress Major Frank Smith led a parade, during a "blinding snowstorm," from the Army barracks on 18th Street and Eighth Avenue to the Academy of Music on 14th Street near Sixth Avenue. Trailing behind him were six mounted aides, one hundred tambourine-"thumping" young women, a brass band, a "War Chariot," and thirty men dressed like "volunteer firemen." Sightseers thronged the parade route, and many marched along to the final destination. But the uneasiness that many spectators felt toward the Army was reflected in newspaper coverage, which, describing Smith at the Congress, reported: "Tall, wiry, nervous with a face like a stage Mephistopheles, he moved about waving his long arms and looking as if he was uttering an incantation."[61]

The reporter's discomfort with a perceived lack of control during the meeting was implicit in his description of events. The Army's "wild" religious display seemed to have little in common with Christian behavior. Smith's followers displayed a "certain morbid ecstasy like that seen on the faces of those laboring under great excitement or on the countenances of the insane." Prayers came forth in "wild, incoherent words," and there was a "wild swaying of bodies, waving of arms, and beating of tambourines." The use of the jungle metaphor culminated in a comparison of Salvationists to African fetishists—an ironic turnabout since the Army deemed "heathen" the unchurched masses whom it hoped to save and since Booth, in *In Darkest England and the Way Out,* would compare London's poor to "African savages." Yet, according to the *Tribune* reporter, it was the Army's followers, caught up in a typical Holiness service, who seemed wild and pagan: "Sometimes, while the speaking or praying was going on, the women would keep up a monotonous and gentle thumping and jingling of their tambourines. It was not like a negro meeting (though there was something about it that reminded one of such gatherings), but more like the fetish worship which those same negroes, in their native African forests, would have performed before some hideous idol, amid the beating of tom-toms and the groans of human sacrifices."[62]

Frank Smith, like Railton, was aware of such commonly held, derisive attitudes toward Africans and African Americans and was eager to bring them into the fold. After a "colored station" in Baltimore failed to attract many converts, he announced "The Great Colored Campaign" to "save the colored people, and to make that a living, practical reality, which the grand deeds of twenty years ago have so far only succeeded in making a written right." Smith's goal was to fulfill the promise of the Civil War through the Army's agency, beginning by integrating Salvationist events and institutions. While planning a sweep through the southern states, he opened a New York barracks for "preliminary practice." That outpost, on West 24th Street, was at the edge of an African-American neighborhood, and officers conscientiously reached out to local residents.[63]

Smith's particular concern for African Americans was rooted in his aversion to slavery, a form of economic exploitation and physical servitude that violated Christianity's teaching not to punish people for circumstances, such as skin color, outside their control. Condemning "the lifeless, formal, wealthy" Christianity of the sixteenth century for reviving the practice of slavery, he criticized nineteenth-century Christians for continuing it. To head the Army's racial outreach, Smith selected Capt. W. R. Braithwaite, a dark-skinned native of British Guyana who had studied medicine, had attended Harvard College, and was an ordained Wesleyan minister. Braithwaite traveled through the Northeast and the Midwest raising funds for the Southern Expedition until sudden, "unexplained charges" led to his dismissal.[64]

Still, the Southern Expedition pushed on as other black officers opened corps in Fredericksburg, Virginia, and planned an invasion of Washington, D.C., and Alexandria and Richmond, Virginia. But the Army was unable to attract a wide following among African Americans. The problem may have been that while individuals were always welcome, institutional practices reflected racial prejudices common to the era, including segregated facilities (Smith's desires notwithstanding). Articles in the *War Cry* played off the social constructions of black and white: saved blacks were washed white and "colored" comrades who glorified God were "blacken[ing] the devil." Similarly, the newspaper printed poetry and prose in "darkie dialect" which depicted African Americans as childlike and naive.[65]

Yet even as the Army accepted and perpetuated racist stereotypes, its leaders kept reaching out to blacks. A contingent of African-American soldiers represented the American army at international meetings in England, Salvationists took an early and courageous stand against lynching, and leaders periodically tried to galvanize work among southern blacks.[66] After one such initiative was announced, Booker T. Washington praised the Army for disregarding the color line and said he hoped its work would succeed among unchurched blacks. Even General William Booth fought for African-American souls. Preaching at an all-black church in Alabama, he brought twenty-two people to the penitents' bench.[67]

As Smith's Southern Expedition demonstrated, the Army was on the march. In 1886 the Salvationist leader met with President Grover Cleveland at the White House and welcomed William Booth to the United States. It was Booth's first trip to the United States and his letters home were enthusiastic. "We must have this," he wrote to his son Bramwell, adding, "I am delighted with the country and the work and the people." Minor irritations dotted the three-month tour. Dwight Moody refused to let the Army use his Chicago auditorium, and his supporters acted "grieved" when Salvationists set up shop nearby. Likewise, when Booth arrived in most cities, he was greeted coolly by the local clergy. But a round of red-hot preaching tended to melt ministerial reserve.[68]

Booth ended the tour in New York, where his forthrightness charmed his listeners. His popularity put the Army on firmer footing and heralded a change in England's attitude toward its New World comrades. Suffering from ill-health, Major Smith requested a return home, and Booth's new appreciation for America made it easy to accept Smith's pleas for reassignment. In his stead, Booth would send his son and daughter-in-law, Maud and Ballington Booth, to lead the forces.

⟿ MAUD and Ballington Booth took over the American Army just as it was beginning to make its mark on New York's public and discursive space. By 1887, the year they assumed command, the Army not only had survived neglect, schism, and persecution but also had gained new legitimacy in the wake of General Booth's successful tour. As the public soon became aware, the Army increasingly addressed themes that were critical to the society at large. What role should Protestant churches play in civic life? What could be done to help the poor? How might men be lured back to the fold? Where did women fit into public service and ministry? What role should religion play in a rapidly changing consumer society?

The Salvation Army was not alone in its attempts to reconcile religion with culture; a postmillennialist outlook still shaded religious thinking, infusing the culture with a positive notion of progress. Indeed, the modernist impulse in liberal religion of this era, according to William Hutchison, sought to dissolve the distinction between the categories of "religious" and "secular."[69] Many evangelicals seeking to redeem the world would have agreed that social regeneration was as important as individual salvation. But Salvationists were different from other religious folk because they consistently used popular media and opportunities provided by the marketplace to challenge the discourse embedded in commercial culture.

As R. Laurence Moore documented in *Selling God: American Religion in the Marketplace of Culture,* Christians have long borrowed business techniques and forms of popular entertainment to communicate the message of salvation.[70] But the Army went further than others and succeeded in grander terms. Interpreting Holiness theology as a way of being in the world, Salvationists made the entire city their mission field. Later, as the Army's outreach expanded to include humanitarian aid, New Yorkers encountered its network of social services in divers neighborhoods. As Army leaders saw that their lower-class constituency could not support such efforts, they realized the need to communicate more than just a message of personal salvation. Rather they needed to promote a vision of social salvation in the broadest terms possible. Salvationists ultimately succeeded because they did just that and, in so doing, defined something to "sell" that New Yorkers of all persuasions wanted to buy. The story of how they achieved this is the story of the city's changing demographics, the growing public recognition of religious pluralism, and changing notions about the role of religion in modern society.

2

THE NEW WOMAN

1886–1896

A STANDING-ROOM-ONLY crowd packed the auditorium at The Salvation Army's National Headquarters. Listeners filled every seat in the orchestra and balconies as latecomers lined the walls and aisles to hear Maud Booth's address on "The New Woman." By 1895 New Yorkers were quite familiar with the New Woman. Her demands for education, economic independence, suffrage, and sexual freedom had been debated in the popular press for almost a decade. On both sides of the Atlantic, supporters praised her bid for autonomy while critics denounced her rejection of marriage, family, and religion—the bulwarks of Victorian society. That The Salvation Army would have something to say on the subject no doubt struck many New Yorkers as odd, since some considered Army women compromised by their public ministry and their "sensational" methods. Thus, drawn by the currency of the issue and the dubious reputation of the organization, men and women who ordinarily would never attend an Army meeting were seated in the 14th Street auditorium on a late summer Sunday evening.[1]

Maud Booth, who shared command of the American army with her husband, Ballington, was familiar to the general public. The daughter of a genteel English family, she had charmed New York's business, civic, and social leaders with her beauty, refinement, and properly plummy tones. She also appealed to young women seeking meaningful vocations yet unwilling or unable to identify with the New Woman.

On this particular evening, Booth had assigned herself a difficult task. In her appearance before the curious crowd she needed to project several different images. As Christian slum worker and Salvationist commander, dignified matron and assertive woman, critic of the media's New Woman and advocate for the Army's "born-again" woman, Booth's performance manifested the Army's vision of a sacralized society in which polarities were transcended. Further embodying the New Testament faith that in Christ there is no Jew or Gentile, male or female, Maud Booth's ministry inverted social conventions by instructing single male officers on house-keeping and transforming Hallelujah lassies into women warriors.

Among Booth's preferred modes of presenting her message was the Chautauqua-style lecture popular in this period. Chautauqua, a retreat in upstate New York, provided Protestant laity with a comfortable compromise between religion and commercial entertainment. For The Salvation Army, seeking to widen its outreach to the middle and upper classes, the Chautauqua format had undeniable appeal, offering an opportunity to speak in a cultural vernacular that mitigated the sensational use of the streets. For Booth, in particular, the use of a familiar medium helped palliate her transgressive message. When the audience, assembled for a religious critique of the New Woman, gazed up at Commander Booth, they saw seated alongside her an all-female platform of officers, band members, cadets, and soldiers.

"This is a woman's meeting," Booth told her listeners. "The women are going to do everything here tonight." She then described a model of womanhood that, while implicitly affirming many of the New Woman's aims, explicitly condemned what the media caricatured as the "mannish" female. Calling her ideal the "advanced woman," Booth enthusiastically supported women's right to education, athletic exercise, and work. But, most important, this new creature must be a "womanly woman" rooted in the love of home, family, and religion.

In her diatribe against the New Woman, Booth suggested turning her "huge sleeves" into dresses for the poor and tossing her cigarettes, gum, and "realistic" literature into a bonfire. Equally dismissive of the New Woman's attitude to men, she reasoned that the best cure for those who spoke of "tread[ing men] underfoot" would be to turn them over to "a strong-willed, self-assertive husband." In conclusion, Booth explained that the truly new woman must be "born-again" since "if any woman be born in Jesus Christ, she is a new creature." Such women, blessed with "a new heart" as well as "new power" would have a "new influence upon the world."[2]

The Ballington Booths' tenure, from 1887 to 1896, marked the Army's initial acceptance by mainstream American society. During this period Salvationists became involved in the issues of the day, especially poverty relief and the changing role of women. Evolving from a strictly evangelical movement to an organization increasingly involved with social welfare work, the Army reached out to slum dwellers, the homeless, and "fallen women." While expanding Salvationist outreach to the poor, the Booths also built up an auxiliary organization for men and women who supported the Army's work but did not wish to be members. As the Booths spread the Army's message and bolstered its financial support, they employed various strategies, from parlor meetings to Chautauqua lectures, to improve the upper classes' perception of the movement.

Woven into the Army's efforts to extend its mission was its role in the debate about women's place in society. One gauge of public opinion on the Army was the secular media's depiction of Salvationist women. In the early 1880s typical descriptions cast the lassies as coarse, uneducated, and morally lax. With the arrival of Maud Booth and the emergence of other upper-class female officers, a new model of Salvationist womanhood began taking shape. Booth played a singular part in constructing and defining that model for both the Army and the society at large. Whether called the advanced woman, the truly new woman, or the woman warrior, this person combined Victorian womanliness with a sense of mission that empowered her to act boldly in the public sphere.

⤳ IN ITS FIRST six years in the United States, The Salvation Army survived one schism, two headquarters, three leaders, and dozens of attacks—from mobs, press, and pulpit. Notwithstanding such setbacks, the Army endured, even flourished, under the leadership of Major Frank Smith. When the Ballington Booths arrived in New York in April 1887, the movement had 654 officers working in 312 cities and towns (totals that would be, respectively, trebled and doubled during the Booths' nine-year tenure). The new commanders brought unity, stability, and prosperity to the fledgling movement. They healed the rift with the remaining Moore secessionists and helped spread the Salvationist message from downtown hovels to the parlors of Fifth Avenue.[3]

The city that Maud and Ballington encountered in the late 1880s was in flux, its social and economic problems more pressing than in previous years. Former certainties, whether economic axioms, social conventions, or religious sureties, were giving way to new realities. Among these were the millions of new immigrants whose foreign ways had a significant impact on the city's social, cultural, political, and economic life. Between 1860 and 1890, 10 million immigrants docked in the New World, and another 15 million would arrive by the eve of World War I. Of those who stayed in Manhattan, many moved into tenement houses—dank buildings in whose dark apartments families slept cheek by jowl. In 1890 almost a million New Yorkers, two-thirds of the city's population, were crowded into some 37,000 tenements. These were the fortunate ones. Almost 14,000 men and women went homeless every night while thousands more sought assistance just to feed their families.

The swelling ranks of new immigrants, most of whom worked long hours for low pay, fed a second reality: the problematic relationship between labor and capital. Socialists and anarchists, the Knights of Labor and the American Federation of Labor cried out for fair wages, safe working conditions, and an eight-hour day. When their pleas went unanswered, organizers turned to tougher tactics, including walkouts and strikes. Across the nation, management responded harshly, seeking to break unions with armed actions, lockouts, and scab labor. Hostilities intensified in the years between the 1877 railroad strike and the 1894 Pullman strike. A culmination of sorts came in 1886 when strikers, police, and anarchists tangled in Chicago's Haymarket Square. Seven died and several dozen were wounded before the violence ended. In the aftermath of this disturbing incident, the United Labor Party candidate Henry George came close to winning the 1886 New York mayoral election. He was narrowly defeated by the Democratic reform candidate Abram Hewitt. Subsequently, the New York state legislature voted to establish a board for mediation and arbitration, a ten-hour working day, and a safety and sanitary code for tenement houses.

Yet another new reality of the period was the expanding opportunities for women. Poor and working-class women, pressed to earn a living, took jobs as domestics, in the needle trades, and in sweatshops. In 1880 some 40 percent of New York's working women were in domestic service, but within the decade new positions opened up in offices, department stores, and large factories. At the same time, upper-class women worked outside the home in volunteer efforts which extended the scope of their "moral housekeeping." But both of these groups, at either end of the economic spectrum, had navigated the public sphere for some time. The women most affected by new opportunities were members of the middle class who were now drawn to a widening range of educational, recreational, and fraternal activities. An increasing number of young women went off to college, while their mothers and older sisters enjoyed browsing in department stores, eating lunch in elegant hotels, and attending ladies' matinees. Leavening this life of leisure were a growing number of women's clubs, where well-to-do matrons met to socialize and plan benevolent activities. Women's expanding sphere did not go unnoticed. The New Woman personified the growing public discussion of women's roles, serving as a popular foil for the cultural anxiety provoked by newly available alternatives to traditional female behavior.

New immigrants, new market realities, and new roles for women were among the many factors undermining the Victorian world view that had previously shaped social relations. Traditional notions of decorum, family life, and religious behavior were challenged by immigrants from different cultures and non-Protestant backgrounds. Long-standing beliefs about women's separate (and domestic) sphere were buffeted by the increased presence of women in public as customers in stores, pedestrians in the streets, patrons at the theater, and employees in a range of occupations. Similarly, the tension between labor and management affected mores. Old social contracts no longer held; the poor and working classes argued that their plight was caused by managerial rapacity, not moral depravity. Likewise, they argued that wealth was not endowed by God and poverty was not a sin. As increasing labor agitation forced the workers' plight into public view, a burgeoning consumer economy brought the classes into closer proximity. Shop girls jostled society matrons at Wanamaker's department store, where both went to inspect the new seasonal styles. But the proliferation of goods and commercial attractions did even more than bring men and women from different social classes into contact with one another; it also called into question conventional notions about pleasure, rewards, and character. Should pleasure be denied or indulged? Were rewards to be postponed until the hereafter or seized in the here and now? Did individuals constitute their identity by producing goods or by consuming them?

Living in a city where the magnitude of these changes altered the very fabric of everyday life, New Yorkers experienced cultural shifts, tantamount to a social revolution, between 1880 and 1900. The contour of the shifts is discernible across the distance of time, but in the moment they gave rise to a desperation born of wildly contradictory impulses, leading one contemporary historian, James Grant Wilson, to describe the era as one of "fear and unrest": "Just as at certain seasons meteors in unusual abundance enter our atmosphere and blaze across the horizon so have new ideas entered—new ideas to be tried or old ideas to be readjusted, by experiment, by discussion, by friction, by strike. The air holds them in combustion."[4]

The Salvation Army benefited from the era's social and cultural upheavals by taking advantage of the opportunities provided by the expanding consumer market and by rapid industrial change. Part of the explanation for growing public acceptance of the movement was the decline of Victorian values and the success of the commercial culture. These factors helped abate criticism of the Army and its lack of decorum. Now its brass bands and blazing banners were deemed entertaining. Its use of advertising appeared shrewd. The Army's style, as well as actions, reflected the times. It aimed to project the same gusto and gaiety as the commercial amusements with which it vied for souls. Like its secular competitors, the Army tried to attract working- and lower-middle-class men and women to an egalitarian setting that emphasized the fundamental facets of consumption—entertainment, emotional stimulation, and personal satisfaction. In the Army's early years this practice had disturbed the churched population for whom religion was a sedate and rational affair. Now such practices appeared prescient.

Critics of Army techniques—which paralleled the consumer culture's eye-catching advertisements, promises of fulfillment, and use of testimonials—were all but silenced by the mid-1890s. Such strategies had pervaded a society whose citizens wanted, even expected, commercial products to enhance their self-esteem and social worth. Even members of the clergy served the Golden Calf. Henry Ward Beecher attested to the virtues of Pear's Soap, while Maud Booth touted Vapo-Cresolene, a fumigating disinfectant. Such flirtations undermined at least one branch of American Protestantism, according to Susan Curtis, who argues that Social Gospelers were absorbed by the consumer culture they had hoped to save.[5] The Salvation Army fared better at survival, in part because of the higher boundaries set by its conservative theology and its institutionalization but also because of its greater visibility and impact on the city streets.

The Marshall and the Little Mother

He was the tall, handsome son of the self-proclaimed Salvationist General. She was the refined daughter of a proper Anglican rector. Her father forbade them to marry, and his father performed the ceremony. Months before Ballington and Maud Booth arrived in New York to take command of The Salvation Army's American forces, the local press had trum-

Maud and Ballington Booth. SAA

peted the story of their romance, informing readers all about the gang of religious zealots who had estranged a wayward child from her devoted father. Indeed, Maud Charlesworth's escapades with The Salvation Army, and the consequences for other parents of young daughters, were duly noted by New York's opinionmakers: "The real moral of this story is that parents who do not wish their children to become officers in the Salvation Army had better forbid attending meetings in the first instance. The part the Army assigns to women has extraordinary attraction in these times. They can in every way be the rivals of men, they can take an absolute equal part in the establishment and building up of the new organization.

By the side of such experiences as this career opens to them, the ordinary routine of home must appear intolerably dull."[6]

Maud Booth's story exemplifies the attraction the Army held for middle- and upper-class women. Raised in London in the last quarter of the nineteenth century, the young Miss Charlesworth was surely aware of popular currents in religion, philanthropy, and gender, which ranged from debates about the New Woman to social work initiatives by pioneer reformers such as Octavia Hill. While the Charlesworths had succeeded in teaching their children the importance of religion, Maud deemed their Anglicanism too remote and, worse, lacking in opportunities for female service. Likewise, her family preached the importance of the biblical mandate to help the poor, but offered few options for fulfilling it other than through friendly visitations. Secular organizations, such as the Charity Organization Society, were equally problematic as they lacked an explicitly religious dimension. Thus The Salvation Army's appeal was twofold: it provided a way to channel spiritual commitments into meaningful work, and it treated women as autonomous human beings who could lead and command. The very act of joining represented a form of the rebellion popular among youthful idealists of all eras. By becoming a Salvationist, a young person like Maud Charlesworth could live out her parents' values—even as the vibrant and exuberant expression of those values shocked the older generation.

The third daughter of Maria and Samuel Charlesworth, Maud would become the self-styled "Little Mother" of the Army's American troops. Samuel Charlesworth, a successful barrister, decided in midlife to become an Anglican clergyman. Even after his ordination the Charlesworths lived well, but a religiously based sense of *noblesse oblige* was also part of the family's values. When Maud was five years old her father traded parishes with a rector who worked in the London slums. Just across the street from Charlesworth's new church, William Booth's Christian Mission opened its own station. Its meeting hall, a dilapidated theater, was a place where the unchurched, attracted by loud outdoor services, might be enticed for prayer. Samuel Charlesworth respected the Mission's work, even offering its members his courtyard when they were forbidden to preach in the streets. But he was not content to let William Booth's followers do everything. The Charlesworths also reached out to the poor: visiting families, holding classes, and opening their own mission for destitute women.[7]

In 1881 Maria Charlesworth took Maud to a Salvationist "Holiness service," an Army gathering for Christians seeking to deepen their faith.

When Bramwell Booth was unable to lead the meeting, his younger brother Ballington stepped in. At six feet, four inches, Ballington was an imposing figure with a slim, erect carriage, dark features, and a mischievous smile. By the end of the service Maud was convinced that her former religious practice had been lifeless; now she would truly devote herself to God. Over her mother's objections Maud began attending Salvation Army meetings. Her interest only deepened when Maria died suddenly. Seeking respite from their grief, Samuel Charlesworth took his daughters abroad in 1882. Arriving in Paris, Maud found Catherine (Kate) Booth (William's daughter) leading the Army's nascent French forces.[8] When Maud begged her father for permission to work with Kate, Charlesworth grudgingly assented. But he forbade her to join the Army or to wear its uniform until she was eighteen. Neither could she preach publicly, sell the *War Cry,* or distribute tracts in cafés. She was allowed only to visit the poor.

Disobeying her father's strictures, Maud participated in all Army activities. But when mob attacks on the Army became dangerous, she and Kate Booth decamped to Switzerland, where they organized a local Army. Assaulted by ruffians and refused permits by the police, the young women persevered. After one service Maud was arrested and escorted out of town. When a private letter to William Booth describing her travails appeared in the *London Times,* Maud's adventures became international news. The British were outraged by Swiss treatment of British citizens, the Swiss were upset by the negative press, and readers around the world were amused by the Army's antics. The publicity humiliated Maud and scandalized her father. He demanded she come home immediately.

But Maud soon returned to the Army. When Ballington Booth proposed to her, she accepted but acceded to her father's request that they postpone marriage until her twenty-first birthday. In the meantime Maud moved into the Booth household and worked with Ballington's sister Emma at the Women's Training Home. Only a teenager herself, Maud instructed future officers in an intensive course of general education, religious instruction, and practical guidance on organizing and leading Army corps. In the spring of 1884 Maud and Emma helped pioneer the Army's social outreach work. Seeking an even lower class of people than were attracted by street meetings, the women dressed in plain clothes and rented lodgings in Hackneywick, one of the city's poorest neighborhoods. Living simply and helping neighbors with their daily needs, they presented a living example of Christian service, which Maud later likened to "the same principle as our workers [who] go to the Foreign Mission field to become natives to the native."[9]

Not long after the Salvationist work began, Rev. Samuel Barnett and a group of Anglican college men started Toynbee Hall, a social settlement house in Whitechapel. Toynbee Hall also brought religiously inspired Christians to live among the poor, but its intentions and activities were quite different from the Army's slum posts. The Toynbee residents were male university students seeking to create a civic and educational institution for the poor, whereas the slum sisters provided practical services and religious witness. The sisters' work was called the "Cellar, Gutter, and Garret Brigade" or, alternately, the "Dive, Tenement, and Gutter Brigade."

While Maud Charlesworth lived with the Booths and worked with the slum sisters, Ballington, known as "the Marshall," was sent abroad.[10] William and Catherine's second son had been baptized by the revivalist James Caughey. A whimsical, fun-loving child, Ballington grew into a talented preacher and gifted musician who played violin, concertina, banjo, steel guitar, piano, organ, and harp. At twenty-three he headed the Men's Training Home, and four years later William Booth commissioned him to consolidate the Army's work in Australia. In 1886 Ballington was called home for the Army's first International Congress. During his furlough he and Maud were wed at an Army hall before a crowd of five thousand. Both wore dark blue uniforms; Maud's only adornments were a white sash and a sprig of white roses and myrtle. Afterward, several hundred guests made a modest donation to attend their wedding breakfast.

The following year Maud and Ballington Booth replaced Frank Smith as head of the American forces. Soon after landing in New York the young couple visited Army outposts across America, invited secessionists back to the fold, and supervised the creation of several Army corps targeting specific nationalities. Work among Scandinavian peoples, begun with a Brooklyn corps in December 1887, was thriving. Similar outreach efforts were organized in New York's German, Italian, and Chinese communities as well as with ethnic Christians on the West Coast.

One indication of Maud and Ballington Booth's successful leadership was the warm reception extended to William Booth on his second American tour. Speaking before packed crowds, the General was introduced by Rev. Josiah Strong in New York, the businessman John Wanamaker in Philadelphia, a United States Supreme Court justice in Washington, D.C., and a United States senator in Chicago. Calling Booth one of the most "remarkable religious leaders in the world," the *New York Tribune* hailed him for creating "out of the humblest and most unpromising materials a great religious force" and noted: "That one man should be able to evolve such a force in this so-called materialistic age is a striking proof of his executive genius."[11]

Whether exhorting new converts or haranguing backsliders, the old General roused crowds from coast to coast. By the end of his five-month tour he had addressed 437,500 people at 343 public meetings in 86 cities. At most venues he spoke for under an hour, explaining Salvationist religion and describing his social program to alleviate urban poverty. Press accounts portray a folksy speaker who entertained while evangelizing: "Getting religion is like jumping in to swim. Some people wet their feet, shiver and dress themselves again; others say 'Get out of the way there and let me jump in.'"[12]

William Booth's tour helped spur growing public acceptance of the Army. Mob violence had hobbled soldiers and officers throughout the 1880s, but the era of physical persecution was reaching an end. Not all Americans agreed with the Army's methods, but most conceded that its efforts to reach the poor and the unchurched were sincere. At the same time, Maud and Ballington Booth had established a firmer financial basis for the organization by diversifying fundraising efforts. The corps' collections paid for their own operations, and anything extra was sent to National Headquarters. An annual Self-Denial Campaign, in which soldiers and officers were asked to forfeit an indulgence for a week, netted $34,586 in 1893.[13] Auxiliaries' contributions brought in another several thousand dollars, about $10,000 in 1892, and the Army's Trade Department, which sold uniforms, bonnets, publications, and printed materials, was yet another source of income. (Sources that would indicate the amount of revenue generated by the Trade Department do not appear to exist.)

From its earliest days the Army was plagued by rumors that its funds were misappropriated by the Booth family and that money collected for use in the United States was sent abroad. Soon after the publication of William Booth's *In Darkest England and the Way Out* in 1890, critics questioned the Army's finances in light of new solicitations to subsidize its "social scheme." An independent panel in England reviewed the Army's accounts and pronounced them sound, even praising Booth's financial acumen and fiscal integrity. Yet rumors of misconduct persisted, and when G. A. Davis wrote a series on the Army for *Frank Leslie's Weekly* in

1893, she questioned the movement's independent auditor, who swore to the "absolute correctness" of the Army's double-entry bookkeeping. Convinced of the movement's basic honesty, Davis observed: "It is hard to understand, indeed, why such questions should ever arise, when one considers the enormous expenses incident to the handling and support of such an organization, and their more or less irregular sources of income, and notes, also, the absolute openness and publicity of the lives of the chief officers, whose habits of poverty and self-denial are as patent to the world as those of any cloistered sisterhood."[14]

Davis, who visited the accountant at the Army's Headquarters at 111 Reade Street, described the premises as a "bee-hive" which was "honeycombed with little offices, most of them airless and gas-lit; the passages are narrow and the stairs steep, and through and up and down them the busy workers are running."[15] By this time the Army had out-grown the Reade Street offices and the Booths were planning to erect a new, more spacious building. Repeated pleas for subscriptions to pay for a new Headquarters honoring the memory of the recently deceased Catherine Booth, had enabled the Army to buy an old carriage factory on 14th Street west of Sixth Avenue where the New York 1 Corps was already located.

"The Rialto," a stretch on 14th Street from Broadway east to Third Avenue, had been one of the city's entertainment hubs, with numerous hotels, theaters, and restaurants. Members of the New York 1 Corps, a few blocks west, regularly saw actors frequenting Union Square's "slave market" looking for work in the surrounding theatrical district. But by the 1890s the area was in decline; the better theaters had fled north, several prestigious concert halls had been demolished, and lower-class entertainments had moved in—most notably working-class vaudeville theaters and concert saloons. When the new National Headquarters opened, 14th Street resembled a bustling market with street peddlers and shopkeepers vying for customers. The hubbub continued until dark, when electric globes cast an eerie light on glove shops, candy stores, and even an exotic Japanese bazaar.[16]

Readers of the *War Cry* learned details of the Booths' building plans when a front-page drawing of the proposed Headquarters appeared in June 1894. The price of the land was $160,000, and the new building itself would cost $200,000. The nine-story structure displayed the architectural embellishments of a medieval citadel. Crowning the building were four turrets, crenellation, and an imposing central tower. The building's entrance, a huge wooden door surrounded by stone, was built on a

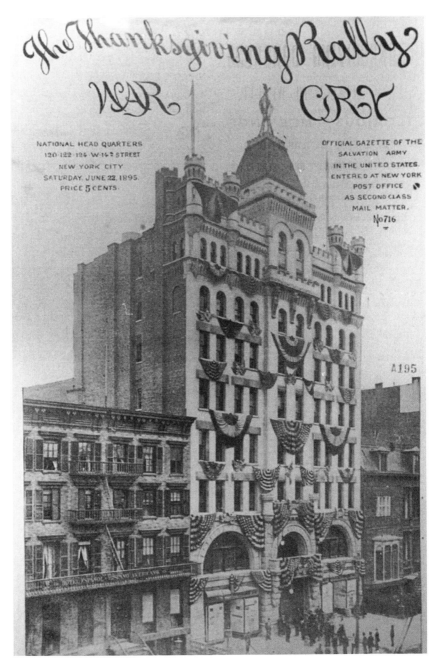

The Headquarters built by Maud and Ballington Booth towered over its neighbors on 14th Street. Patriotic bunting decorated the building for its dedication. AWC, June 22, 1895, 1, SAA

scale appropriate to a castle or fortress, complete with vaulting arches, insignia, and additional turrets.[17] This brick-and-mortar embodiment of the Army's institutional persona exemplified its difference from existing churches. While the Army's spiritual center, the cathedral of the open air, was an invisible canopy covering the entire city, its strategic base, the 14th Street Headquarters, resembled a mighty fortress, an apt materialization of God's kingdom.

When the finished product was dedicated on June 4, 1895, the *New York Times* called the results "architecturally quite pleasing"—despite being "a cross between a skyscraping office building and an armory." It further observed that the blending of the two styles caused the building to lose "the ugliness of both" with ungainly corners transformed into "diminutive turrets." The dedication ceremonies were heralded by a "picturesque" parade—complete with brass bands, colorful banners, and eye-catching floats. But the high point of the day occurred when the Army demonstrated its theatrical savvy and technological dexterity with an electrical light display. By the mid-1890s Broadway was aglow with electrical signage, and some churches, feeling lost amid burgeoning skyscrapers and electrified theater signs, had put up incandescent crosses and lighted displays of their own. Now The Salvation Army joined them: "An electric button was pushed and upon the summit of the central tower appeared a device of incandescent lights. The letter 'S' in white lamps was entwined around a cross of scarlet lamps; underneath was the letter 'A' in white lamps. It was asserted that this electrical combination can be seen from the Narrows."[18]

Combining elements of the skyscraper, New York's signature building, with the armory, a heroic structure that provided office space, drill halls, and storehouses for the military, Salvationists built a monument that signified that they had, indeed, made themselves at home in the city. The armory captured their militant spirit, but it was also a familiar urban presence. The skyscraper symbolized the Army's utilization of the culture's new technology and cutting-edge design. For Salvationists, Headquarters was a safe haven, a place of refuge and inspiration that welcomed all. Though it resembled a fortress, it was not meant to keep out the world; rather it provided a stronghold and staging ground for the new Millennium.

This type of creative appropriation of contemporary forms and symbols enabled the Army to grow as a cultural force when other religious crusaders were marginalized. Yet Maud and Ballington Booth's particular approach to synthesizing the Army with American culture—intentionally promoting American officers, displaying the American flag alongside Blood and Fire, and leaving the eagle atop the *War Cry* crest—angered William Booth. He was displeased by the "Americanization" of the Army, and he railed against the "Yankee Doodleism" in letters to his daughter Emma.[19] The General's disapprobation culminated in a decision to transfer Maud and Ballington to another post. When the Booths learned of the orders, they wrote to Bramwell Booth, the Army's Chief Secretary, asking him to reconsider. They argued that the work in the United States needed continuity and that large debts were still outstanding on the new Headquarters.

When Bramwell refused to let them stay, the Booths announced that they would retire from the Army rather than leave the United States. Emissaries sent from London, including Ballington's siblings Eva and Herbert, only inflamed the situation, which by this time was a running newspaper story. While press accounts blared tales of bad faith and British tyranny, Ballington and Maud tried to negotiate a graceful departure. Loyal officers urged them to declare an independent American Army, but they insisted that they did not want to split the ranks.

The auxiliaries soon joined the fray. Chauncey Depew, president and chairman of the board of the New York Central Railroad, presided at a Carnegie Hall meeting at which several hundred people, including Josiah Strong, Frances Willard, Lyman Abbott, and William Strong, the mayor of New York, expressed support for Maud and Ballington Booth. The international situation in 1895 and 1896 only intensified the problem. England had refused to arbitrate a border dispute between Venezuela and British Guyana. The United States asked Britain to step in, citing the Monroe Doctrine as a cause for its concern, but the British still declined. At the end of 1895, when the American government announced that it was prepared to set and maintain the borderline, public sentiment for England was at a low ebb. The decision to recall the Salvationist leaders, rumored to be a result of William Booth's displeasure with the Americanization of the Army, infuriated local supporters as yet another example of British arrogance.

By the end of February Maud and Ballington had quit the new Headquarters, and soon afterward they founded the Volunteers of America, a religious organization initially similar to the Army. Over the years warring members of the Booth family released letters about the conflict seeking to bolster their side, yet no single explanation suffices. Susan Welty, Maud Booth's biographer, suggested that the source of the trouble was Ballington's refusal to obey the General's order to mortgage Salvationist properties to pay for work in India.[20] But other factors were also involved. Several of Bramwell's siblings resented his position as second in command. Ballington, for example, questioned Bramwell's decisions and resented his authority. Moreover, William Booth was suspicious of a strong American Army that seemed increasingly autonomous from International Headquarters. Americanization had affected Maud and Ballington, too. They questioned the international Army's autocratic form of government, which gave the General total control and allowed him to select his own successor. Ballington believed that a representative government and elected leaders would better ensure the future of the movement. Events a generation later, when his sister Evangeline led the charge to reform the international Army's governance, proved him right.

Do Something!

During the Ballington Booths' tenure The Salvation Army extended its outreach into what it termed "practical religion": religiously motivated social programs. True, this was the same practical religion that had inspired Emma Booth and Maud Charlesworth to work in the London slums, just as it motivated other Army officers to start homes for "fallen women" in England, Australia, and the United States. But until the late 1880s such social initiatives had been ad hoc and informal. Then, according to Army lore, William Booth was crossing the Thames one cold night when he discovered packs of homeless men sleeping in the shadows of London Bridge. Learning that his son Bramwell already knew of the problem, Booth directed him to "do something!"—specifically, to acquire a warehouse where men could eat and sleep but would not be "coddled." The Army's first men's shelter opened in London in 1888 and was followed by two more within the year.

The drama of this tale notwithstanding, Booth's interest in social problems did not spring full-blown from his encounters with squatters under London Bridge. In 1870 his Christian Mission had opened several inexpensive food shops in London, but the enterprise had been too costly to maintain. In 1885 Booth participated in the journalist W. T. Stead's "Maiden Tribute" campaign to raise the age of sexual consent.[21] To demonstrate the ease of "buying" girls for sex, William Booth asked a Salvationist who had formerly owned a brothel to procure a thirteen-year-old from her own mother. After the girl was medically certified as a virgin, Stead went to her room but had no sexual congress with her. His subsequent articles shocked Londoners and led to changes in the law. But the girl's mother later claimed her child had been abducted and filed charges against Stead, Bramwell Booth, and the Salvationist who had set up the transaction. The Salvationist was sentenced to six months in prison, Stead to three months, and Booth was acquitted. While William Booth advised his followers to avoid controversy, the "Maiden Tribute" campaign was one time he did not heed his own advice. (He also supported striking London dockworkers in 1889.) Although American Salvationists also tried to eschew controversy, they aided striking Pullman workers (1889), denounced lynching (1895), and supported Prohibition—among other causes.

But the problem of the poor seemed less a political controversy than a public shame, and the General, spurred on by Frank Smith and W. T. Stead, developed his "social scheme" in 1890 in *In Darkest England and the Way Out*. There is some debate about who actually wrote the book. Some scholars say Booth wrote the first draft and Stead edited it; others maintain the work is largely Smith's and Stead's with Booth providing a religious gloss. The *Darkest England* plan proposed setting up "salvage stations" where the urban poor could work and from which, once saved and skilled, they would move to farm colonies in England and overseas. (Booth talked to Cecil Rhodes about locating a colony in Rhodesia.) Riding on the popularity of Henry Stanley's *In Darkest Africa* (1890), Booth compared heathens abroad with the poor in England. Readers would have understood that many of the poor, at least in London, were indeed heathens—of Jewish and Catholic origin. The "savage" motif was not new in Britain, but Booth pushed it harder than other social commentators. "The Equatorial Forest traversed by Stanley resembles the Darkest England of which I have to speak, alike in its vast extent—both stretch, in Stanley's phrase, 'as far as from Plymouth to Peterhead'; its monotonous darkness, its malaria and its gloom, its dwarfish de-humanized inhabitants, the slavery to which they are subjected, their privations and their misery."[22]

Booth's racialized discourse, which spilled into the American Army's "darkie dialect" and its oppositional use of "black" and "white," was typical of the times. A Christian imperialist, Booth intended his Army to be the religious shock troops of the British Empire. Declaring that "The Sun Never Sets on The Salvation Army," the cover of the 1892 Christmas *War Cry* featured colorful illustrations of Army work on four continents. While Booth's book followed in the tradition of works by British reformers such as Charles Booth's *Life and Labour of the People of London*

(1889), Andrew Mearns's *The Bitter Cry of Outcast London* (1883), and Henry Mayhew's *London Labour and the London Poor* (1851), it differed in presenting a religiously based solution to the problem of urban poverty. After improving their economic circumstances, the poor would be ready for the moral and spiritual conversion manifest in accepting the value of family, work, and sobriety.

In Darkest England was also a bestseller in the United States, where its publication coincided with Jacob Riis's *How the Other Half Lives* (1890). The felicitous timing and ambitious scope of Booth's book won it (mostly) positive reviews on both sides of the Atlantic; it sold well—115,000 copies in its first year and 100,000 in its second. Lyman Abbott predicted that in the future the state "will do by law what Gen. Booth endeavors to do by private charity. It will assist the vagrant who cannot support himself; it will provide him with food, clothing, shelter and *work*." Others praised the book's breadth and its cool admixture of religious compassion with practical relief efforts tied to work. Rescued women would be transformed into domestic servants, unemployed urban men would form salvage brigades, and the truly saved would emigrate to overseas farming colonies.[23] But others criticized Booth for exaggerating the problem, seeking to compete with existing charitable organizations, supporting indiscriminate charity, spreading his religious system in the guise of philanthropy, and squandering money. Many of his contemporaries wondered, and scholars still debate, whether Booth launched the social scheme to revive his flagging evangelical efforts or whether he truly saw the need to link the two to hasten the coming of God's Kingdom. Most likely it was a little of both.

In the United States the Army's social outreach paralleled developments in England. In 1889 Maud Booth supervised the beginnings of a "Cellar, Gutter, and Garret Brigade," and two years later Ballington opened the New York Lighthouse, a men's shelter at Bedford and Downing Streets in Greenwich Village. The Lighthouse was located in the basement of a former Baptist church where the New York 2 Corps met on the ground floor. Advertising itself with two lettered signs and a picture of a lighthouse, the shelter provided a washroom, sleeping space for thirty-six men, and a small restaurant which served simple fare prepared by a converted "colored brother." Amenities were reasonably priced: a bed was seven cents a night and food cost between a penny and a nickel. Men who could not pay were expected to work, either chopping wood or cleaning the shelter.

The Army sought to keep the premises orderly; drunken men were not allowed to stay, and good conduct, keeping clean and behaving properly, was required. Moreover, the shelter's primary mission was always in sight. Religious mottoes such as "Remember Your Mother's Prayers" lined the walls, and visitors were encouraged to attend the nightly meetings that the New York 2 Corps held upstairs. In less than two months 100 men said they had been converted and 6 were working full time at the shelter.[24]

During the depression of 1893, 8,000 businesses and 360 banks failed in the United States. Almost 20 percent of the industrial workforce went unemployed, and nowhere were the ranks of idle men more evident than in New York, where between 100,000 and 200,000 vainly searched for jobs. The Army continued its social outreach through slum posts, which provided crèches, or day nurseries, for working mothers, and an expanded Lighthouse, relocated to 243 Front Street and accommodating 154 men.[25] Salvationists were opening social programs across the nation. Shelters, slum posts, and rescue homes appealed on multiple levels: they provided an outreach to the destitute, an opportunity for the wealthy to support charitable work, and a vindication of the General's social scheme, which, in economic hard times, appeared more prescient than ever.

At the same time, Army outreach to the upper classes flourished under Maud Booth's leadership. Revitalizing the auxiliary movement became a priority soon after she and Ballington settled in New York. The auxiliaries, established by Major Moore in 1883, were non-Salvationist supporters who donated $5 yearly to the Army's work and pledged to promote the Salvationist cause. Hoping to secure financial backing and sympathetic support from social elites, Maud held parlor meetings with society matrons to discuss the Army's philanthropic work. At a gathering in Washington, D.C., hosted by Mrs. John Wanamaker, the spouses of several senators and congressmen came to see the anomalous sight of a well-bred English gentlewoman in a Salvation Army uniform. *The New York Times,* reporting on a gathering of the rich and powerful in the Fifth Avenue drawing room of Mrs. Courtlandt de Peyster Field, noted that "the Booth contingent of the army is evidently aiming to work in an entirely new field" and that Maud Booth "made an excellent impression."[26]

Booth's successful small gatherings soon expanded into "by-invitation-only" meetings in large halls. In these settings she shared the platform with female officers from the slum and rescue brigades, who described their crusading work. Contemporary press accounts noted Maud's "angelic face," "petite figure," and "graceful manner" as if surprised to see a Salvationist woman so resemble a lady. But Booth's refined demeanor masked a steely determination. By 1893 the auxiliaries numbered 2,000, and three years later that figure had tripled. Among their ranks were religious notables such as Frances Willard, Josiah Strong, and Lyman Abbott, as well as society families like the Vanderbilts, the Dodges, and the Depews.[27]

In 1892 the Booths launched *The Conqueror,* a monthly magazine for well-to-do readers. More sedate than the weekly *War Cry,* it featured reports on the Army's social work interspersed with testimonials from well-known auxiliaries and human interest stories. Neither the *War Cry* nor *The Conqueror* resembled anything else in the religious press. The *War Cry,* in particular, looked like a cross between a daily newspaper and a popular magazine. Its editors employed all the aesthetic conventions of the day: color covers, bold use of display type, etchings, photographs (by the mid-1890s), and a mix of stories including news, human interest, and fiction. There were features for women, a children's page, and contests. Blending a Victorian visual aesthetic with a penny-press news sensibility, the sixteen-page broadsheet aimed for mass appeal. It offered religion without the stultifying formality that characterized a good deal of the religious press.

One genre of story that regularly appeared in both the *War Cry* and *The Conqueror* described the difficulties of publicly supporting the Army. In "Five Steps: An Auxiliary Story," Mrs. Melville is deeply stirred when a "sweet-faced" lassie describes latter-day Army "martyrs" to a crowded meeting at her local church. Swept up by enthusiasm, she pledges a "paltry" $5 to become an Army auxiliary. But the next morning she regrets her action. The auxiliary badge looks "gaudy" and her husband is appalled. He doesn't want her "mixed up" with The Salvation Army. Mrs. Melville never pays her $5, but the broken pledge haunts her prayer life. When another lassie speaks at her church, she weeps inconsolably: "She did not mention the Auxiliary League. But Mrs. Melville thought of little else through the entire service than of the way in which she had betrayed and deserted our blessed Lord in shrinking from allying herself with a people despised and persecuted for His sake, and for the first time it dawned on her that she had, in so doing, cut herself off from a personal means of grace."[28]

The story makes two suggestive points. As late as 1897, some people still perceived the Army as a disreputable organization. Their distaste appeared to be based on class prejudice (the "gaudy" badge and the

RENDER PRAISE UNTO THE LORD OF THE HARVEST.

This Thanksgiving *War Cry* cover illustrates how the Army integrated a popular style of design with a subliminally religious message. A cross can barely be seen if the eye follows the "T" up through the turkey's breast feathers, and the knife and fork echo the military motif of crossed swords. AWC, Nov. 28, 1891, 1, SAA warning not to get "mixed up" with it). Playing into the stereotype while simultaneously combating it, the Army identified itself with other outcasts and social pariahs, specifically Jesus and the Christian martyrs. The reader is reminded that just as Jesus was despised and persecuted by the establishment of his era so is The Salvation Army today.

Although Mrs. Melville was only a fictional character, she reflected sentiments that were real enough to middle- and upper-middle-class women. Such inclinations led some women, including Maud Charlesworth and Florence Soper—a physician's daughter who married Ballington's brother Bramwell—to join the Army. American women, too, fell under the Salvationists' spell. The Vassar girls Suzie and Elizabeth Swift interrupted their European tour to join the Army after attending services in Scotland. The *War Cry* was full of stories describing young women who became soldiers after seeing an Army parade and sneaking off to services. Although the Army competed with a growing number of occupations newly opened to women, it was one of the few purely religious endeavors that welcomed them as the equals of men. Several Protestant denominations were ordaining women by the 1880s, but few females entered the ministry because it was nearly impossible to find a congregation willing to hire one. Other alternatives for the religiously motivated were to become deaconesses, a predominantly Methodist vocation for service in church-based institutions, and to participate in para-church groups such as the Women's Christian Temperance Union. For those interested in service, but not necessarily within a religious context, the settlement house movement was one option and working as a friendly visitor was another.

For the right kind of woman, one who was both religious and adventuresome, The Salvation Army was an exciting prospect. Stories in Army publications suggested that most female officers came from small towns where career choices were limited. These recruits tended to be from farming families or the petite bourgeoisie rather than the wealthier classes. When a daughter of the upper class did fall under the sway of the Army, the event was news, as in 1892 when Emma Van Norden, the offspring of an old New York banking family, became a Salvationist. For months afterward reporters followed the young recruit—even to an Army encampment in Staten Island. There the *New York Times*, still reflecting (or perhaps constructing) a picture of Salvationist womanhood as lower-class and unrefined, found Van Norden nonpareil among the lassies: "An air of breeding [makes] her conspicuous among her coarse-faced companions in spite of the tendency that the army uniform has to neutralize the attractions of its wearer and make them all as much alike as peas in the pod."[29]

Joining the Army required more commitment than most women were willing to make. For the somewhat sympathetic but mainly curious, an easier solution was to investigate and write about the movement. From the late 1880s on, the Army's work received increasingly in-depth and engaged coverage from female journalists, who attended prayer meetings, followed slum sisters on their rounds, and even donned bonnets and uniforms to experience the life of a "persecuted people."[30] Undercover reporters were a feature of the age, especially after Riis's work on poverty. Everyone wanted a first-hand look at how the other half lived. Even Army reporters even disguised themselves as tramps and fallen women to ascertain how Army institutions treated their clients. Crossing class boundaries was provisionally permissible as long as it provided the powerful with access to the powerless (Salvationists had more status than the poor to whom they ministered). But the learning experience did not go in both directions; there are no press accounts of the underclasses going "mansioning" to learn how that other half lived.

One of the most comprehensive "insider" accounts of Army life was written by a *Chicago Tribune* reporter who went undercover for several weeks. "Nora Marks" spoke for many of her contemporaries when she observed at the outset of her project that the Army seemed "a class of fanatics, bizarre and picturesque, and exciting only wonder and ridicule." Echoing the prevalent perception of the lassies, Marks noted that the common features of its "lower-class" women were only minimally offset by their simple blue uniforms.[31]

A tepid churchgoer herself, the young reporter yearned nostalgically for a religion that preached old-fashioned notions of heaven and hell. Attending a large rally at which the Ballington Booths spoke, she was struck by twenty-three-year-old Maud's "pure and holy" face. The very next day Marks joined a small corps in a working-class Chicago suburb. Her commanding officer, Captain Bertha Leigh, struck her as the embodiment of beauty, compassion, and grace. Indifferent to money or physical comfort, Leigh was passionate only for saving souls. Marks, who found it excruciatingly painful to be seen in Army uniform—"People put down their papers to look at me," she wrote—was most impressed by the Captain's utter disregard for society's opinions.[32]

After a week, Marks had not yet adjusted to the privations of Army life, which included crowded beds, plain fare, and the awful uniform, but she had begun to respect the group's mission. When she was suddenly transferred to the Chicago 8 corps, her old doubts returned. The women stationed there were coarse, ignorant, and vulgar. Captain Wheeler falsified her financial records, and her cadets pined for worldly pleasures. "If I had jewelry, I bet I'd wear it" said one cadet, who spotted the reporter's hidden baubles."[33] After a short stay Marks left the post and wrote the classic good news/bad news story: The Army was neither as fanatical as its detractors believed nor as holy as its supporters would have liked.

Marks's account reflected the public's ambivalence toward the Army. For Christians who sought spiritual conviction in an age when religious liberalism was on the rise, Salvationists offered certainty. They preached a literal heaven and hell and offered followers a guide for Christian living. Yet the spiritual model of a Bertha Leigh was mitigated by the hypocrisy of the embezzling Captain Wheeler. Moreover, many, like Marks, judged the Army by their own class biases: Wheeler's coarseness was less surprising than Leigh's refinement, which, Marks explained, was the result of religious devotion lifting up one of the common folk. Many Army women would have disagreed with such conclusions. Class consciousness seemed to be as pervasive among Salvationists as it was within the larger society. In several *War Cry* articles, female officers pointed out that they and their colleagues were from good Christian homes and not the lower classes.[34]

For Marks and many readers, it was not the Army's rejection of class and gender norms that rankled most. Rather, the group's major transgression was the ease with which it turned religious commitment into a spectacle. Christians who called attention to themselves by parading in the streets and encouraging the lower classes to shout about God might intrigue but could never truly attract female writers whose own career decisions demonstrated more of a willingness to accept the dominant social order.

Cherry Street Slum Work

In the summer of 1889, some eighteen months before the publication of Riis's *How the Other Half Lives,* Maud Booth asked Staff-Captain Emma Bown if she would work with the poor on the Lower East Side. When Booth first mentioned the plan to longtime New Yorkers, she was told that the city's slums were much better than those in England and that the work she proposed was unnecessary. Believing otherwise, Booth asked Bown, the thirty-one-year old, British-born head of the Women's Training Home in Brooklyn, to investigate. Following the example set by the

Major Emma Bown dressed in slum clothes, from an illustration in
Frank Leslie's Weekly (1893). SAA

Army's English slum workers, Bown wore simple clothes that would not distinguish her from her neighbors. In an interview twenty-two years later Bown recalled her preparations: "We purchased enough calico to make dresses for ourselves and an apron each. We bought little brown sailor hats and trimmed them very plainly with black and green. These we purposed to wear instead of the regular uniform, which we laid aside entirely until at some future day it would seem appropriate to wear it again. Our 'ammunition to war' consisted of a broom, a scrubbing brush, a pail, and a Bible."[35]

Bown and her assistant, Cadet Martha Johnson, set up housekeeping in two small rooms in a rear apartment on the ground floor of 65 Cherry Street. More than a century before, Cherry Hill had been a fashionable neighborhood: John Hancock lived on Cherry Street and George Washington resided nearby. But by the middle of the nineteenth century the neighborhood had become a waterfront slum. Just two blocks from the East River and in the shadow of the Brooklyn Bridge, Cherry Hill was a favorite haunt of sailors, streetwalkers, and tramps. The street itself was piled high with rubbish; painted women openly plied their wares; and small, raggedy children darted through alleyways sloshing buckets of beer. Sharing the street with the Salvationist slum post were saloons, brothels, and tenements packed with the poorest of Irish, German, Swedish, Norwegian, and Italian immigrants.[36]

Settling in, the two women scrubbed down the dark apartment before moving in their meager furnishings: a three-legged stove, six wooden chairs, a plain table, some cooking utensils, a bedstead, a mattress, and bedding. Their routine was simple. During the day Bown and Johnson, known as "Em" and "Mat" to their neighbors, went from door to door, offering their help. They cleaned apartments, tended the sick, and prepared food. They rarely mentioned religion lest they offend the people whose trust they sought to gain. At night Bown and Johnson visited dives, dance halls, and saloons. There they passed out short tracts and tried to talk to patrons about their souls. Their efforts were usually ignored, but sometimes they made an impression. One Sunday afternoon, for example, they visited a tavern that was open despite the city's blue laws. Since the bar and adjacent tables were packed, men and women sprawled on beer kegs and barrels. Passing out tracts, the Army women expected to be harassed or even ejected. Instead they found a surprising welcome:

When we distributed the tracts we announced that we would sing a song for them, which we did, and when they discovered it was a

SLUM LASSES IN ACTION.

Slum sisters visited bars and saloons, where they pleaded with patrons, especially young women, to leave with them. AWC, Mar. 23, 1895, 7, SAA

religious song some of the men sitting around, in a shamefaced sort of way, slipped their caps off. At the end of the song, I told them that we wanted to pray with them, so we got down on the filthy bar-room floor, and I noted that the head of almost every man and woman in the place bowed and the hats of the men came off when they saw us kneel. At the end of the prayer we told them that we wished to leave so the door was again carefully unlocked and we went out, but we saw tears on many faces.[37]

In this, as in their other accounts of slum life, slum workers meticulously described their surroundings to readers of the *War Cry* or other Army publications. Since their audience embraced Salvationists, auxiliaries, and the general public, writers strove to be descriptive along the same lines as the secular press. Writing graphically about illness, over-crowding, malnutrition, and drunken brutality, Salvationists rarely senti-mentalized their subjects. Yet the stories in the *War Cry,* whether depicting wizened babies, dying crones, or abandoned mothers, were incorrigibly melodramatic. Army workers never reported meeting intact and upwardly mobile families despite their door-to-door canvass of a neighborhood. Moreover, these early slum workers never looked further than the evils of drink to explain the cause of poverty and degradation. Unlike Socialists, trade unionists, members of the nascent social work profession, or even General Booth, Bown and her colleagues did not delve into the social and economic causes of poverty or formulate a systematic plan to relieve it. Their belief was simple and straightforward: people lived sinful lives and needed salvation. According to Maud Booth, provid-ing temporal relief was important only because it enabled Salvationists to develop trusting relationships which, over time, would bear spiritual fruit. The slum sisters understood this intuitively: "Reforms which aim only at educating, giving employment, or improving the environment will not prove a permanent cure for the terrible social degradation and misery of the people; for where vice, crime, disregard to cleanliness, and utter immorality exist, they will make chaos of your order, filthy ruin of your improved dwellings, and merely use your higher education in the perpe-trating of cleverer crime and more extended mischief."[38]

Their spiritual ardor notwithstanding, slum workers were sensitive to religious differences among the people they encountered. William Booth's *Order and Regulations* counseled officers to be tactful rather than con-frontational when dealing with people of other faiths, especially Catho-lics and Jews. In the early days of the work, slum sisters rarely prayed or proselytized unless they were asked about their religion. Over time they grew bolder, and by the late 1890s they routinely asked the people they visited if they were saved. If the visit looked to be a short one, the slum workers tried to start with prayer.[39]

Salvationists believed that their actions were the best advertisement for Christianity, and when dealing with members of other traditions they stressed their commonalties. Maud Booth recalled visiting a household with Bown and Johnson where they encountered a "virago" who, calling herself a good Catholic, tried to throw them out. Her husband showed them the family's crucifix and the slum workers said that He was their Lord, too. When the woman asked whether Booth and the others could bless themselves in Latin, she was told: "We don't say anything about your priest or your religion, except that you should do as your priest tells you. He does not tell you to get drunk and sin and to live like this. You are not a good Catholic. That's the trouble. We want to help people be good and to serve God; and we don't say that it is the name that's wrong but the life."[40]

During their first years of operation the slum sisters rapidly expanded their scope. Taking over two more floors on Cherry Street, Bown began a day nursery and a training school. For several cents a day, working mothers left infants and toddlers with Salvationists who bathed, fed, and tended the children from dawn to dusk. The staff for the nursery came from the Army training school, whose program devoted extra time to visitation and saloon work. Bown also opened a second slum post on Manhattan's West Side near the Battery and secured a meeting hall on Chambers Street. During meetings a policeman stood watch outside in case the crowd, which was predominantly male, turned unruly. The audience rarely got out of hand, but neither was it polite. Several months passed before Bown could hold listeners' attention for more than a minute or two. A reporter noted the ruckus caused by a "mob of half-grown boys," who displayed a proprietary interest in the lassies. The boys were quiet until Bown stood to speak. During the ensuing melee a visiting soldier ran to assist the Captain, who was carrying on despite the noise:

> "Now boys," he cried. "look-a-here. You're in God's house an' ye just orter be ashamed o' yerselves. Don't ye know it's God's house? Ain't ye afeared?"
> "Rats!" yelled the boys.
> "You're no good!" "Let the sisters alone!" "The sisters can manage us!" came forth a chorus of voices.[41]

The slum work spread from New York to other large cities. By 1895 there were posts in Philadelphia, Boston, Chicago, Brooklyn, Buffalo, and St. Louis. The work proved popular with the media. After Riis's book appeared there was widespread interest in the condition of the poor. Society "slummers" and newly minted reformers traipsed through tenements and back alleys to see conditions for themselves. Eager to differentiate its work from the newly popular pastime of "slumming," the Army stressed the rigors of its members' shared existence with the poor. In an article for *Scribner's Magazine,* Maud Booth contrasted the Army's "practical slum work" with misleading accounts of "slumming" by popular writers. She derided stories of wealthy women who moved to the slums and decorated their rooms with "fragrant flowers" and "peacock feathers" in order to provide "a little oasis" for their neighbors. Contrasting such "lady-like" heroines with her stalwart slum sisters, Booth insisted that "no child's play is the life of the woman who wishes to consecrate herself to the reclaiming of the lost."[42]

Women reporters, in particular, portrayed the slum workers as "slum angels" who toiled selflessly amid the urban squalor. Such accounts often began with the journalist "disguising" herself in a plain frock and patched apron so she, too, could pass unnoticed in the city's bleakest streets. In an article for the *New York World* Julia Hayes Percy began her night of revelation ("revelations of such misery, depravity, and degradation that, having been gazed upon, life can never be quite the same afterward") by sharing tea and plum cake at the Army's Brooklyn barracks with "Maud" and "Em." The women took a ferry to Manhattan, where Hayes, overwhelmed by the "vile stench," breathlessly compared the "dirt and garbage" with the Salvationists' abode of warmth and cleanliness. In another *World* piece, "Em," Captain Bown herself, appeared saintly: "She is tall, slender, and clad in a coarse brown gown, mended with patches. A big gingham apron, artistically rent in several places, is tied about her waist. She wears an old plaid woolen shawl and an ancient brown straw hat. Her dress indicates extreme poverty; her face denotes perfect peace." Even more rhapsodic was G. A. Davis's description of Bown in *Frank Leslie's Weekly:* "In the fourteenth century, this dark-eyed, mobile-featured Englishwoman would have been a rapturous ascetic, seeing visions and dreaming dreams; here in the nineteenth, she brings to practical uses the same spirit of self-abnegation and takes the slums and the alleys for her cloister and her cell."[43]

Through the mid-1890s, many newspapers, magazines, and journals published accounts of the Army's slum work, citing the dedication of its workers on a desolate and deserted mission field.[44] But praise for the slum work was not uniform. Critics contended that the Army, despite all the publicity, was not the only player in the field. The Reverend John Devins, a Presbyterian minister who worked in the New York slums, charged Salvationists with doing their most aggressive work among the wealthy who filled their coffers while true outreach, accomplished by unsung missionaries, went unfunded. Citing the good work accomplished by men and women at the Catherine Street Mission, the Mariner's Temple, The Tabernacle, the Florence Mission, the Industrial Christian Alliance, and the Bowery Mission, Devins accused the Army of "slumming," the very sin Maud Booth had ascribed to others: "The devotion shown by the young women who try to make the people believe that by wearing patched clothing and living in bare rooms, they are on the same social level with the frowzy, dirty women who live next door to the one occupied by these refined women, is pointed out as a special mark of grace. But there is no heroism and no devotion, and this without hypocrisy, displayed by the men and women who dress in a becoming manner and live and work among the same class of people."[45]

In 1890 the Army claimed to be the only mission group in Cherry Hill except for McAuley's workers. But Devins was correct that a growing number of religious outreach efforts began in lower Manhattan during the decade. By 1894 representatives of churches and benevolent associations, including the United Hebrew Charities and several Catholic organizations, formed a Federation of East Side Workers to study needs and to improve delivery systems. Later that year the *New York Tribune* chided William Booth and his officers for suggesting that the Army single-handedly battled poverty in England and America. Citing money and manpower deployed by Catholics, Protestants, and Jews, the *Tribune* noted the work of the Five Points Mission and McAuley's Water Street Mission. It also questioned, as Devins had done, the Army's claim that it reached those whom the church did not: "Attention is never called, so far as my information goes, to the fact that many of the soldiers and attendants who sing so heartily the Army songs have left their own churches for this purpose."[46]

Norman Murdoch and Glenn Horridge have since reached the same conclusion about the Army's work in England: rather than winning the poor, unchurched masses, Salvationists had more success with working- and lower-middle-class Protestants. Although the Army did not publicly agree with this evaluation, its increased emphasis on social welfare work enabled leaders to report on how many poor people were helped rather than how few heathens were saved. Moreover, the Army maintained that its Christian witness made an impact on those who received its services. Writing about slum work for *The Conqueror*, Adjutant Ida Turpin made this case: "Though not so very many people have been saved directly through our house-to-house visitation, yet indeed hundreds have been indirectly saved through it. You ask, 'How?' Our daily work in the homes of the people, the watching by sick and dying, and the loving service in trying hours, have given us a weight and influence with our people that no amount of charitable gifts of money and food would ever have done."[47]

The Army's slum work never expanded to the degree that its other social services, such as rescue work and industrial homes, did. Weekly notices in the *War Cry* advertised for "good, devoted girls" willing "to sacrifice everything and go and live among the poor," but few answered the call. Slum work was among the most grueling of the Army's activities, and women attracted by the Salvationists' promise of gender equality found few opportunities for public ministry and leadership in the tenements. Those who chose slum work were primarily single women whose simplicity and deep faith made toil and privation possible. Yet the very characteristics that drew workers to the field were the cause of its shortcomings, according to an early observer of the Army's social work. The Columbia University student Edwin Lamb, who in the early 1900s wrote a doctoral dissertation on the Army's social programs, argued that the slum missions' failure to thrive was due to the intellectual limitations of their workers: "The slum officers are imbued with the idea that personal salvation according to the doctrines of the Army is the all-essential need. They would not be engaged in this work themselves were it not for the hold these doctrines have upon them . . . But, in a community almost entirely Catholic or Jewish, such aggressive evangelism is not likely to increase the influence of its advocates. Many settlements have learned with grief, this very same lesson. Another reason for the lack of success is the mental calibre of those engaged in the work."[48]

Just as the slum sisters saw themselves bringing God's love to the "poor creatures" they tended in the slums, they felt equally impassioned to save the more hardened sinners they encountered in dives, brothels, and dance halls. An 1891 article in the *War Cry* saluted ten cadets who visited 1,025 saloons in one week. The reporter described the range of reactions elicited by the lassies, including a dousing with warm liquor and cold beer. More often, articles recounted the life-changing experiences that Salvationists spurred among the denizens of demimonde. The tone of these articles, at once hortatory and comfortably colloquial, appealed to the paper's varied audience. Not only did the *War Cry* need to satisfy Army supporters seeking confirmation of continuing conquests, it also had to snag sinners leery of self-righteous sanctimoniousness. The lassies were excellent agents for saving lost souls and attracting new readers. Unlike their portrayal in the secular press, the *Cry*'s lassies were modest and refined, emboldened only by their religious zeal. An article of 1892 described a typical night. The group started out at a dance hall, where patrons wept when the women "dealt earnestly and tenderly with them about their souls and salvation." Next they visited a brothel, where lewd songs, violent brawls, and pervasive profanity approximated Salvationist notions of Hell. But no sooner did the lassies begin a hymn than they were surrounded by listeners who, falling to their knees, joined in "Room for Jesus."[49]

Women Warriors

As articles in the *War Cry* demonstrate, Salvationists were aware of popular prejudices toward the lassies and countered them with their own constructions of Army womanhood. Thus, even if the *New York Times* declared that "whoever joins the Salvation Army from the nature of the case bids good-bye to respectability as much as if he went on the stage of a variety show," the example of Maud Booth suggested otherwise.[50] Booth's words and deeds, her Army persona, challenged the notion that becoming a Salvationist meant an end to a woman's respectability. Booth forcefully articulated women's abilities and rights without compromising her "refined" and "angelic" demeanor. While serving as a role model for young women seeking lives of holy service, she also inspired trust among the hundreds of auxiliaries she addressed in parlor meetings and public forums. Early in her tenure Maud Booth began a weekly *War Cry* column to encourage women officers. In these columns, sometimes written in epistolary form, she endeavored to buoy the spirits of young women who frequently defied social convention by joining the Army and then struggled, often alone, to start corps in unfamiliar towns. Between the late 1880s and the mid-1890s the *Cry* also ran many articles, letters, and columns that addressed the Army's deployment of women. Did Salvationist activities—such as selling newspapers in saloons, preaching outdoors, and serving as religious leaders—undermine a woman's natural modesty and render her unwomanly?[51] Such activities, at odds with traditional norms of female behavior, antagonized critics and created anxiety for some of the women expected to perform them. Writing to her officers, Booth argued that the desire to save sinners and the determination to "crucify" self by disregarding "taste, worldly opinion, and natural obligation," bestowed the "power to rise above" one's circumstances:

> Do you think that God's women warriors should think that it looks unwomanly to do this or that, such as selling *War Crys* in the saloons? This is the heaviest cross I have to bear. Often I think that the idea of a young girl going in a crowd of rough men to sell papers

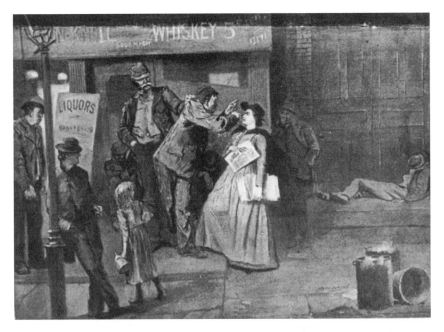

Selling the *War Cry* often provoked hostile confrontations. In this illustration from *Harper's Weekly* (1894) a vagrant accosts a lassie but is held at bay by an onlooker, who, like the others in the scene, appears amused. SAA

goes against our nature; don't you think so? Must salvation destroy a woman's sensitive nature?

I do not think for a moment that God wants his women to be anything else but modest but I cannot see that they in any way endanger their modesty by entering a saloon as God's messenger. That would be Christ's mission were He on earth today. Nor do I think that salvation must destroy a woman's sensitive nature. Jesus Christ's sensitive nature was not destroyed.[52]

Although she preferred to communicate individually with her "girls," writing on robin's-egg-blue Salvation Army stationery, Booth's busy schedule necessitated group letters in the movement's weekly newspaper. Nevertheless, in these missives she aimed for a personal touch. Booth signed her letters "Your Mother in the War," aware that for some girls, disowned by disapproving parents, she was indeed a surrogate mother. Her columns, intended to encourage her officers' spiritual fervor, also offered practical advice: on health, "Take cold baths!"; on child care, how often to bathe a baby; on public speaking, "Never shout."[53]

Even before she attained the rank of Commander Booth appreciated the opportunities the Army offered women. Salvationists believed that God gave each woman "talents, capacities, abilities" to use properly. "Therefore in opening the way for women to talk and sing and pray for God and souls, in public and otherwise, the Army does not give them any privilege, but merely puts them in the way of exercising their rights." Moreover, the Army respected female autonomy, noting that "every woman has the right to be the proprietor of her person, her time, her powers, and all else that belongs to her." Yet alongside Booth's spirited defense of women's rights was an understanding of gender differences endemic to the era. In a speech at the 1893 World's Fair in Chicago, Booth praised the Army for upholding "the rights and privileges" of women's ministry when most Christians opposed it. But even as she sought to vindicate women's equality in all spheres, she upheld certain distinctions such as feminine modesty and masculine chivalry. Anticipating critics of women's rights, Booth argued that women's tender nature ensured that they would not seek mastery over the opposite sex.

> We make no difference between the men and the women. We do not give her a separate sphere in the work nor organize her work as though she were in any way disqualified for standing shoulder to shoulder with men at the battle's front.
>
> But on the other hand we do not want it to be surmised that by rising to their right sphere and position the women in this organization have in any sense desired or endeavored to push into the background or tread beneath their feet the influence and power of men in the battle for righteousness . . . In past years it is true that women have been kept down, ignored and slighted but let her not wish in any sense to forge upon the hands and feet of man the shackles she has cast off.[54]

Booth was not always consistent. She believed that in order to succeed Salvationist women needed to mingle some masculine qualities with their feminine nature. The result was the "Woman Warrior," a term coined within the Army as opposed to the "Hallelujah lass," a demeaning epithet hurled by detractors before Salvationists adopted it as their own. The woman warrior wed "tender, gentle, loving attributes" to "courage, strength, action, sacrifice, and loyalty." While some scholars have suggested that religious groups like the Army used religion to instill middle-class notions of respectability among the poor and working classes, Booth's pronouncements on women warriors complicate this conclusion. Booth did not always hold herself or her female followers to conventional standards; rather, a spiritual mission often conflicted with society's notions of ladylike behavior. Not content simply to challenge the notion of separate spheres, Booth also contested concomitant class assumptions. "I presume all officers have had the good sense to discard gloves altogether in this hot weather," she wrote in a column. "I have always looked upon this as one of the emancipations the Salvation Army has brought to women. The opinion of the world on what is ladylike dressing does not enter into Salvation Army dressing." How could the Army be a vehicle for embourgoisement when its female leader preferred the word "woman" to "lady"? Booth clearly believed that the Army's concept of female behavior was not dictated by social convention or class expectations but by religious instrumentality: "Woman, I think, is a beautiful name. I cannot bear to hear an Army warrior called a 'lady.' It always seems to me to be so out-of-place, such a come-down from the holy, natural, unaffected name of woman, and besides that it savors always to me of the world."[55]

Not all Salvationist women were ready to abandon the notions of respectability implicit in the image of the lady. Aware of the popular belief that most Army women had been saved from the dregs of society, and thus represented a degraded version of the sex, some officers sought to clarify their actual social status. According to one Army wife, all the women warriors she knew had been saved since childhood and raised in "refined" settings. Noted another in the *War Cry*: "To those of our readers or critics who have 'with the larger majority' always held that the ranks of the Salvation Army are altogether made up and recruited from the riff-raff and bob-taildom of society, we say, 'Hold it a bit!' Perhaps they will be surprised to find that Major Chatterton and a great many others have been gathered in, not from the slums or the haunts of shame, or the purlieus of iniquity but from the ranks of upper tendom and aristocracy."[56]

The Army appealed to the "upper tendom," a popular term for the wealthy, because it took advantage of the historical moment. Expectations of women's capacities were changing, yet few professional options, as opposed to wage-earning jobs, were available to them. For the wealthy woman who was not content to be just a friendly visitor, but who was more evangelical than the average settlement house worker, the Army held appeal. Moreover, female Salvationists flourished. Most well-to-do women who joined rose rapidly through the ranks. Some were promoted to ensure the visibility of respectable women, others succeeded because their education and background prepared them for leadership roles. Such women, when confronted by hostile characterizations in the media, ardently defended themselves or, as Maud Booth did, turned the criticism on its head—embracing the very qualities that were derided. Thus, in Booth's ears, the term "lady" rang worldly while "woman" sounded unaffected and holy.

In general, privileged women who joined the Army were the daughters of professional men from large towns and cities. Most had strong religious feelings untapped by the churches they attended. Alice Terrell, a New Yorker of "Puritan-Knickerbocker" descent, discovered the Army when it took over the downtown church that her congregation had abandoned. "Little Alice" became a soldier in 1882 and served with corps in New York, New Jersey, and Pennsylvania. The Swift sisters were traveling through Europe when they encountered the Army in Glasgow. Both enlisted; Suzie became the first female editor of an Army publication, and Elizabeth married Samuel Brengle, the Army's leading Holiness writer. Emma Van Norden, the daughter of a wealthy New York banker, wrote for the *War Cry* under the byline TAO (for trust and obedience). Carrie Judd Montgomery, a bestselling author of books on faith healing, became a Salvationist when she and her millionaire husband became convinced that Army missions were the most effective way to reach the unchurched.[57]

More typically, however, women warriors came from more modest backgrounds. Actual profiles as well as the stories in Salvationist periodicals indicate that many grew up in small towns. In fictional accounts, a worldly young woman realizes the emptiness of her life when she is confronted by the Army. The story's tension arises when the protagonist's attachment to the world, especially its things (such as dress and fashion) and its conventions (regarding women's roles), conflicts with her desire for a service-filled, God-centered life. In some stories the heroine dies before she is saved and, with her last breath, regrets her ill-spent years. Most real-life stories were less dramatic. Recruits were the daughters of farmers or small businessmen; they had been baptized in a church, often Methodist or Episcopal, but had either fallen away or found their religious practice cold and formal. Although the 1880s and 1890s were a time of expanding opportunities for women, these late teens and young adults were not part of the tide. Few careers were open to them unless they left home. But absent the press of financial need, many lacked the impetus to strike out on their own. Opting instead to follow the social and domestic rounds of their mothers and grandmothers, some wondered if this was all life had to offer.[58]

With the Army's appearance came a whiff of wider possibilities. A young woman attended a Salvationist meeting where, amid the red jerseys and poke bonnets, she found radiant faces testifying to a vital faith. If she decided to join the Army and her family disowned her, she had little time to grieve. Officers were sent to "open" new corps every few months. Like Nora Marks's heroine, Captain Bertha Leigh, an officer was expected to move to a city with few resources and quickly build a corps and make it self-sufficient. Within a few months she would be sent somewhere else.

Writing about her own "eventful life," Captain A. Y. Dixon began: "My birth occurred in Western Pennsylvania where also I was reared—a farmer's daughter." Dixon said she was willful and selfish until, at age eighteen, she lost both her husband and her mother. Seeking forgiveness for past sins, Dixon found salvation and joined the Army. She served corps in her home state, in Connecticut, and in Massachusetts, where she was attacked and imprisoned. Sentenced for the crime of marching in the streets, Dixon spent sixty days in a state workhouse toiling at "arduous" labor and surviving in "loathsome" conditions. Yet she never lost sight of her mission: "Notwithstanding the fact that the soft soap ate the skin off our hands and our 'inner man' fairly revolted at the sight of the prison food, the peace of God filled our hearts and we found exceeding great recompense of reward talking to the poor, sinful, despairing creatures."[59]

Like A. Y. Dixon, many women who joined the Army were young, idealistic, and mobile. When Minnie Myers first saw the Army members in her hometown of Alpena, Michigan, she disliked them, "but underneath it all I loved them because their lives were so pure." She became a soldier and was sent to Detroit, where she was horsewhipped and battered by persecutors. May Harris grew up in the Connecticut hills, the daughter of a Danbury furrier. Although her father was not religious, he took the family to an Army meeting, where Harris was converted. After enlisting she was stationed in a small town where an angry mob burned down the corps building and threatened to throw her, too, into the fire.[60]

Lassies like A. Y. Dixon, Minnie Myers, and May Harris met Maud Booth's expectations for women warriors. Unlike their more privileged Salvationist sisters who held administrative and editorial positions, these women did front-line work which often provoked local resistance. While officers serving in New York slum posts were rarely attacked after the

early 1880s, lassies in small towns and cities experienced physical violence throughout the decade. Such attacks indicate that female Salvationists were not considered respectable women in many communities. That
men felt no compunction about horsewhipping or beating them suggests
that the lassies' role as public religious figures placed them beyond the
pale of acceptable gender behavior. Among the Army's responses to these
attacks was a rhetorical strategy that linked the lassies to more conventional feminine imagery such as angels, refined homes, and Christian
families.

But the Army wanted it both ways. If all the lassies were from upstanding families, then Salvationists weren't doing a very good job of converting the masses. Therefore, when a *War Cry* headline trumpeted "The
Extraordinary Career and Conversion of Lt. Maude A. Harris," the subsequent story was a true page-turner. When Harris was three, her mother
gave her to a circus to be trained as a bareback rider. After enduring years
of punishment among the most "unwomanly of women," she ran away to
become an actress. Harris toured around the world and later worked as a
baseball player, a champion rower, and a jockey. Surviving several
brushes with death, she succumbed to a dissolute life: "I was among the
most reckless of my circle; an incessant smoker, the fastest among fast
women. I had completed nineteen years of a wild and depraved life."
When she fell ill and nearly died, a well-meaning doctor read scripture to
her. The words touched her heart, and after she recovered she found
religion. She soon became a Salvation Army officer.[61]

War Cry narratives aside, however, few women like Maude Harris
found their way to the Army. The Army was not the fastest route to
respectability, and its tang of adventure held little allure for women
whose circumstances had forced them to be independent and self-supporting. Lower-class women already had the freedom and mobility that
accompanied being wage earners; they did not need the Army to provide
it for them. Moreover, a significant number of these women were Jews
and Catholics who had no interest in the Army's brand of evangelical
religion. As a result, comparatively few soldiers and officers were recruited from the very classes that the Army most wanted to reach.

While the Army offered women equality of opportunity tempered by
traditional notions about woman's sphere, it offered men a religious experience shaped and defined by the rhetoric of combat and masculinity. By
its own definition, the Army defended the godly, if old-fashioned, virtues
associated with manhood: courage, loyalty, and discipline. Its very institutional structure—a hierarchical, no-questions-asked command—coun-

terbalanced any hint of effeminacy that stemmed from its egalitarian treatment of women. Steeped in the masculine discourse that critics said the churches lacked, the Army initially had almost equal numbers of male and female recruits. (The ratio of women to men would increase over time.)

By the century's end many American church leaders were dismayed by what they saw as the feminization of religious practice. Looking out at their pews, clergymen noted an absence of male congregants, and they decried the recreational pursuits that had superseded Sunday services.[62] Men's fraternal movements had soared in membership, sports were increasingly popular, and even social movements, such as labor unions or the Grand Army of the Republic, offered alternative locations for ritual, fellowship, and meaning.

At the same time, a wave of Christian militarism and muscular Christianity had struck both Britain and the United States. Tracking the development of Christian militarism in mid-Victorian England, Olive Anderson attributed its growth to the popularity of the British army following its celebrated exploits in the Crimean War and the Indian Mutiny, the growth of the civilian militia movement, and the popularization of military metaphors in the militant, evangelical rhetoric introduced in England by traveling American revivalists. Muscular Christianity, which had been a force within the Anglican church since the mid-1800s, hailed Jesus as the Prince of War as well as the Prince of Peace. Celebrating physical strength and competitive sports, its exponents urged Christians to use their bodies as well as their minds to fight the devil. In the United States themes from the two movements coalesced in initiatives aligning religion with sports and the military. The YMCA was the best known of these endeavors, but boy brigades and quasi-military groups were also popular in local churches. Janet Forsythe Fishburn has even argued that the Social Gospel's emphasis on Christian manhood was a reaction against changes in gender ideology and the feminization of religion.[63]

The Salvation Army was not wholly typical of either militant or muscular Christianity. Its openness to women and its lack of interest in sports were among the reasons it did not fall squarely in either camp. But in drawing on the rhetoric of battle to define its mission, the Army did offer American men (and women) who had missed the Civil War an opportunity to participate in their own holy crusade. The *War Cry* occasionally made this connection explicit, as in the story of a Civil War veteran who became a drunk and was saved by the Army. Like many young women attracted by Salvationist fanfare, many male officers had grown up in small towns and farming communities. For these boys the Army's arrival was a spectacular event. Edward J. Parker, who headed the American Army from 1934 to 1943, always remembered the Army's "grand bombardment" of his hometown of Elgin, Illinois. It was 1885 and Parker was a "skinny" and "callow" sixteen-year-old. He and his friends "had expected an army with guns and banners," but instead found a man, a woman, and a child "feebly" singing in the town square. Until then the circus had been the most exciting event in the teenager's life, but, following this ragged army to its "free-and-easy"—an indoor service that featured singing and testimonies—Parker discovered a new world. He returned nightly for meetings, sold the *War Cry*, and testified to finding Jesus. Several weeks later, he became a soldier: "The next day, still thrilled from that proud moment of being sworn in beneath the Army flag of yellow, red and blue, I ordered my soldier's insignia . . . I wanted to show everybody that I had joined the Army."[64]

Parker and many others found purpose, structure, and meaning under the Blood and Fire flag. The feminization feared by established churches was hardly a concern for a crusade whose very language witnessed to the glory of war. Salvationists favored an exuberant use of military terminology to designate their religious activities—prayer was "knee drill," daily devotionals were "rations," shouting "Amen" or "Hallelujah" was "firing a volley," a planned revival was a "siege," new converts were "captives," vacation was "furlough," and short testimonies were "small shot." Moreover, there was nothing effeminate about Army life. Opening a corps was a courageous act: Salvationists risked not just ridicule but also persecution. In the best of times, officers lived modestly; they owned few possessions because they were constantly on the go. Everyday life was a frugal affair governed by the *Orders and Regulation,* the Army manual whose rules covered everything from dress and courtship to prayer times and account-keeping.

But the masculine bias inherent in the Army's explicit rhetoric, and in its policy of promotion, was mitigated by Maud Booth's *War Cry* columns to male officers and soldiers. In 1894 Booth began alternating the "Women's Warrior Column" with articles for Salvationist men. Just as she offered practical advice on topics such as leadership and public speaking to women officers, Booth instructed men on becoming self-reliant by mastering the basic domestic arts:

Why should men be obligated to depend on women for so many things as if they were still small children? Why should they make and keep a house in upside down, untidy condition because they have not a woman's ability to keep it clean and tidy? They ought to have it . . . You have the notion that it is not manly to do anything or to know anything about such matters.

Is not the lack of common sense one of the reasons some of my bright, useful women warriors are persuaded to give up a single career three or four years before they ought to think of such a thing, by men who are not nearly so concerned about finding a good capable co-captain as to get someone to do their cooking, washing, etc.[65]

In subsequent columns Booth dispensed suggestions on what household items to buy (washing soap, scrubbing brushes, dustpan, broom, dustcloths, and carbolic acid soda), how to clean (use the same cloth for dusting and washing dishes), and what to cook (a week's worth of breakfast recipes).[66] It is impossible to know whether Maud was more interested in preserving the independence of her women warriors or in engendering self-sufficiency among the men. But it is possible to speculate that she was trying to build independent, self-reliant warriors of both sexes. The Army was unusual for expanding women's options, but few of its leaders—Maud Booth was an exception—realized that assuming new roles required both sexes to develop new skills.

Slaves of Fashion

For many young women eager to join the Army, wearing the blue uniform and the plain poke bonnet was the ultimate test. Salvationist garb was an obstacle for both sexes; but for women, to whom a burgeoning commercial market promoted fashion as status, identity, and self-expression, donning regulation issue was particularly difficult. At a time when women's zeal for new and better clothes was stoked by mass production and spurred by the proliferation of catalog houses and department stores, Salvationist writings demonstrated that the Army made the rejection of fashion a test of spiritual commitment.

Not that the Army was alone in eschewing such temptations. The Quakers also advocated plain and simple clothes, as did most branches of the Holiness movement. Similarly, members of the Protestant clergy and Catholic religious orders wore distinctive dress. The function of religious clothing to instill modesty, to set wearers apart, and to make visible one's inner commitment was not unusual. But using clothes to advertise the peculiar metaphor embedded in the Army uniform was. Despite a long history that identified Christians as God's soldiers, no other sect had turned the trope into a literal designation. But William Booth had directed his soldiers to attract attention; and, in an age of marketing, the uniform served as a label for the Army's brand name.

In its early years, the brand was not one that most people wanted. When Suzie Swift, the Vassar girl turned Army editor, decided to visit home, her mother's response was unequivocal: "Do not come back to me in attire which, however fit it may be for the London slums, is suitable nowhere else. Spare me that pain." Writing in the *War Cry,* Swift said that before her conversion she had never heard of "altering one's dress on account of religion except when people went to convents or sisterhoods." But when she was saved at an Army meeting, an officer told her she now "belonged to God," who would "give her new ideas about little things in life." One such idea occurred to her that very night. Swift had been at an outdoor service and heavy rains had drenched her fashionable Sunday suit. When her sister asked how she felt about spoiling a good outfit, Suzie said she was glad: "Tonight it flashed upon me that [Jesus'] garments were rough and poor and I hated the touch of my velvet and lace. He taught me to despise them even before I could put the reason into words."[67]

In the 1880s, when Suzie Swift was ready to renounce her "velvet and lace," the Army's uniform was not fully regulated. Women's hats had been standardized since the early 1880s—a plain, black straw Quaker bonnet with black silk around the brim and black strings to tie under the chin. But until 1891 men wore "pith helmets, toppers, cowboy hats, derbies, sailor hats, and discarded military band helmets." Clothing style was also diverse, though garments were always in the Army's colors: blue for purity, red for Christ's blood, and yellow for the fire of the Holy Spirit. By 1882 both sexes began wearing blue jerseys, later manufactured in red, with "Salvation Army" written in yellow letters across the chest. Later in the decade men and women wore simple dark blue suits with Norfolk jackets that were devoid of any decoration except an "S" at either end of the collar.[68]

From the beginning, William Booth wanted his followers' clothing to embody Christian witness, to identify them as believers, and to eradicate class distinctions. But it was not until Railton's party embarked from England in 1880 that an officer appeared in an official Army uniform. The group's distinctive dress was not lost on the American journalists who covered their arrival. The *New York World* noted Railton's "dark blue suit," "cutaway coat," and "high peaked hat" as well as the women's "short blue dresses" and "blue coats trimmed with yellow." The *Tribune,* too, described the Army's "peculiar uniforms . . . with red bands around their hats" and "The Salvation Army" inscribed in gilt letters.[69]

Such press coverage confirmed William Booth's assessment of the uniform's value in raising public awareness of his mission. In the early days the uniform invited persecution; those who disliked the Army's open-air services and resented its anti-liquor stance frequently threw refuse and rotten food at the blue-suited Salvationists. But Booth foresaw that such easy identification would eventually work to the Army's advantage, and in an order to his soldiers in 1883, he noted "the greatly increased value of uniform with every fresh growth of the Army's publicity . . . when so many would fain stop our public processions how important for every soldier to be so dressed as to make a public demonstration every time he crosses his threshold."[70]

Booth's adoption of the uniform, like many of his stratagems, demonstrated an astute appreciation for public relations. To the Victorian eye the uniform symbolized service. It distinguished wearers as members of a special profession, usually one that assisted others. Uniformed women were either nurses or religious, Quakers or Roman Catholics; uniformed men were civil servants or military. In Victorian England the military uniform reflected British pride in the Empire's preeminence. In the United States uniforms were redolent of the high-minded principles in terms of which both North and South had cast the war between them.

All these factors—the uniform as religious garb, badge of service, and embodiment of imperial might—reinforced The Salvation Army's self-perception and the image it sought to project. Their "peculiar" uniforms set Salvationists apart from the rest of society—a theme that echoed in many of the *War Cry's* articles. "It separates one not only from the world but from the old self," wrote Suzie Swift. The uniform, like a religious habit, was a "costume," a social skin that signified the wearer's commitment to God. Many new recruits approached the role with trepidation. The uniform bestowed spiritual authority, yet it also signaled the wearer's repudiation of social norms.[71]

Still, given a choice, many young female Salvationists would have preferred to mediate between Christian conviction and social convention. When Elizabeth Swift enrolled in the London Training School, she was given a plain, dark blue uniform. She wore it dutifully until, when it was "stretched with wearing," she asked for permission to "go over to Paris and have a uniform fitted properly." Advised instead to have her outfit made locally, Swift found a fashionable tailor in the West End. She took him an expensive piece of broadcloth and had him style it as a princess gown with a modest pannier (the wire framework used to puff out a skirt at the hips) and silk ruching (pleated trimming) at the neck and sleeves.[72]

When an officer at the school asked why she wore silk ruching instead of the standard linen collar, the young American ardently defended her choice. But a few days later "the spirit of God put the questions to me and I had to answer straight." Convinced that God had instructed her to stop spending "His money" on frivolities, she stripped the trim off her uniform and afterward stuck to plain skirts and narrow sleeves. Some years later, writing under her married name, Elizabeth Brengle, she explained that the uniform helped her hew to a godly path. It strengthened her resistance to worldliness, and it increased her humility. Most important, it deepened her religious conviction: "I am more and more convinced that uniform wearing must be an affair of the heart; that, in order to please God or profit our own souls, we should recognize the fact that His Word commands a distinctive dress for His followers, and then put it on and keep it on for Jesus' sake only."[73]

As Elizabeth Brengle's words suggest, the uniform served as both a beacon to outsiders and a benchmark of personal commitment. The number of articles in the *War Cry* decrying fashion indicated its strong hold on contemporary women. (Uniform wearing did not seem to be as much of an issue for men.) Fashion was repeatedly denounced as antithetical to authentic Christianity. Struggling to overcome her reluctance to put on the sober blue suit, Mrs. Captain Gally realized she "had become such a slave to fashion although I had been a professing Christian for years."[74]

Fashion, celebrating consumption and individual autonomy, represented a set of values contrary to the Army's. Its lure was so strong that fashion was among the few facets of secular culture that Salvationists could not redeem. Wearing the uniform required women to renounce the trappings that society deemed essential for a sexualized female identity, in effect compelling reflection on one's relationship to God, self, and society. These very fundamental relationships—especially between self and society—appeared highly negotiable in the late-nineteenth-century city. Urban anonymity permitted individuals to reinvent themselves in ways that would have been impossible in smaller, tightly knit communities. Clothing facilitated reinvention, obscuring class and regional markers. Shop girls wore copies of *haute couture,* matrons donned rags to tour the slums, and former farm boys traded overalls for crisp shirts and ties.

Salvationists reinvented themselves, too, casting off old identities to be "born again." Clothes made the man, but the uniform made a soldier.

Throughout the 1880s and 1890s the *War Cry* devoted a great deal of space to uniforms. Much of this copy was written by and about women. Like Suzie Swift's story, these were personal accounts of a believer's struggle to wear the distinctive dress. A second genre was made up of letters from outsiders telling how the uniform enabled them to recognize a Salvationist and ask for assistance. A third type was official missives explaining what the uniform meant and why certain accessories were not part of regulation wear. These three types of text illustrate the aesthetic, moral, and ideological dimensions of clothing, and they are all important to understanding the uniform's meaning for Salvationists and the larger society.[75]

The uniform's aesthetic function obliged the wearer to take stock of her relationship to God by owning her fixation on fashion. Ideally she would repudiate fashion's false values—as well as the shallowness of those who measured one's worth by one's clothes—and recognize the spirituality inherent in the Army's garb. An article of 1889 described this process:

> The Hallelujah bonnet was laying on the side of the bed while she sat looking at it. Should she wear it or shouldn't she? "It was not necessary," a voice whispered in her ear, but another voice said it would glorify God and disappoint the devil. But it meant separation from her relatives and friends and perhaps exile from the home of her childhood. Just then she noticed that the strings of the bonnet which she had carelessly thrown on the bed formed a cross, hanging down the side. It was a new revelation to her. "My cross," she said. "Dear Jesus, help me to deny myself and bear it, and wear it henceforth for thee."[76]

The uniform's moral function expressed the wearer's relationship to society. When public hostility diminished, uniformed Salvationists were recognized as Christian soldiers dedicated to service. Army lassies traveled freely in slums, saloons, and brothels because they were immediately identifiable as religious workers. For women the uniform was a source of power, a protective shield around their person. Citizens seeing the uniform felt free to ask for material aid or religious succor. When a drunken "wretch" spotted Lieutenant John Buckland's uniform, he demanded to know "if there was any hope for him." Buckland assured him that there was, and they knelt praying together on the streetcorner until the old drunk was saved.[77]

From an ideological standpoint, the uniform underscored the wearer's allegiance to the Army. Regulations detailing what was and was not part of the uniform suggest that loyalty was hard won. The need to counter fashion's pervasive pull was evident in the Army's regulation of 1889 that officers must wear the full uniform at all times and that soldiers must don it fifteen times each week. But fashion's devotees still devised little ways to make the uniform more distinctive. Cognizant of the problem, Maud Booth wrote in the *War Cry,* "I know that the wearing of the uniform has always been, and will always be, to a certain extent, a cross." But since the Army's good intentions were now widely recognized, its official attire was, at least, no longer an object of ridicule and persecution. If all Army women would wear the uniform, "what a mighty power should we, as women, become."[78]

Emphasizing her point, Booth reminded readers why they wore the attire: it demonstrated a commitment to God and "a religion of which they are *not* ashamed"; it freed them from worrying about their dress; it protected them on visits to saloons, and it identified them as God's helpers. But wearing a version of the uniform was not enough; their dress had to conform to regulations because "it is absurd on the face of it to have the brass 'S' of a Salvationist stuck on the collar of a velvet waist, or to see the Army bonnet worn above bangs."[79]

Besides prohibitions on bangs and velvet waists, Booth enumerated all the fashion trends that Salvationists must forgo. Proscribed items signaled worldly attachments and violated notions of simplicity. No jewelry was allowed except a simple gold wedding band. No lace, velvet, or silk. No broad belts or buckles. No silver, bronze, or metal buttons. No kid gloves or high sleeves. Uniforms were to be "the very darkest shade of navy blue"—not light blue or black. Bonnets were to be trimmed with dark navy blue silk—not velvet. Hair was not to be crimped or frizzed. And shoes were to be of the "sensible low heel" variety—not high-heeled or pointy-toed.[80]

The uniform was not the only "costume" Salvationists wore. When William Cox, editor of the *War Cry,* wanted to investigate conditions at The Lighthouse, the Army shelter for men, he put on old clothing and pretended to be a tramp. Ballington Booth found a tattered outfit to be a helpful disguise when he toured the nether regions of the Lower East Side for his book *New York's Inferno Explored.* Dressed to blend in with the

Bowery gangs, Booth easily slipped into flophouses, saloons, and opium dens.[81] Changing their dress was strategically important when Salvationists wanted to work among people resistant to the uniform's religious and cultural signification. When Major Frederick St. George Lautour Tucker "invaded" India in 1882, he adopted native customs and costumes in order to develop a rapport with the local population. Likewise, his followers traded uniforms and boots for sandals and saffron-colored robes. When Maud Charlesworth and Emma Booth ventured into the London slums, they exchanged their uniforms for the ragged skirts of local residents. The London slums, like those in New York, were populated by many Catholics and Jews. Rather than signal the religious specificity and cultural implications that their uniforms represented, Salvationists wore old clothes that made them look the same as everyone else.

Yet even as the slum worker's torn calico skirt and mended shawl enabled her to pass unnoticed in the city's bleakest streets, the humble dress came to represent Christian service and commitment when it was worn as a "costume" at public events. In this guise, the slum workers' clothes symbolized the Army's mission and tacitly presented a powerful argument for its support. Appearing in patched skirts and tattered shawls at Asbury Methodist Church in New York City, slum sisters were praised for "com[ing] near to living the ideal life of Christ." When they marched in Army parades "dressed in slum costume with a red sash around on which was printed the one word 'Slums,'" the modestly attired women always attracted attention.[82]

For Salvationists, attuned to the importance of drawing and keeping a crowd, clothes were crucial to their performances. The uniform emboldened wearers to take part in the drama of parades, streetcorner evangelizing, and personal testimonies. Participating in what had once seemed bizarre behavior became possible because the individuals identified, by virtue of the uniform, with a cause greater than themselves. But even when Salvationists went native, their plain clothes concealing what the uniform had revealed, they still acted from a soteriological script. Whether it served to reduce or increase the distance between performer and audience, dress was crucial to the Army's ultimate goal: saving souls.

Clothes and costumes occupied a central role in the Victorian imagination for a variety of reasons. Mass production had made fashion accessible across class and regional lines at the same time that mass transportation and communications enabled Americans to see what people were wearing beyond previously well-kept boundaries. Moreover, a new consumerist ethos promised self-actualization and well-being through things. As Jay Mechling has noted, many Americans viewed "the pursuit of consumer goods as a way of discovering and displaying one's emerging identity." In an age when class distinctions were becoming more defined, clothing made boundaries appear permeable. Poor girls could dress up like their wealthy sisters, reporters regularly went undercover, and society swooned for masquerade balls. Mechling explains: "The growing inability to interpret the relationship between external appearances and internal states was rooted in the accumulating social and historical forces that were changing the cultural experience of Americans at the end of the nineteenth century." By seeking the full integration of the inner and outer person, Salvationists underscored the totality of their spiritual commitment as well as the role clothing played in constructing social identity.[83]

In a dramatic example of just how much clothes make the man, the Army held a "Dressed as We Were" meeting in 1895. Army members wore outfits from their former lives, while the standing-room-only crowd tried distinguishing the real lawyers and laborers from the Army's costumed ranks. Dressed in an academic cap and gown, an Army captain recalled the uproar she had caused at Wellesley College when she pinned a Salvationist badge on her lapel. A "bartender" demonstrated his preconversion skills, and a "sailor" shimmied down a rope that hung from the ceiling. According to the *New York Times*, "No play at the theatres was more thoroughly enjoyed last night than was the Dressed as We Were meeting given by the Salvation Army." But underlying this entertaining charade was the Army's awareness that clothing was a "costume" creating and maintaining social identity just as the Salvationist uniform created and maintained a religious identity.[84]

When necessary, Salvationists were willing to play into society's own uncertainties about the relationship between clothes and costumes, personhood and role. When her employer offered Jennie Skanberg two tickets to the Cercle Française de l'Harmonie, an annual masked ball at Madison Square Garden, the young Salvationist soldier eagerly accepted them. This ball, according to Timothy Gilfoyle, "was probably the most significant event for testing the boundaries of urban sexual behavior," as several thousand people indulged in licentious activities. Skanberg invited another Salvationist lass to accompany her to the revels, and the pair took along one hundred copies of the *War Cry* to distribute. Once inside the Garden, the smartly dressed soldiers were asked if they were indeed Salvationists or just in clever costume. When they replied that they were the

The Army lassies almost blend into the crowd of costumed revelers at the Cercle Française de l'Harmonie ball. While those to whom the lassies speak look serious, the other partygoers seem quite merry. AWC, Mar. 14, 1896, 1, SAA

real thing, the ball's organizers asked why they had come. Said Skanberg, "Our place is here just as much as in the saloons for you are doing the devil's business in both places."[85]

While Salvationists demonstrated a great deal of ingenuity in deploying clothes to accomplish religious ends, they were indisputably opposed to using the uniform for secular or recreational purposes. This taboo found fictional expression in a *War Cry* story about the consequences of blaspheming a sacred symbol. "A Ballroom Tragedy; or, The Fatal Consequences of Trifling with Religious Things" recounted the sad tale of a beautiful but spiritually adrift young woman. Although she had been inspired by a young Salvationist soldier who worked for her father, she tried to deny her feelings. Seeking to mock her own impulses, the girl decided to dress as a lassie for a masquerade ball. Her unusual costume, true even to the details of banner and tambourine, won first prize. But she was overcome by guilt and remorse: "She knew she had knowingly and willfully wronged and insulted God." That night she went mad, and she never spoke again.[86]

The message finally got through to the ranks. After the late 1890s the *War Cry* ran only an occasional article on the uniform. The Army was well established in the larger society, and its distinctive clothing was understood to symbolize charitable service and religious commitment. In fact, the uniform was so ensconced in Army culture that officials perceived its utility as a marketable commodity in and out of their ranks. In the early decades of the new century uniforms were avidly advertised in the *War Cry*'s back pages, where the Army's Trade Department extolled "perfect fitting, well made garments" at "most attractive prices."[87] An advertisement by the Trade Department in 1916 asked "Are You Interested in Good Clothes?" and reprinted letters from satisfied customers. Army officials had discovered there was money in encouraging at least a little clothes-consciousness among the troops. And after World War I Salvationists also realized the uniform's potential for fundraising.

    ᪥ IN RECENT years historians have argued that gender roles were in flux during the late Victorian period as industrialization shifted the definition of masculinity from its earlier foundation in labor, physical strength, and aggression to a new base of mental acuity, financial success, and entrepreneurial zeal. Initially, as families moved from domestic-based production to participation in commercial economies, women became responsible for the home and dependent on a cash economy. But by the last quarter of the nineteenth century women, too, were engaged with the new commercial economy as workers and as consumers. The influx of women into the public sphere spurred debates about their social and political equality, which same-sex groups, ranging from clubwomen to suffragists, raised with varying degrees of zeal. While increasing numbers

of women entered the workforce, educational institutions, and the political arena, men sought ways to retain their power, to differentiate their identity, and to develop a more satisfying vision of masculinity than that presented by contemporary mores and institutions. The Salvation Army tried responding to both sexes in ways that offered a balance between the old and the new.

As the first Christian group in modern times to treat women as men's equals, the Army offered a compelling, if sometimes contradictory, vision of gender. The Army was praised by women's advocates, and the Reverend Anna Howard Shaw called it "the best field at this time for comparing the services of men and women in the regeneration of humanity." And, except in the upper echelons of Army administration, Salvationist women did have equal opportunities. It is equally true, however, that women often performed tasks associated with the domestic sphere, and in some ways slum sisters were the apotheosis of "True Womanhood."[88] These selfless women modeled Christian virtues by "mothering," that is, by nursing, cleaning, cooking, and tending children. Their adherence to social norms may explain why their ministrations received more media attention than the exploits of women warriors, who tended to receive coverage that, in the case of jailings or beatings, ensured their notoriety. To the public, slum angels were conflated with the "True Woman" while women warriors represented the New Woman—desexed, aggressive, and coarse. This was never the intention of Maud Booth and other Salvationist leaders, but at a time when women's roles and behavior were increasingly contested, the notion of women warriors was too unsettling for mass appeal. After Booth resigned there were no more columns for women warriors and few articles providing domestic assistance for men. Her female successors, sisters-in-law Emma Booth-Tucker and Evangeline Booth, proved more conventional. They accepted both the Army's stated goal of equality for women and the limitations imposed on it by contemporary society.

3

THE RED CRUSADE

1896–1904

EASTER SUNDAY 1900 dawned brightly in New York City, the spring sun penetrating even the Bowery's darkest corners. As the morning hours passed, lower Manhattan came alive: tramps and vagrants headed to illicit saloons, while young swells made their way to Fifth Avenue. Amid the throng, a trumpet blast and a bellowing drum suddenly smothered the buzz of pedestrian activities. Down the street came a column of marching soldiers; at the head of the line strode a slender woman in red with a scarlet scarf across her brow. The medieval insignia on her scarf and dress, a white Maltese cross, marked her as a latter-day Crusader. Emma Booth-Tucker, known as the Consul, was leading a procession of lassies, officers, and band members down the Bowery and into the London Theatre. In their wake, a large crowd scrambled for the vaudeville house's atypically free seats. The Salvation Army's "Red Crusade," an evangelistic campaign that used medieval imagery to dramatize its mission, was about to begin.

Emma Booth-Tucker, who commanded the American Army with her husband Frederick from 1896 to 1904, led the packed house in prayer and song. But she did not hold the stage alone. The Booth-Tucker's Red Crusade had a touch of vaudeville about it, too, as religious "acts" performed a Christian version of the theater's regular fare. The Staff Band played a variety of tunes, two "saved variety actors" sang duets, and "the converted whiskey bottles leapt into the affection of the crowd." The crowd was well entertained: "'Say,' said a boy in the top gallery with a strong odor of garlic about him and not overdressed, 'this 'ere is a cinch. It beats the theatre holler—and all seats free! You people must be awful good!'"[1]

The Army was good—particularly at adopting the vernacular of the audience it wished to reach. Just as Maud Booth presented Chautauqua-style lectures to attract the comfortable classes seeking uplifting entertainment, Emma Booth-Tucker mounted a religious variety show that drew clientele who normally flocked to see the dancers, singers, jugglers, and comedians who were among vaudeville's main attractions.[2] By the turn of the century The Salvation Army was not the only religious group using popular forms of entertainment to impart a religious message, but it was noteworthy for the scale, diversity, and sophistication of its productions.

The Red Crusade exemplified all of these facets. (The Army named its evangelistic campaigns and organized them thematically. The Red Crusade, signifying the saving blood of Jesus, had a medieval flair.) The Easter Sunday service at the London Theatre was the "revival" portion of the crusade. During the five years in which the Red Crusade toured the country, it was usually preceded by "Love and Sorrow," an illustrated lecture on the Army's social programs. Accompanied by a series of stereopticon views of Salvationist caregiving at home and abroad, the two-hour lecture was punctuated with living tableaux and choral numbers from the Yankee Songsters and the American Staff Cowboy Band. To build an audience, the Army piqued interest with articles and advertisements in local newspapers. Then, before the lecture was to begin, a brass band marched through the streets tootling loud, military music. Frequently several thousand people sought admission.[3]

The very success of such publicity stunts encouraged Army supporters who desired alternatives to commercial entertainments. As one *War Cry* correspondent noted: "As a Christian and as a lover of my country my heart had often ached as I had watched the dense crowds pouring in and out of the theatres, the music halls and saloons. When I had compared their nightly thousands to the meager audiences that gathered once a week for the purpose of worship, I had been tempted to wonder whether something more could not be done to turn this ever-increasing tide of humanity in an opposite direction."[4]

When all were seated, Commander Frederick Booth-Tucker welcomed the audience and introduced his wife, Emma. After offering a brief prayer, Emma Booth-Tucker lectured on "sorrow," the suffering that Salvationists encountered daily, and "love," the work the Army did to

THE DAYS OF THE CRUSADERS HAVE RETURNED

The Red Crusade made use of medieval imagery, as in this *War Cry* cover. While Salvationists are arrayed as knightly Crusaders riding to battle, the upper-right-hand corner reveals their true aim—saving souls. AWC, Oct. 1, 1898, 1, SAA

alleviate it. As she spoke, slides of the despondent and the degenerate flashed on a large screen behind her. Next the audience saw pictures of Salvationist relief programs: slum sisters in action, unemployed men working in Army woodyards, smiling residents of the Army's farm colonies. Interspersed with the Consul's dramatic narrative were living tableaux that depicted characters such as "the Madonna of the Slums," "the Drunken Rag-Picker," and the missing father who came home for Christmas.[5]

The Consul excelled at dramatic flourishes. She often appeared in an Indian sari, its soft folds artfully draped around her slender body. The Booth-Tuckers had served in India, where their decision to adopt native dress and customs had won the Army local support. Appearing in a sari before American audiences telegraphed the Consul's own role in the Army's international campaign and also appealed to audiences intrigued with the exotic. Not surprisingly, the secular press praised "Love and Sorrow." The *New York Observer* called it a "remarkable example of eloquence." The *Boston Herald* noted: "It was a form of entertainment—if the term is not, indeed, a misnomer—unique, forceful, and realistic."[6] In tune with the times, the Booth-Tuckers had taken the Ballington Booths' lectures on social problems one step further. By expanding the performative aspect of these talks with drama, slides, and song, the Booth-Tuckers broadened their audience beyond those interested in a straightforward lecture.

"Love and Sorrow" continued the Army practice of suffusing theatrical performances with spiritual meaning. But it was noteworthy because it separated the purely evangelical side of the work from the social mission. Ideally the lecture laid the foundation for the revival work of the Red Crusade, but those who chose not to attend the second meeting at least were exposed to the Army's outreach to the poor. For those who questioned whether helping the poor was the correct course for a religious group—social workers and charity societies claimed to have a better understanding of the realities and the remedies for poverty—"Love and Sorrow" dramatized the Army's vision of the problem. Simply put, the sorrow of the poor could be alleviated materially, but the only real cure was the power of God's love.

WHEN THE Booth-Tuckers began appearing in venues such as the London Theatre, the American stage was booming. Theater seating capacity in New York doubled between 1890 and 1900, and the number of shows extending New York runs to national tours increased tenfold, from about fifty to over five hundred, between 1880 and 1900.[7] This newfound popularity had many sources. By clearly differentiating work time from leisure, the process of industrialization had stimulated a demand for recreation as a reward for and break from the routinization of work. At the same time, promoters and theater operators were seeking to expand their audiences. For most of the century New York audiences had been segregated by class and gender. The wealthy attended opera, lectures, and concerts; men from the lower and working classes went to concert saloons and variety theaters, and the middle classes stayed home. But as women increasingly ventured into public spaces and the pursuit of leisure became a respectable pastime, savvy entrepreneurs redesigned theatrical performances to suit the tastes of women, families, and the middle class. Vaudeville proved to be the wedge. Promoters gathered a wide variety of acts that appealed across class and gender lines. Prices were lowered, theaters cleaned up (besides refurbishing, owners ejected prostitutes who catered to clients in the upper tiers), and newspaper advertisements ballyhooed special acts. Army productions like the Red Crusade and "Love and Sorrow" took out ads in newspapers' entertainment sections targeting the same patrons.

Vaudeville was not the only popular attraction that the Army added to its arsenal. Its parades became more spectacular, with ever more elaborate floats and costumed battalions. Similarly, its evangelical street workers invented ever more dramatic ploys to attract spectators. Loud bands remained the first line of attack, but Salvationists also circulated handbills advertising staged "trials" of the devil, "John Barleycorn," and even Robert Ingersoll, the most famous atheist of the day.[8] Army officers preached from coffins, held marathon hymn-singing contests, and appeared as "specialty" acts with names such as the Golden Minstrel, the Saved Cowboy, and the Converted Pugilist. Army advertising became more sophisticated, too. The Trade Department expanded its line to help fund the growing array of social programs. Since many of its offerings, such as teas, fountain pens, and bicycles, were also sold in secular outlets, trade officers had to devise marketing strategies that borrowed from but did not fully partake of the consumerist ethos.

An Age of Condensation

The Booth-Tuckers steered the Army through a period of rapid social change as business mergers, technological advances, and the advent of scientific social work intersected with the movement's outreach and image. Commander Booth-Tucker, intent on remaining in the vanguard of social and cultural innovation, adopted practices that had been forbidden just a few years before. The Ballington Booths, for example, disparaged

The "Hustle" *War Cry* cover captured the Army's desire to be both up-to-date
and effective. AWC, Oct. 10, 1896, 1, SAA

bicycling as a popular fad deemed unseemly for Salvationists. But by September 1896, five months after their departure, the *War Cry* was hailing the Bicycle Brigade as "the very latest" strategy for soul-saving. Booth-Tucker himself led troops on a "hallelujah spin" from the 14th Street Headquarters up to 110th Street, where he held an open-air in a vacant lot. Illustrations depicted women cyclists, and the reporter described the brigade as "rejoicing that there is at least one spiritual organization which is sufficiently alive to the interests of the Master as to utilize the most up-to-date appliances of civilization to push them upon the attention of the masses."[9]

The stereopticon, Edward J. Parker's gadget of choice, was another example of the deployment of modern technology to serve God. Parker, who headed the Trade Department during the Booth-Tuckers' tenure, helped them prepare the slide show for "Love and Sorrow." Likewise, the wireless telegraph, invented by Marconi in 1895, turned up on a *War Cry* cover of 1896 illustrating the theme "Hustle." The motif began with the masthead, where the usual typography for the *War Cry* was replaced by the wavy script popularly identified with Western Union. Below the flag, a pulsating telegraph sent an electrical charge to Salvationists busy saving souls, cleaning slums, feeding the hungry, and collecting money. The electrical charge, dividing the illustration into fourths, created a cruciform design that imposed a religious frame on the otherwise secular images. As a design depicting religious activities energized by the current of faith, the message was creative and effective.[10]

While secular society adapted to new forms of corporate organization, with mergers peaking between 1897 and 1904, the Army's leaders strove to apply the meaning of such changes to their own circumstances. Describing the 25th Anniversary Congress, held at Carnegie Hall in 1904, a *War Cry* reporter dubbed the contemporary period an "age of condensation" and described the Army's resonance with the spirit of the times:

> This is an age of condensation—tabloid news service; compressed fuel and fodder; evaporated, peptonized, predigested foods with the possibility not out of reach of carrying around a capsule containing ingredients for a square meal in one's vest pocket. Huge businesses are largely conducted by means of the telegraph and telephone. Lightnings are harnessed and Niagaras held in leash to serve the purpose of the human race. Advocates of "The Simple Life" are greatly in the minority. The saving of five minutes, as well as the saving of $5, stands for so much added to one's assets, for time is

money. Compression is therefore freely admitted as a business principle, nowhere more than in The Salvation Army. The faster the expansion—and what an extraordinary growth ours has been!—the
greater the need for compression.[11]

By compression the Army reporter meant improving organization and
efficiency, a trend that was to continue well after the Booth-Tuckers'
tenure. The Booth-Tuckers, however, sought to make their message of
organization and efficiency clear through every available means of com-
munication—the *War Cry*, secular newspapers, theatrical performances,
and evangelical crusades. One of the key points "Love and Sorrow"
illustrated was the Army's efficient delivery of social services. The Ballington Booths had opened shelters, food depots, slum posts, and rescue
homes, but the Booth-Tuckers quickened the pace and increased the number of outlets. Within a year of their arrival the number of social
institutions the Army operated rose from nine to twenty-one and
accommodations for the homeless tripled. The new programs reflected
the social schemes delineated in William Booth's *In Darkest England*.
Booth-Tucker was a staunch supporter of Booth's social program, especially the establishment of farm colonies. These farming communities
would house the rehabilitated urban poor, uniting, as Booth-Tucker frequently said, "the landless man to the manless land."[12]

Yet the Booth-Tuckers' emphasis on social programs also may have
represented a tacit admission of the Army's lack of success at slum evangelism. Contemporary Army sources celebrated their soul-saving work,
but the numbers of conversions cited in Army sources are so varied as to
be unreliable. Actual success at winning the unchurched masses, especially those in urban slums, appeared small. *War Cry* accounts typically
profiled converts from rural communities or small towns, who tended to
be tepid or lapsed Protestants from petit bourgeois homes. An occasional
article described a converted, slum-dwelling Jew or Catholic, but these
"trophies," as converts were called, were rare. Even Salvationists admitted that their slum work set an example for the poor rather than spurred
their conversion.[13] But while the Army may have failed at saving slum
dwellers' souls, it was able to ease their physical needs, allaying the worst
ravages of a rapidly advancing industrial economy beset by severe cycles
of unemployment and depression. Under the tenure of the Booth-Tuckers
the Army began calling itself a religious and philanthropic organization,
as opposed to an evangelical mission that also attended to dire physical
needs. That difference, initially one in emphasis, betokened a more sig-

The Tenderloin, which stretched from 23rd to 57th Streets and from Fifth to Eighth Avenues, was an entertainment and commercial hub by 1900. Besides theaters, hotels, and department stores, the neighborhood was home to many bars, brothels, and concert saloons. In this street scene, a Salvation Army band reaches out amid the crush of shoppers, newsboys, and theatergoers. SAA

nificant shift in orientation that would culminate when Evangeline Booth succeeded her sister and brother-in-law.

As THE Booth-Tuckers expanded the Army's philanthropic work they joined the public debate over pauperism and poverty. By the late 1890s a growing number of groups were addressing the problems of the urban poor. Some of these were religious in orientation: in addition to the Army there was a surge of church-related outreach during this period. Secular organizations were also busy: settlement houses, the Charity Organization Society, and an emerging cadre of professional social workers developed strategies for relieving human suffering. Among the fundamental issues of the era was deciding whom to help and how best to provide assistance. "Love and Sorrow" was among the Army's tools for informing the public about its particular form of religious philanthropy.

During the nineteenth century the American perspective on poverty was far from static. Each generation decided anew why there were poor people and what to do about them. Several theories circulated in and out of fashion, popular in one age and, when proven insufficient, unfashionable in the next. These theories pivoted around four basic themes: fatalism, morality, environment, and heredity. They posited respectively that (1) the poor were part of God's plan; (2) the poor were ignorant and, through moral suasion, could be uplifted; (3) the poor were products of the environment, and if social conditions were changed poverty would disappear; (4) the poor were victims of heredity, and their inherent depravity could be controlled only by coercive measures.

Throughout the century, discussions on poor relief were framed by these notions of poverty and pauperism and, by extension, constructions of the "deserving" and "undeserving" poor. Most writers and reformers were less concerned with poverty as such than with pauperism, that is, the creation of an idle and dependent underclass through indiscriminate charity. Robert H. Bremner argues that after the depression of 1873–1878 the movement for scientific philanthropy arose to address this concern.[14] Reformers believed that too much of the money raised to assist the poor had actually supported impostors, and that funds which did reach the truly needy did more to degrade them than to relieve their suffering. These new reformers castigated religious philanthropists whose "sentimentality," or warm-hearted view of human nature, commingled with evangelistic zeal to result in indiscriminate aid. Scientific philanthropists called for an end to such pauperizing charity and proposed guidelines on whom to help and what types of assistance to provide.

Among their primary goals was an end to "outdoor relief," assistance provided outside institutional settings by soup kitchens, breadlines, and free (or very cheap) lodging houses. Scientific philanthropists preferred sending the needy to poorhouses, almshouses, and asylums—institutions designed to be as inhospitable as possible lest they attract lazy schemers seeking a free ride. Central to the reformers' thinking was distinguishing between such frauds, who were the undeserving poor, and the truly helpless (widows, orphans, accident victims), who were the deserving poor. The distinction between the two groups had been drawn since the antebellum era, but later reformers zealously embraced it. In their view the undeserving poor—lazy, idle, and immoral—corrupted the worthy poor while at the same time draining taxpayers' pockets and deceiving religious sentimentalists.

To prevent unworthy citizens from beating the system, scientific philanthropists investigated every charity case before giving assistance. Even those deemed "worthy" were rarely given direct aid. Reformers preferred to send in "friendly visitors" who helped the poor become better stewards of their resources. These volunteers, usually well-to-do women, saw themselves as mentors and role models. Seeking to build character by exemplifying proper behavior and attitudes, friendly visitors instructed the poor on budgeting, housekeeping, cooking, and child care. They were instructed to offer direct aid only as a last resort, and many recipients viewed their efforts as patronizing and insensitive.

Scientific reformers did not agree on the solution to the problems of poverty and pauperism. They were divided over the efficacy of individualistic versus social remedies. For example, despite its secular rhetoric the Charity Organization movement took a moralistic and individualistic view of the poor, classifying most as vicious and depraved. Accordingly, Charity Organization Societies focused on rehabilitating individuals rather than on improving their environment. Other "scientific" groups— socialists and anarchists, on the one hand, and social workers and Progressive reformers, on the other—believed the environment was the root of the problem. They hoped to eradicate poverty by improving the living conditions of the poor or by creating a more egalitarian social and economic system.

By the late nineteenth century many religious reformers advocated a two-pronged approach as they increasingly saw the city as an important mission field. Dubbed by Josiah Strong, an influential minister and social critic, "the Gibraltar of civilization," the city was vital to the development of culture and society.[15] Encompassing elements of both good and evil, the city required a strong Christian influence to determine if it was to be Jerusalem or Babylon, and the struggle was no less than a war for the urban soul. At a popular level, religious (like secular) rhetoric focused on the corrosive influence of foreign immigrants, who, unfamiliar with American culture, language, and mores—not to mention Protestantism—threatened the very fabric of Christian civilization. Housed in miserable hovels, refugees from Europe were accused of breeding degenerate children and squandering their income on alcohol and other vices. Yet beneath these gross stereotypes, which were convenient tags for racial, religious, and ethnic prejudice, many Christian social critics held a more complex perspective.

Strong's book *The New Era* (1893) argued that the city's ills resulted from corrupt municipal government and insufficient evangelization, a position more nuanced than the anti-immigration stance of his earlier book *Our Country* (1885). Foreigners were not necessarily evil, Strong said, but many fell prey to immorality because they were victimized by the deleterious conditions of slum life. By the 1900s Strong presented an even fuller picture of the situation. The city was a "menace" to itself because its "intellectual and moral development is not commensurate with its physical growth."[16] Again, Strong faulted municipal government for its venality and shortsightedness. A "new patriotism," invigorating democracy and civic pride, was needed to save society, just as a reinvigorated home and church were crucial to saving individuals. Strong cast a critical eye on the city's environment and found it wanting. The new industrial economy had contributed to an alienated labor force; the absence of wholesome leisure-time activities created clientele for saloons and dance halls, and the exclusion of religious instruction from the public schools impaired the moral development of the next generation.

Worst of all, many contemporaries felt the church had withdrawn from the fray, all but conceding the outcome. One city investigation found five times as many churches in New York's uptown neighborhoods as in those downtown. Between 1868 and 1888, 200,000 people moved in below 14th Street; but in the same period, seventeen Protestant churches moved out. In the years after 1888 another eighty-seven churches followed suit. Many of the congregations that remained, unwilling or unable to adapt to new circumstances, had no influence on the surrounding population. Thus, while criticizing the churches, Strong and other Protestant activists praised The Salvation Army.[17]

The Army not only aimed to reach the masses, it also experimented with new strategies. Acting out of a theology of service and love, officers improvised in an effort to discover what worked. Pragmatic rather than doctrinaire, Salvationists shied away from the extremes of the philanthropic world. They rejected the businesslike efficiency of scientific charity, but they were equally leery of religious groups that provided handouts. In line with the "social Christianity" that Strong advocated, the Army operated on two fronts. Although Salvationists sought spiritual conversion first and foremost, they tended the body as well as the soul. The Army provided emergency relief to those who were most needy and, under the Booth-Tuckers, launched a variety of programs and institutions for the urban poor. To be sure, other groups, such as city missions, institutional churches, and social settlements, did similar work. But the Army operated on a larger scale than most, and its national network of institutions served a broad spectrum of human need.

By the late 1890s many Christian leaders considered the Army to be the church's best hope for the city, combining the can-do spirit of the times with the Protestant call to establish the Kingdom of God. Moreover, its emphasis on nonsectarian social services enabled Salvationists to speak to a wider audience than either Catholic or Jewish charities doing similar work. But while the Army's social mission was indeed nonsectarian, open to anyone regardless of race, color, or creed, the Army itself remained a sectarian movement, an evangelical church based in the Holiness and Wesleyan traditions.

The Consul and the Commander

Building the Kingdom of God was second nature to Emma Moss Booth, the fourth child born to William and Catherine. The qualities that so impressed her American contemporaries, a serious intellect commingled with a maternal heart, were evident from childhood. Emma's intensity compensated for a reserved and withdrawing nature which, according to her intimates, resulted from an avid dislike of public attention.[18] Though skilled at handling crowds and a renowned orator, Emma Booth, unlike her brother Ballington or her sister Evangeline, did not enjoy the limelight.

From her youngest days Emma was an inward-looking child. Like most of the Booth family, she was susceptible to frequent bouts of ill-health and nervous debilitation. She also shared with her siblings an early interest in

Emma and Frederick Booth-Tucker. SAA

spiritual matters. As a toddler she joined her mother in prayers for strang-
ers, and when she was a small girl she mimicked her father in nursery-
room revivals. At age seven Emma professed conversion, but, concerned
that she had not given her whole heart to God, she offered herself again
four years later.[19]

During her teenage years Emma started a class for converts who
wanted to become evangelists. She soon began preaching publicly, but her

real love was teaching and training. When William Booth asked her to head the Army's International Training School in London, she was delighted. While Emma looked after the women, Ballington supervised the men. Later, when Ballington went to Australia, Emma worked with her future sister-in-law Maud Charlesworth. Emma was Maud's favorite among the Booth girls, and just as Emma styled herself as the "mother" of her cadets, Maud adopted the same conceit when she came to the United States.[20]

In 1887 Emma married a widower, Frederick St. George Lautour Tucker, the Salvationist officer who had "invaded" India. The couple were wed in a large hall where 5,000 spectators contributed a total of $25,000 for the privilege of watching the ceremony. Tucker, following the custom of the men who married into the Booth family, adopted a hyphenated surname. Instead of going on a honeymoon the newlyweds sailed to India to resume work, but Emma fared poorly in the hot climate. She returned home so ill that her doctors expected her to die. When she did recover, "Fritz" (as she called her husband) moved back to London and the two served jointly as the Army's Foreign Secretaries.[21]

When the Ballington Booths resigned in 1896, William Booth asked the Booth-Tuckers to take over the American command. Ballington and Maud's forced departure had upset the Army's rank and file as well as their American supporters, and the General wanted leaders he could trust to smooth out the situation. Emma, always dear to him, had become especially precious after Catherine's death in 1890. Of all his daughters, Emma was most like her mother, possessing a rigorous mind and a generous soul. William Booth referred to Emma as his "left hand," while Bramwell, his eldest son and Chief Secretary, was his "right." Frederick Booth-Tucker, too, had proved himself capable of adapting to new environments. Unlike many of the early male converts to the Army, he was a "gentleman" from an upper-middle-class family. William Booth probably understood that he would need such a leader to reassure American auxiliaries, many of whom sympathized with Maud and Ballington.[22]

Emma Booth-Tucker arrived in New York at the end of March 1896. One reporter present for the debarkation noted the weariness in her "tall, slim figure" and her "sharp, prominently outlined features." Another, who interviewed Booth-Tucker while the ship was in quarantine, offered a fuller description:

She is about thirty-five years old, tall and slender, and of frail appearance. She wore the familiar Salvation Army costume. Her face is striking and intellectual. Her features are regular, the nose long, and when she smiles there is displayed a row of remarkable white, even teeth. She has large, blue eyes, wears glasses, and arranges her thick brown hair in a fluffy style about her forehead. She speaks with a decided English accent. Her countenance, naturally rather sad, lights up with subdued animation when she talks, and her words flow smoothly.[23]

Emma projected a more subdued style of female leadership than her sister-in-law Maud. Unlike Maud, who had grown up in a conventional Victorian household, Emma may not have felt the same need to differentiate herself from her upbringing. Catherine Booth provided a ready exemplar of a working mother, and Emma easily followed her example. During her six years in the United States she not only shared command with her husband but also experienced six pregnancies. When Booth-Tucker addressed female Salvationists specifically, she focused less on their public roles and responsibilities than on the difficulties of balancing work and family.[24] Constantly in the public eye, Emma traveled as much as, and often independently of, Frederick. But wherever she was and whatever she did, she projected a "mother's heart"—a nurturing image resonant with the cult of domesticity.

In fact, Emma Booth-Tucker came to represent the epitome of the "womanly woman," a favorite construct of the era and a foil for the more provocative New Woman. Unlike that aggressive, self-centered creature, the womanly woman embodied the domestic, feminine traits of wife, mother, and helpmeet. Her moral authority guaranteed her a place on the public stage, but she was never aggressive or confrontational. Frances Willard, head of the Women's Christian Temperance Union and a long-time supporter of The Salvation Army, exemplified the type. Both she and Booth-Tucker legitimated their public roles with an explicit and active commitment to their Christian faith. Later public figures, such as Jane Addams and Florence Kelley, built on the figure of the womanly woman in their work as secular reformers.

In her attempt to balance work and family, Emma Booth-Tucker resembled a late-twentieth-century career woman. She led a national movement, traveled extensively, and looked after seven children. Press coverage of her speaking engagements placed her all around the nation—presenting "Love and Sorrow," leading the Red Crusade, and visiting the expanding network of social service programs. Nor did the pace slacken when she returned to New York. "A Peep in My Diary," a *War Cry* story by Brigadier Alice Lewis, depicts the Consul juggling interviews, speaking engagements, and correspondence while visiting the sick, leading worship services, and coordinating volunteers. Even so, feature stories in the secular press described Booth-Tucker's reserve and her dedication to her family. Zealous about the care and upbringing of her children, she held traditional ideas on childrearing which were impervious to the American predilection toward permissiveness. Methodically overseeing even the smallest details of family life, Booth-Tucker made certain her children had plenty of outdoor exercise, a proper diet, and an appropriate course of studies. She cut their hair, sewed their clothes, and regularly led them in Bible study.[25]

Emma's husband, Frederick St. George de Lautour Booth-Tucker, was born in India in 1853 to a financially comfortable and prestigious family.[26] Frederick's father served as Deputy Commissioner for the British Civil Service, and although the boy was sent back to England for school, he aspired to return to India to follow in his father's footsteps. He passed the Civil Service qualifying exams after college, around the same time he was saved at an evangelical crusade led by the American revivalist Dwight Moody. Tucker's embrace of evangelicalism dismayed his proper Anglican family, and their discomfort only grew when he wed his first wife, a woman eighteen years his senior whom he had met at a temperance campaign.

Tucker and his new bride traveled to India, where he served as assistant to the Deputy Commissioner in Amritsar, the holy city of the Sikhs. There, to the chagrin of his superiors, he started religion classes for the natives. Keeping current with evangelical doings at home, Tucker learned about The Salvation Army from a Christian journal. He liked what he read and sent a donation. When he received the *War Cry,* an engaging cross between the penny dreadfuls and the religious press, he was intrigued. Requesting a leave of absence, he sailed home to investigate. Upon encountering William Booth and his Army, Tucker soon enlisted. One of the few "gentlemen" recruits in the Army's early days, he was valued as a special prize, although the General wryly doubted whether someone from the "dangerous classes" could succeed in his Army.[27] Booth placed Tucker in the Legal Department, overseeing Army cases for civil disobedience as well as administering bequests and acquiring property. But the saved sahib yearned to return to India. When Railton went to the United States, Tucker proposed another international initiative.

Tucker's campaign was among the most sensational of the Army's early overseas ventures. When his party of four landed in Bombay, they were met by a large contingent of police, who believed that thousands of Salvationists had come to "attack" their country. In the days that followed the fledgling Army inflamed civil authorities by parading in the streets. Undeterred by arrest and prosecution, Tucker successfully defended the Army's right to process peacefully in public. He argued that British law forbade local authorities to interfere in religious worship and that it also mandated equal and impartial protection for all religious groups. In the end the Army was granted permission to parade everywhere except in Muslim areas. The Salvationist victory was celebrated by all Christian missionaries, whose activities had previously been restricted.

But Tucker's forces did not attract non-Christian converts. After observing other missionaries and conferring with natives, Tucker decided the group would have more success if it adopted local dress and customs. He took the name Fakir Singh and exchanged his uniform for the saffron-colored robes of a holy man. His officers did likewise, dressing in native clothes, living in huts, and eating local food. In time the movement began to attract some Hindus and Buddhists.

In 1887 Tucker was back in London advising International Headquarters about his work. His wife had died the year before, and Emma Booth was serving as his assistant. Her efficiency won his respect, and his admiration soon turned to love. They wed, went to India, and then returned to London. In 1896 William Booth reassigned them to the United States. When Emma sailed, Frederick stayed behind with Tancred, their ailing infant. Once the baby seemed better, he was ready to depart for America, too. But was New York ready for Frederick St. George de Lautour Booth-Tucker? The Army's antic days were over, replaced by Maud and Ballington's cultivated charm. Lassies still paraded on the streets and brass bands roused downtown neighborhoods, but the Army—at least until the Ballington Booths' resignation—was seen as a force for public good rather than a sensationalist sect. In short order the new Commander changed all that. Tall and lanky with long, silver-blond hair and a walrus mustache, Booth-Tucker had a striking appearance. Guided by his own sense of publicity, as well as a personal press agent, he designed his activities to be equally conspicuous.[28]

Less than a month after his arrival in New York City the new Commander was arrested for disorderly conduct. Twice in one week he visited the city's slums in an outlandish disguise. The first night his outfit was so ragged that several newspapers reported that he had been thrown out of a Bowery lodging house. Booth-Tucker's account of the evening, accompanied by an illustration of "The Commander in His Slum 'Toggery'" (re-printed from the *New York World*), appeared on the May 23 cover of the *War Cry* as well as in the secular *Sunday Herald*. Booth-Tucker recounted his escape from "the army of lynx-eyed reporters" at Headquarters, his journey through downtown back alleys, and his Bowery resting spot. (In his version, two men in the lodging house spoke rudely to him, but no action was taken and he was not ejected from the premises.)[29]

On his next trip to the slums Booth-Tucker was accompanied by Steve Brodie, a Bowery saloonkeeper notorious for his publicity stunts, includ-ing an alleged jump off the Brooklyn Bridge. Brodie, who offered his services as a tour guide to New York's netherworld, undoubtedly saw the possibility for printer's ink in a midnight jaunt with the Salvationist leader. Booth-Tucker appreciated the publicity value, too—as well as the chance to snare an awfully big sinner: "The very audacity of the idea of going slumming under such an escort, and the hope, I must confess, of winning the notorious bridge-jumper and saloon-keeper one day to the Cross, had a special attraction for me. The bit of risk it involved seemed a thousand times worthy of the cause. Here was at least a man who desired to help the poor, and if in doing so he wanted, at the same time, to advertise himself, I knew of a good many saints who had a leaning in the same direction."[30]

Booth-Tucker's disguise on this occasion was even more preposterous than before. In addition to tattered clothing he donned phony whiskers and a wig. As the two men walked through Chinatown they were stopped by a policeman demanding to know Booth-Tucker's identity. Protesta-tions notwithstanding, the Salvation Army leader was hauled off to the nearest police station, where he was arrested for disorderly conduct. Brodie paid the $500 bond, Booth-Tucker's press agent notified the local newspapers, and the two continued their inspection of Bowery lodgings.

The next day the secular press lambasted Booth-Tucker's activities. The *New York Tribune* questioned his methods of gathering information, suggesting that such escapades, "drawing public ridicule upon himself," were likely to cause more damage to the Army than Ballington Booth's defection. He was chastised for choosing Brodie, "one of the most dis-reputable men in the city," as a guide, and his explanation for wearing a disguise to dodge reporters was ridiculed. "Nobody seemed more keenly alive to the advantages of publicity and advertising than Mr. Booth-Tucker," noted the *Tribune*, adding that he had set up a press room at Army Headquarters that was comfortably decorated with "a pile carpet, a highly polished table and chairs."[31]

Booth-Tucker made headlines again the following year, when he was indicted for maintaining a disorderly house. Neighboring landlords were aggrieved by all-night prayer meetings at the 14th Street Headquarters. They charged that worshipers made so much noise that tenants were forced to leave their boardinghouses and they themselves were deprived of sleep. Booth-Tucker was unrepentant. The day after the indictment was handed up he led a dedication service for his month-old son and declared that he was not at all sorry for holding religious meetings. In fact, he promised, if he was sent to the Tombs, New York City's infamous jail, he would hold all-night meetings there, too.[32]

Having fought a bitter campaign for the freedom to parade publicly in India, Booth-Tucker understood the political and cultural significance of defending religious liberty. He also realized the public relations benefit of espousing such a cause. The new charges provided him with an occasion to ask why religious worship was prosecuted when saloons and dance halls flourished. He also demanded to know when and where the working man, unable to attend regularly scheduled services, was supposed to pray, and he berated citizens for caring more about their sleep than about the welfare of the "dangerous classes" (Booth-Tucker, unlike his father-in-law, meant the poor and working class).[33]

A. Oakley Hall, a former New York City mayor and a crony of Boss Tweed, defended Booth-Tucker at his trial. Hall quoted the Bible to establish a precedent for boisterous, music-filled worship, but the judge instructed the jury that the basic question was whether or not the defendant maintained a public nuisance. In other words, did 2,000 worshipers playing music from 8 PM to 4:30 AM make the "enjoyment of life uncomfortable for other residents." The jury said yes and found the Commander guilty. Booth-Tucker was released on bail of $25, and his sentencing was postponed indefinitely. In a subsequent statement he warned that the religious liberty of thousands of Americans had been jeopardized by the jury's decision.[34]

Despite the negative publicity generated by Booth-Tucker's trial, the Army leaders won the sympathy of the public. Booth-Tucker developed relationships with several important politicians, including Mark Hanna, the Ohio senator and political power broker who later backed the Army's plans for putting the poor to work in salvage centers and on farm colonies. It was an age of action and activity, and Booth-Tucker displayed both in abundance. He and the Consul helped shape the image of the Army into one of an activist organization with practical solutions to vexing social problems.

Cross of Shame

The vexing social problems of the era were rooted in economic changes that were reshaping the nation. The depression of 1893–1897 had brought more men than ever to the cities. An unemployed army, they strained already thin resources and sparked a backlash against aiding the able-bodied. Jostling with this wave of native-born new arrivals were European immigrants, of whom more than 11 million came to America between 1870 and 1900. For many New York was the destination of choice; at times more than 80 percent of the city's population was foreign born. Packed into urban ghettos, these Old World refugees tried to reconcile golden expectations of life in America with the grim reality of slums and sweatshops.

Even when the depression ended and the economy improved, life remained a struggle for those at the bottom. The increase in wages was not commensurate with the rise in prices. More women and children than ever worked in factories and mills. According to a survey in 1900 by the United States Industrial Commission, between 60 and 88 percent of Americans were poor or very poor. At the same time, big business was booming. Between 1897 and 1904 merger activity peaked, producing an aggregate capitalization of more than $7 billion. Yet, while principles of "scientific management" improved production, factory life was nearly intolerable for workers reduced to repeating the same mind-numbing tasks hour after hour, day after day.

New York, a magnet for the poor and the unemployed, was frequently characterized as the prototype of urban menace. Paul Boyer has noted that cultural commentators, as well as fiction writers, depicted the city as the embodiment of social chaos and moral corruption. But The Salvation Army never expressed such pessimistic sentiments. Rather, the city was just another battleground in its holy war, and urban social structures, no less than souls, cried out for redemption. By the 1910s this perspective was widespread among Social Gospel activists. Walter Rauschenbusch, one of the towering figures of the Social Gospel movement, advocated Christianizing the social order, a plan of social and political change that was much more radical than The Salvation Army's stance.[35]

Like other social activists of the day, Booth-Tucker did not expect the poor to embrace religion when their material needs were overwhelming. But he did believe that once men had work and could support their families God would step in and bring about their redemption. That difference in emphasis or agency has led many historians to distinguish the

Salvationist social vision from that of the Social Gospel, describing the former as conservative and ameliorative and the latter as progressive and comprehensive. But Booth-Tucker's ideas were similar to those of contemporaries such as Josiah Strong, Washington Gladden, and Lyman Abbott. These pioneer Social Gospelers also believed in the primacy of individual conversion while affirming a Christian responsibility to relieve the suffering of the poor. Effecting these goals in tandem would revolutionize the social order by initiating the Second Coming. In fact, it was the later Social Gospelers like Rauschenbusch who diverged from the original mission that the Army shared with other evangelicals.

The Salvationist plan was based on strengthening families and putting people to work. Booth-Tucker encouraged Salvationists to develop a network of city-oriented institutions such as shelters, salvage stations, and hotels for single people seeking to escape or to avoid poverty. But he was adamant about the need to find additional strategies for poor families. He railed against domicide, "the annihilation of home and family life," which occurred when men were forced to seek employment away from their homes or when breaking up a family became a prerequisite for philanthropic aid. Critical of scientific reformers who split up parents and children, Booth-Tucker argued that the family unit was the basis of a strong society: "The most alarming feature of our modern civilization is its wholesale disregard for and disruption of the family. Domicide is to the nation what suicide is to the individual. It is as false economy for society to destroy the home as it is for a man to blow out his brains so as to save the expense of feeding his body. And yet almost all modern pauperology is based upon the destruction of family ties."[36]

Booth-Tucker's solution for domicide was the farm colony, since he believed there were more opportunities for work and more wholesome conditions for childrearing outside congested urban areas. To prove his point he set up three colonies: Fort Herrick near Cleveland, Fort Amity in eastern Colorado, and Fort Romie in northern California. Despite initial public enthusiasm, all three failed within ten years. A variety of factors contributed to their demise, including insufficient funding, inhospitable land, and a shortage of experienced workers.

Nevertheless, the farm colonies were the apogee of the Army's systematic social vision for the era. Enthusiastic about possibilities of land irrigation in the American West, Booth-Tucker developed a proposal, which later became the basis for a congressional bill, to create a federal colonization bureau. The legislation proposed assisting the settlement of the deserving poor on some 100,000 acres of newly irrigated western land under the (implied) supervision of The Salvation Army. While many labor groups and newspapers endorsed the plan, "the biggest piece of real charity ever undertaken in the United States," one editorial called it admiringly, westerners disparaged it. Despite Booth-Tucker's best efforts the bill never left committee and the opportunity for governmental support of his grand social scheme came to naught.[37]

That scheme, an expression of "practical religion," addressed the whole man. For Salvationists the farm colonies provided a positive environment that sustained family, work, and spiritual development. They also answered the larger issues of the day—the problems of labor and of the cities—by offering an alternative to the specter of unemployed, urban masses. Much of the plan's appeal lay in its boldness. Few religious or philanthropic groups proposed as comprehensive a scheme. That the idea intrigued so many of their contemporaries suggests the Army's skill at melding a popular consensus of Protestant and Progressive values into a social platform.

The farm colonies may have been at the summit of the Army's social scheme, but Salvationists also provided intermediate steps for the arduous climb from urban tenement to vine-covered cottage. The Booth-Tuckers established a range of institutions and services, including industrial homes, book binderies, and hotels, to foster self-sufficiency.[38] In 1896 they created a new position, National Social Secretary, to oversee the expected boom in social services. That same year the "League of Love" began reaching out to women employed in saloons and brothels, while the "Knights of Hope" was organized to assist the criminal classes. At the center of the Army's urban strategy were its salvage operations. Collecting discarded household items for reuse and resale was already a familiar practice. William Booth had proposed it in *In Darkest England,* and during the Ballington Booths' tenure a San Francisco shelter had briefly dealt in salvage. Seizing upon the idea—which had the potential to subsidize Army activities, employ men willing to work, and provide cheap goods for the poor—Booth-Tucker made it a national strategy.

The first New York salvage brigade operated out of the basement of an Army shelter for men. Workers supplied with a yellow wagon emblazoned with the red "Salvation Army" logo went from door to door picking up household junk: old clothing, furniture, paper, scraps, and other waste. Since municipal trash collection had only begun in 1895, it was at a rudimentary stage and housewives had many items to give away. While one group of workers collected junk, a second crew sorted the take—mending, repairing, and baling. Rags and paper were sold to dealers;

clothing and household items were offered at minimal prices to the poor. The business was so successful that the Army soon transferred its salvage operations to a site near the Cherry Street slum post. As business grew, this site too proved inadequate.[39]

Salvage workers were recruited from the shelters that Salvationists established near local corps. Officers encouraged men housed in the shelters to attend worship services at the corps, since conversion was, after all, the Army's explicit goal. But by the end of the 1890s officers were admitting that the shelter clients and the corps soldiers did not mix. The latter tended to be members of the respectable poor and the working class, while the former were vagrants, tramps, and drunks. The decision was made to separate the shelter and the corps, but since conversion was still paramount, a new model for integrating the social and spiritual work was needed.

The solution was the "industrial home," a center that provided food, lodgings, work, and evangelistic activities under one roof and would eventually supersede shelters, workingmen's hotels, woodyards, and salvage brigades.[40] All residents of the homes were put to work. The Army paid them a subsistence wage to cart off and recycle middle- and upper-class waste for sale to businesses and to the poor. In this tidy urban ecology, the victims of the new commercial society found their place as scavengers and bottom-feeders.

As opportunistic and exploitative as this scheme sounds, it dispensed with the moralizing and scrutinizing attendant upon distinguishing between the deserving and undeserving poor. If a man was willing to work, then investigating his past or present circumstances was irrelevant. From the Salvationist perspective converting to a profitable life, just like a spiritual conversion, wiped the slate clean. "Inquisitorial" policies, Booth-Tucker said, dehumanized the poor. Rather than shame people by endless interrogations or by shuttling them from one program to the next, he proposed that private agencies (not the government) experiment with a range of (amply capitalized) programs that would engender self-sufficiency. Employing a leitmotif that echoed William Jennings Bryan's well-known "Cross of Gold" speech, Booth-Tucker disparaged "nailing poverty to a cross of shame": "The policy must be consistent with the dictates of mercy, humanity, morality, and Christianity. While firm, it must not be brutal. Poverty must not be nailed to a cross of shame or treated as a crime. The sense of self-respect must be cultivated rather than destroyed. What is needed is to put more backbone into the pauper rather than to take out of him what little may still be left."[41]

Many of Booth-Tucker's contemporaries applauded this outlook. At a time when charity workers often advocated institutionalizing the poor, the Salvationist plan was a humane alternative. Yet even though the Army positioned itself as, even acted as, an advocate for the poor, its social vision—based on a belief in individual conversion and increasingly financed by middle- and upper-class money—seemed to support the status quo. In a rapidly industrializing, economically polarized society the Army's programs offered a form of social triage. Both the farm colonies and the industrial homes provided a place for those who were outside the new economy but able and willing to work, while Army shelters and orphanages housed those who were either truly desperate or incapacitated. Moreover, since all Salvationist institutions espoused traditional values regarding family, hard work, and sobriety, those in power—politicians, the press, and business leaders—lauded their work.

The Army's vision, its emphasis on religion in action and providing work for the poor, was well attuned to the Progressive spirit of the times. The Army shared with the burgeoning Progressive movement an emphasis on getting things done; indeed, the Progressives' animating religious concerns resonated with Salvationist leaders. Theodore Roosevelt was a warm supporter of the Army, as was Jane Addams. The Army's organizational patterns increasingly reflected the Progressives' concern for efficiency and results. Numbers, always important barometers of Salvationist success, were displayed in abundance. In 1899 Booth-Tucker noted great increases in the Army's social work. In the nation there were forty-nine men's shelters and five women's shelters; fourteen rescue homes; twenty-three food depots; twenty-three workshops, factories, and labor yards; twenty slum posts; three farm colonies; three hospitals; and two homes for waifs and strays. To humanize the numbers, Salvationist photographs of the period depicted such scenes as neatly attired young women sewing at the New York Rescue Home; an Army "department" store in Chicago stocked with handsome secondhand goods, and the cozy, gingerbread exterior of the Children's Home in San Francisco. These images underscored the Army's success at transforming the heathen masses into productive classes. Even if evangelicalism was not an explicit part of the picture, Christian faith still provided the motivation for philanthropic activities.

In addition to creating institutional resources, Booth-Tucker was responsive to special needs. The winter of 1896–97 was a bitterly cold season and the tail end of the depression that had begun in 1893. During

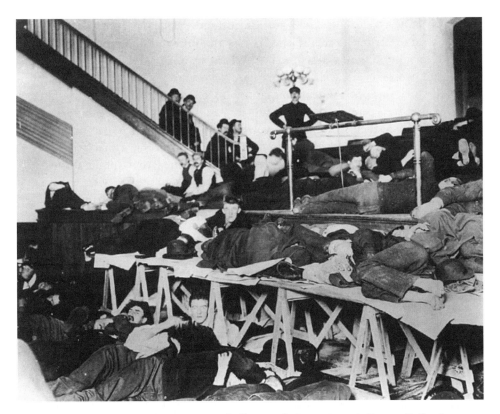

Homeless men in a Salvation Army hall on 14th Street (1897). Byron Collection, Museum of the City of New York

a particularly chilly period Booth-Tucker saw an opportunity to promote the Army's vision of philanthropy and, at the same time, attract good press. The *New York Journal,* investigating how many destitute men had families and homes and thus needed food and fuel, found many more homeless men than it expected. Gathering them at Madison Square Park, at 23rd Street and Madison Avenue, representatives of the newspaper marched a motley assemblage of 400 down through the Ladies' Mile, the city's preeminent shopping district, to the Army's Headquarters on 14th Street.[42]

Once seated in the Army's warm auditorium, the men were interrogated by the *Journal's* representatives "on the political economy line, both pertinent and impertinent," as to why they were homeless in midwinter. Most of the men patiently explained that they were unable to find work and, as a result, could not afford food or shelter. Further inquiry satisfied the *War Cry* reporter, who was also on hand, that almost all the men supported the Army's farm colony scheme and "agreed to a man that if they were given such an offer they would gladly go at once and quit New York forever." When the questioning ended, the Army held a religious meeting, provided supper, and invited an additional 200 homeless men to spend the night on the benches in the auditorium.

The following week's *War Cry,* excerpting an article from the *New York Herald,* illustrated the popular reaction to the Army's philanthropy. Noting that the city's poor turned to the Army as a "refuge" where there were "no questions asked," the reporter added that all of the Army's halls had been opened to the poor and as many as 3,000 had found shelter in them. Validating Booth-Tucker's criticism of the glacial speed of organized charity, the story described the sad spectacle of "more than fifteen hundred men, homeless through lack of labor; hungry, because organized charity, in its multitudinous work, does not provide food for those whose names are not on its registry lists."[43]

Throughout the winter the Army improvised as needed. Free breakfasts were provided at a different downtown location each week. The hearty meal, consisting of meat stew, bread, jelly, and coffee, was served on china to uplift the spirits and affirm the dignity of recipients. A labor bureau opened at National Headquarters to match job seekers with prospective employers. Rescue homes began classes in bookbinding and millinery skills so that residents, once discharged, could find work other than in domestic service.[44] When the weather improved, slum families were offered free excursions on boat rides up the Hudson, visits to the New Jersey shore, and short stays at fresh-air camps. A maternity home provided services for poor women, and an orphanage, the Cherry Tree Home, took in strays and waifs.[45] By the late 1890s the Army's brightly painted wagons were a fixture in the city's poorest neighborhoods, selling ice in the summer and coal in the winter. In 1901 the wagons distributed 5 million tons of ice as part of the Army's "Penny-Ice Philanthropy." Two years later the "Cheap Coal for the Multitudes" program ensured that 1,000 pounds of coal were distributed among the city's neediest.[46]

To pay for its ambitious program of social and spiritual work, the Army needed to enhance its image and devise new funding strategies. The two were often interconnected. Seeking broad public support and even governmental assistance for its social schemes, the Army stressed its humanitarian, nonsectarian nature—relief was given to all regardless of race, religion, or creed. At the same time, Salvationist narratives began to change, reflecting the new sociological studies of poverty characterized by ethnographic investigation and dispassionate observation. The *War Cry* mirrored urban journalism, reporting on foreign immigrants in stories that were investigative and descriptive rather than moralistic and prescriptive. In 1897, when clothing trade employees in New York went on strike, a *War Cry* reporter examined sweatshop conditions. The subsequent article expressed support for the workers, praising their deportment and communal solidarity as exemplary. Although Salvationists were prohibited from becoming involved in politics or controversial issues, the writer's sympathies and his awareness of capitalism's harsh toll was apparent: "It is difficult, in some respects, to see what advantage the sweatshop system . . . has over the serfdom of Russia. The vision dims in contemplation of its damning effects, and one is led to wonder at the glaring falsity of a system of commercial ethics which permits the sacrifice of human flesh and blood for the sake of producing ultra-cheap articles of clothing."[47]

In 1900 the *War Cry* began an occasional series called "Strange Corners of New York," which included reports on different ethnic communities.[48] Descriptive prose portraits, these articles were intended to familiarize readers with seemingly exotic neighborhoods. Even though reporters wrote as if they were urban anthropologists, their articles focused on Army concerns, such as a community's treatment of women, its work ethic, and its moral code. Some ethnic groups fared better than others under such scrutiny. Jews and African Americans received respectful treatment; Italians and Chinese less so.

In "Hell's Kitchen: A Study in Black," the reporter observed how racist attitudes stigmatized "the negro." Despite the writer's own stereotyping—Negroes allegedly were prone to gambling and lacked a commercial outlook—the correspondent depicted the dark-skinned denizens of Hell's Kitchen as honest citizens and devout churchgoers. Commenting on the "Peculiar Customs of the Descendants of the Chosen People," the *War Cry* offered similarly well-honed characterizations. In describing the Lower East Side the newspaper noted the unsettling feeling evoked by the Jews' "grimy appearance" and the "babel" of their guttural, foreign tongues. But also included was a sympathetic, if somewhat envious, account of the Jews' emphasis on family and their devotion to their faith: "What a bitter commentary it is upon the namby-pamby, wishy-washy flabbiness of a million diplomatic Christians!"[49]

A Church of the People

War Cry correspondents preferred Jews and Negroes to Italians and Chinese because they deemed the former hard workers. By Salvationist standards, willingness to work constituted a moral baseline. But work was just the first step in the journey to the Millennium. Once humanity's material conditions were secure, its spiritual condition had to be addressed. For the Booth-Tuckers individual and social salvation were inseparable. Maud and Ballington Booth had sounded the same theme, but it took on new valence during the Booth-Tuckers' tenure as the search to find solutions for social problems intensified and more programs competed for public support. In staking out their position, Salvationists aligned themselves with adherents of Social Christianity. These men and women, unlike their counterparts of an earlier era, believed that environmental factors bred poverty and that vice—liquor, prostitution, crime—was a symptom, not a cause, of destitution. Advocates of Social Christianity believed that every person should have a decent place to live, nourishing food, and a fair-paying job. But the unconverted were unlikely to benefit from the opportunity to become self-supporting because they lacked the inner resources that accompanied religious conviction.

Social Christianity, more commonly known as the Social Gospel after 1900, took shape as a growing number of clergy felt compelled to address the nation's problems. Chief among these problems were the treatment of labor and the squalor of the cities—two interrelated issues. In New York Protestant leaders had railed against the corrupting influence of the city—its sinful stew of commercialism, vice, and foreigners—since the early years of the nineteenth century. Propelled by postmillennial perfectionism, evangelical crusaders had sought to reform prostitutes, close saloons, and convert heathen immigrants from the 1810s on. With the passage of time, urban life had grown more complex: cities were larger, populations more diverse, and the economy more captive to business. Many Protestant leaders, caught between the desire to hold on to their increasingly affluent native-born congregations and the urge to reach the unchurched masses, chose the path of least resistance. They moved away from poor neighborhoods and discouraged the destitute from attending their uptown churches. Opinionmakers like Andrew Carnegie and Henry Ward Beecher provided a rationale: hallowing the achievement of financial success, they blamed poverty on the inherent depravity of the poor.

In the last quarter of the century, religious reform efforts gathered new impetus. Social Christianity suggested an alternative model. By replacing the Gospel of Wealth with the Gospel of Jesus Christ, leaders sought to uplift society as well as individuals. The message was compelling to Christians across a broad theological spectrum; the hardening into ideological camps of liberals and fundamentalists had not yet occurred. A multiplicity of groups, alliances, and federations formed—linked together through journals, membership, and meetings. Although The Salvation Army was not an active participant in the movement, its work was frequently cited as a model for what committed Christians could do. In the bestselling *The Failure of Protestantism in New York and Its Causes* (1896), Thomas Dixon Jr., a Social Gospel minister, praised the Army as one of the few religious groups trying to reach the urban poor.[50]

Similar encomiums came from activist leaders such as Washington Gladden, Lyman Abbot, and Josiah Strong. Strong, in particular, cited the Army for its foresight and compassion. In the introduction to Helen Campbell's study of city life, *Darkness and Daylight,* he noted that the Bureau of Charities had a woodyard and a laundry where the poor could work for their keep, but that "Gen. Booth in his Salvation Army has sketched a larger scheme and a wiser one. To the woodyard he has added the workshop. For work done he will give food and shelter to every tramp who applies. For admission there is but one condition—the tramp must be willing to do any work assigned to him. Smoking, drinking, and bad language are not allowed on the premises . . . The principle of the Army is—Never give something for nothing. To do this is to rob man of his manhood. Gifts that pauperize never truly remove poverty."[51]

For Strong the Army was praiseworthy because it never lost sight of its primary goal: saving the masses. But its very attentiveness to the needs of the unconverted had turned evangelists into philanthropists, and that, from Strong's perspective, was the correct course: "The Army made a wide departure from the churches, which have been careful to separate religion from philanthropy, and, in so doing, they have put asunder what the Master joined together."[52]

Strong, Campbell, and others also wrote about the city missions, institutional churches, and settlement houses that were active in the period. Among the city missions, Jerry McAuley's was still the best known. McAuley had died in 1884, but his efficient work continued. Nondenominational missions like his received support from businessmen and from large uptown churches seeking to stem criticism of their flight from lower Manhattan. Primarily concerned with soul-saving, most city missions also helped with basic needs: supplying food, shelter, and baths. Beginning in 1886 city missionaries met annually at the Convention of Chris-

tian Workers to discuss evangelical strategies; at their 1887 gathering in
New York, Ballington Booth presented an address entitled "The Rise and
Methods of The Salvation Army."[53] A familiar form of outreach, missions
provided a comfortingly conservative program of evangelism and humanitarian aid. But they met with little success. Underfunded workers,
often operating out of storefront churches and slum apartments, failed to
win large numbers of immigrants or even the native poor. Their resources
were too limited and their appeal too parochial to attract much interest
from those they sought to help.

A new and more dynamic variation of the city mission was the institutional church, a local congregation that served as a community facility
with classes, clubs, clinics, and recreational activities. Among New York's
best-known institutional churches was St. George's Episcopal, once a
fashionable parish but by the 1880s located in a decaying East Side neighborhood. Rather than relocate, St. George's lay leaders invited an innovative young rector to direct outreach efforts to the poor. Seizing the
opportunity to create "a church of the people," the Reverend William S.
Rainsford accepted the challenge, with the proviso that his evangelistic
work be amply bankrolled. From his base on East 16th Street, Rainsford
established St. George's as a neighborhood center to which local people
came for education and recreation. Between 1883 and 1899 the church
spent more than $3 million on religious and philanthropic projects. The
venture paid off: Sunday attendance skyrocketed from 200 worshipers to
more than 4,000 each week.

Although Rainsford's social program proved unappealing to some of
his original parishioners, his success spawned many imitators. To the
north of St. George's, another Episcopal congregation, St. Bartholomew's,
received nearly $400,000 from the Vanderbilt family to build a parish
house that would provide space for classes, clubs, a working girls' summer home, and a children's home. The church also established a medical
and surgical clinic, an employment bureau, and a loan association, and
hired staff fluent in Near Eastern languages to serve immigrants from
Turkey, Syria, and Armenia. Institutional churches served African-American communities, too. St. Phillip's Episcopal, originally a mission church
for black congregants of Trinity Church, began offering community services as early as 1875, and its outreach expanded in subsequent decades.

The Episcopal Church was not the only denomination to experiment
with this new form of mission. Presbyterians, Baptists, and Methodists
followed suit. In an article entitled "The Progress of the Institutional

Church" (1897), some dozen churches in New York City were cited as providing philanthropic and humanitarian work alongside their religious efforts.[54] And the trend was spreading across the nation. In 1894 the Open or Institutional Church League held a founding meeting at the Madison Square Presbyterian Church of New York. By the turn of the century some 200 American churches had adopted the institutional model. Institutional churches proved more successful at attracting the masses than did city missions because they provided services that people wanted. But critics argued that their appeal owed more to their social programs than to their religious teaching.

As the leaders of the institutional church movement sought to improve upon the model of the city mission, so did the pioneers of the settlement house borrow what they perceived to be the best aspects of the institutional church. The settlement movement had begun when an Anglican rector serving in a destitute London neighborhood turned his home into Toynbee Hall, a community center where university men could live and work among the poor. A similar experiment, the Neighborhood Guild, was started in New York in 1886, and Jane Addams's Hull House in Chicago soon followed. By 1900 more than 100 settlement houses had been established in slum neighborhoods, providing dedicated young men and women with a practical program to help the urban poor.

Few settlement houses had an explicitly religious orientation, though the outlook of the staff and workers typically was shaped by an evangelical understanding of mission, service, and the Kingdom of God. More ambitious than The Salvation Army's slum posts, settlement houses provided a wide range of services, including clubs, classes, and recreational activities. Rather than share their religious faith with local residents, settlement workers tried to express their values in the way they lived. Extending the concept of the "friendly visitor" to its logical conclusion, settlement workers modeled middle-class beliefs and behaviors with their constant presence in the community. Young and progressive, they differed from older practitioners of scientific philanthropy in their estimation of the causes of poverty. This new generation was much more apt to blame environmental causes than to cite inherent depravity. The difference prompted settlement workers to be more interested in investigating neighborhood and community conditions than in looking into the worthiness or unworthiness of individual sufferers. It also motivated many settlement workers to become involved in political and social reforms, specifically through the Progressive movement.

A Radically Different View

In addition to religious reformers, the "scientific" school of philanthropy was at work among the city's poor. Among its leaders was the Charity Organization movement, which originated in London and arrived in the United States during the late 1870s. The movement's main objective was to end indiscriminate aid that pauperized recipients. Its strategies were to organize charitable resources and institutions and to promote cooperative and efficient operations. Local charity organization societies typically co-ordinated diverse public and private relief efforts and enlisted "friendly visitors" to investigate the poor so agencies would know whom to help. Over time, charity organization societies began dispensing aid, but they preferred to provide services rather than cash gifts.

By the 1890s more than 100 charity organization societies existed in the United States and several journals spread their message. The head-quarters for one of the larger societies was in New York, and its director, Josephine Lowell Shaw, was among the movement's most influential lead-ers. Shaw founded the New York Charity Organization Society in 1882 and directed its work for twenty-five years. Her outlook was tough-minded; she believed in controlling, not coddling, the poor. Although the economic crisis of the mid-1890s spurred some philanthropists to view poverty as a systemic problem rather than an individualistic one, Shaw was slow to renounce her moralistic analysis. She and Booth-Tucker, representing two distinct poles of philanthropic thought, clashed publicly over methods and goals for helping the poor.

Their disagreement began as soon as the Army expanded its number of shelters. During their first year in New York the Booth-Tuckers started a women's shelter on the Lower East Side which welcomed anyone who needed a bed. The new facility accommodated sixty women and charged a small fee for room and meals "in order to prevent the demoralizing effects of pure charity." The officers in charge also screened "fallen women," since any who were truly repentant became candidates for the more intensive program at the Army's uptown rescue home. A few months later the Dry Dock Hotel, a men's shelter, was set up nearby. At the opening ceremony Booth-Tucker announced that it was the first of many shelters the Army planned to establish in New York and across the nation. The shelter's prices were competitive with those of most Bowery flophouses. A dormitory bed with mattress, pillow, sheets, and blankets was ten cents; supper and breakfast were five cents apiece; delousing facilities and baths were free. If a man couldn't pay, he was asked to work for his keep. A four-story brick building with 108 beds, the Dry Dock provided clean and comfortable lodgings for a low cost. But its goals were not roundly applauded. The Committee on Vagrancy of the Conference of Charities, chaired by Lowell, warned that the Army's plans would attract vagrants to the city. When a delegation visited Booth-Tucker, the Salvationist leader promised to consider their concerns.[55]

But the Commander had no intention of desisting. Exemplifying what a later era would call "tough love," Booth-Tucker believed in helping any man who was ready to help himself. While announcing that the Army planned to convert some of its barracks into a free shelter for women, Booth-Tucker revealed the contents of a secret correspondence between himself and Lowell. Noting the charity committee's aim to investigate all applicants for relief, Booth-Tucker explained to Lowell, and reiterated in an address to charity workers in New York, that the Army held "a radically different view." Army policy held that "If a man is willing to work he is worthy of being helped."[56]

> Mrs. Josephine Shaw Lowell, chairman of the committee, told me a man had no right to be homeless. What can one say to talk like that? I told her men were homeless and would always be so . . . Men starve while their agents are spending money finding out who they are. We settle that by dividing the homeless into two classes—those who are willing to work and those who are not. If a man is willing to work we do what we can for him. We can't find work for men and women in many cases, but we can relieve distress, and that's what we'll go on doing while they go on investigating.[57]

Booth-Tucker fundamentally disagreed with Lowell's claim that shelters encouraged vice, and he argued further that the Army's scheme was more economical than plans put forward by either public or private philanthropies. The city spent $11 million annually to take care of 150,000 poor people, and the charity committee's plan, if implemented, would cost $15 million. The price tag for the Army's scheme was a mere $7 million. Booth-Tucker never made clear why the Army plan was cheaper. One differential may have been labor costs; the Army's workers probably received less pay than either private or public employees.

"Keep the Pot Boiling" quickly became the Army's Christmas fundraising slogan. Here a Salvationist lassie and an elegant matron share an understanding look while a young girl gazes wistfully at the well-dressed woman. The three female figures—donor, doer, and recipient—cluster around the tripod, bound together in the act of charity. AWC, Dec. 13, 1902, 1, SAA

Christmas Kettles and Boozer Parades

Although Salvationists believed that a man should work for what he received, there were times, such as the bitterly cold winters of 1897 and 1899, when the Army provided emergency relief. Similarly, summer excursions organized primarily for women and children were free, although collections were taken after the day's requisite religious service. But the biggest giveaway in the Salvationist year was the Army's annual Christmas banquet. Whether motivated by shrewd public relations or by the belief that everyone deserved a chance for Christmas cheer, the Booth-Tuckers institutionalized and expanded the free holiday meals that previously had been served at local corps and slum posts.[58] The resulting extravaganza, at which several thousand people dined at long tables festooned with linen and china, was criticized by some charity movement leaders as redundant, pauperizing, and little more than a staged spectacle for Army contributors. But the banquets were popular with the public, and the Army's seasonal fundraising apparatus, the Christmas kettle, became emblematic of its vision of service.

The kettle made its debut in San Francisco in 1891. To finance a free Christmas dinner for the poor, an energetic soldier named Joseph McFee borrowed a large crab pot and hung it from a tripod on a busy street. Posting a sign, "Fill the Pot for the Poor—Free Dinner on Christmas Day," he collected enough spare change to feed more than 1,000 hungry citizens. McFee's innovation quickly spread across the country. In New York the Army had provided free Christmas dinners on a modest scale during the Ballington Booths' era. In 1893 the New York 1 Corps fed 250 people, and just two years later the corps provided meals for some 1,100 people with money donated by soldiers and friends. The Booth-Tuckers significantly enlarged the scale during their first American holiday season. They decorated a fifty-foot Christmas tree at National Headquarters and distributed 632 pairs of shoes and 132 pairs of stockings to needy children. Afterward youngsters received a free dinner and a chance to see Santa Claus. When Santa, who sported an Army band around his fur cap, was asked if he was saved, he enthusiastically replied, "You bet!"[59]

Santa Claus, kettles, and free food became the nucleus of the Army's Christmas fundraising scheme. The mix proved popular, as The *New York Press* noted: "Three gallon pots of money appeal to the imagination. None of the plans for raising funds for the Christmas of the city's poor seems to be more effective than these kettles on tripods with Santa Claus on guard, which the Salvation Army has placed in many conspicuous sidewalk positions." The kettles' appeal worked on several levels. The pot itself reminded passers-by of hearth and home, conjuring up warm images of winter nights, sturdy stews, and an older frontier generation. Moreover, it was not associated with a particular religious group, and its nonsectarian identity was reinforced by the presence of Santa Claus. The kettles also acted as a corporate logo, which standardized giving across space and time so that donors knew where their money was going whether they contributed in New York in 1898 or San Francisco in 1998.

Army leaders also understood that the kettles operated as a multivalent symbol. The author of "At the Sign of the Tripod" (1916) noted that "the boiling kettles, signifying plenty" were a "symbol" for the poor, for the rich, and for the spirit of Christmas. "In the tripod is focused the genius of The Salvation Army; in it concentrate all the high and holy impulses and moods in which the Spirit has manifested Himself in us."[60]

Contributions of nickels, dimes, and quarters fed some 20,000 people at the Army's first Christmas gala. The dinner, "the largest Christmas feast ever in New York City," was held at the Madison Square Garden. Chosen for its size and reputation ("the reputation of the Garden will give the scheme a certain dignity," noted the *War Cry*), the Garden was able to encompass all the holiday banquets that previously had taken place in local neighborhoods. By selecting a central and secular space, Army leaders sought to demonstrate that "the unsectarian character of the undertaking" was worthy of "help from every source." Before the dinner began, some 3,200 baskets, each filled with food for a family of five, were distributed to the "deserving poor without regard for race or creed." These recipients, who "would rather starve" than go to a public dinner, had received tickets from officers familiar with their situation. Those with less pride lined up for admittance to the Garden's large hall decorated with holly and mistletoe, flags, and banners. Seated in shifts of several hundred, diners enjoyed a splendid holiday banquet served by Army soldiers and officers. The abundant menu included turkey, beef, mutton, lamb, chicken, pork, potatoes, celery, turnips, onions, plum pudding, apples, oranges, bananas, and coffee.[61]

For the guests' entertainment, the Army's staff band went through its paces and a stereopticon show, illustrating Salvationist social work and the Oberammergau Passion Play, was screened. Meanwhile, even as the honored guests were treated to a festive holiday performance, they themselves provided entertainment, of a similarly uplifting variety, to spectators whom the Army invited to fill the hall's upper tiers. The *Times*, in the next day's lead story, noted the thousands of "well-fed and prosperous" onlookers, bedecked and bejeweled, "who looked on in happy sympathy." Some of these invitees, who included politicians, philanthropists, clergy, and society folk, were solicited by "pretty lassies" for donations. Others watched the feasting hordes with a jaundiced eye: "Some seemed to look upon this feeding of the ravens as a spectacle and whispered and pointed at poorly clad men and women who ate ravenously or smiled when a piece of turkey was surreptitiously slipped into a capacious pocket."[62]

Salvationist leaders hoped that the Christmas banquet would arouse sympathy for the poor and generate support for the movement's method of philanthropy. But in some quarters the banquet raised mostly criticism. In 1906 the charity official Edwin D. Solenberger, reiterating what others had said, faulted the Army for refusing to cooperate with other churches and agencies. As a result, he averred, its Christmas giveaways were redundant and its banquet a crass public relations ploy: "We cannot approve of the tendency to make such dinners public spectacles. At the big free dinner given by the Army at Grand Central Palace in New York City last Christmas, the boxes and balconies were thronged, according to the *War Cry* with well-dressed men and women who had come to see what a Salvation Army dinner was like. Does not this come dangerously near to exploiting the poor for the sake of advertising the Army?"[63]

The Army was undeterred by such charges. In 1900 its leaders increased the number of people fed and broadened their efforts to entertain. Flags from all nations hung from the Garden's ceiling and large banners proclaiming "Merry Christmas" and "Happy New Year" decorated the ends of the hall. At the head of a line that stretched several city blocks, the Commander and the Consul handed out some 3,500 Christmas baskets filled with "a fowl, four pounds of potatoes, an equal amount of turnips, beets, etc., a load of bread, coffee, sugar, salt, pepper, and apples." When Booth-Tucker realized there were many more people in line than there were baskets, he sent officers to scour neighborhood stores for food and directed them to assemble additional provisions. That evening some 4,000 guests dined at fifty long tables and were treated to music, speeches, stereopticon slides, and a visit from Santa Claus.[64]

In subsequent years the venue was changed to Grand Central Palace, and clothes and toys were also distributed. The connection between Christmas and the Army kettle became established in the public's mind, and the oft-repeated slogan "Keep the pot boiling" telegraphed the Army's intention to spread holiday cheer among the needy. As a philanthropic endeavor seeking broad public support, the Army continued to stress the nonsectarian nature of the banquet. Both secular and Salvationist press accounts signaled the diversity of the diners by printing names and imitating dialects that were clearly identifiable as Jewish and African American as well as ethnic Protestant and Catholic. Concomitantly, the press downplayed the religious component of the banquets. Accounts mentioned hymn-playing and speech-making, but little intentional proselytizing. Still, in an effort to assure *War Cry* readers that the banquets did have a spiritual aspect, the 1904 edition reported that the "religious end" of the celebration—hymn-singing and stereopticon views of the life of Jesus—resulted in 150 penitents. Espousing the "practical religion" that found its mission in the city streets, the writer celebrated the Army's ability to reach people where they were: "This is the religion of The Salvation Army, the creed deeper than dogma, whose vestments and ritual is righteousness, and whose theology is brotherly love, its pulpit the streetcorner and gutter, its pews and busy aisles the curb and pavements where surge the common people on whose backs are reared the pillars of all society."[65]

The Booth-Tuckers' positioning of the Army as a Christmas charity was a strategic coup. The bell-ringing lassie, the kettle, and the tripod symbolized love, service, and compassion amid the consumer frenzy. It was not an accident that the Army stationed soldiers and kettles near stores, theaters, and commercial centers. On one level the Army's presence was an attempt to redeem the holiday marketplace by placing religious claims alongside the acquisitive spirit that marked the season. But on another level the Army sought to profit from that very spirit of acquisition. The humble kettle was a silent reminder of what the holiday was really about. Tossing in a few coins was an easy way to assuage an uneasy conscience.

Just as Booth-Tucker linked the year's most significant holiday to the Salvationist cause, he also found a way to identify the Army with one of the era's most important social movements—the temperance crusade. From the Army's beginnings it had prohibited members from imbibing alcohol. Soldiers and officers were required to be teetotalers, and William Booth had ended the practice of Communion, citing as one reason that newly converted drunks might be tempted by wine. In England the Army's temperance stance had incurred the wrath of the liquor industry, which supported the Skeleton Armies' harassment of Army operations. No similarly motivated actions against Salvationists occurred in the United States, where the Army's anti-alcohol policy attracted little attention. Frances Willard, the head of the Women's Christian Temperance Union, was an early supporter of the Army, but Salvationists did not offer any official support either to her work or to her efforts to organize the Prohibition Party.

Nevertheless, the Army considered alcohol to be the cause of untold misery. *War Cry* stories explicitly condemned drinking as a blight on family life: inebriated mothers neglected children while drunken husbands beat their wives. Drunken men also seduced and betrayed young women, and, once fallen, women were prey to the bottle and tumbled further still. In Army narratives alcohol was evil and the remedy was individual conversion. The political goal of the temperance movement—banning the sale of liquor—was rarely mentioned. Thus when Booth-Tucker was asked in 1903 to address the Chautauqua Society on temperance, he admitted that although the Army had always "waged a ceaseless war against drink," he had never, in his twenty-two years as an officer, given or heard a temperance lecture.[66]

It was inevitable that the Army would be drawn into the temperance debate. During the 1890s Frances Willard won popular support for the Prohibition Party and came close to negotiating a merger with the Populists. When Willard lost momentum because her movement espoused causes other than temperance, the Anti-Saloon League, organized by churches in 1895, stepped into the political breach. At the same time, a growing number of states began passing prohibition laws. Booth-Tucker, keenly aware of opportunities for advancement, became more vocal in his denunciation of alcohol in the late 1890s. After all, The Salvation Army was, according to William Booth, the world's largest temperance organization.

In his Chautauqua address Booth-Tucker called the Army's work itself "a temperance lecture" and described the organization's zeal at pursuing drunkards in dives, saloons, and brothels. Moreover, he claimed, the Salvationists' strategy for redeeming alcoholics was successful; in the last ten years 10 percent of the Army's 400,000 conversions had been former drunks. But Booth-Tucker grounded the line of individual conversion in a larger social strategy. Distinguishing between cause and effect, he argued that alcohol was a problem when people lacked work, shelter, and food as well as salvation. The Army's solution was to open industrial homes where men could be rehabilitated and start anew. After Booth-Tucker's lecture the Army began to identify more with the temperance movement and to develop new strategies to help alcoholics. In 1904 the Army's hotel at Chatham Square in lower Manhattan opened a free clinic for alcoholics ready to fight their addiction. That same year the Drunkards Rescue Brigade began using stretchers to pick up drunks asleep on city streets and to bring them to a shelter where they could be helped.[67]

Under the leadership of Evangeline Booth, the Booth-Tuckers' successor, the Army expanded its fight against alcohol and actively supported Prohibition. Although the Army refused to publicly endorse the Prohibition Party or any other political group, Booth's words and deeds left no doubt about where her sympathies lay. In lectures and articles she emphasized repeatedly that a ban on liquor would diminish crime and other social evils.[68] Some observers even criticized her for being too vocal in her support for Prohibition. But the Army's efforts to help drunks kept pace with Booth's anti-alcohol platform. In the early 1900s some 75 percent of the men at the industrial homes were habitual drunkards, and Salvationists continuously sought new ways to help them.

In 1909 Colonel William McIntyre organized the first Boozers' Convention on Thanksgiving Day. Borrowing several of the city's double-decker buses, Salvationists collected drunks along the city streets. With the buses forming a parade, McIntyre enlivened the procession with several "bona-fide bums" chained to a water wagon, a ten-foot-tall walking whiskey bottle, and five brass bands. The parade ended up at National Headquarters, where a free dinner and a revival meeting led by converted drunks capped the day. In later years special efforts were made to include women among the boozers the Army brought in.

In an interview in 1915 McIntyre explained that Thanksgiving had been chosen as Boozers' Day because it was an important national holiday and a time when many people drank too much. But he was motivated as much by concern about existing soldiers as by solicitude for drunks. While visiting local corps McIntyre was struck by the absence of "up-to-date, striking conversions." Hoping to "kill two birds with one stone," he directed soldiers to round up drunks in the hope of stirring "mighty conversions." The subsequent meetings justified his plan. Converted drunks offered "thriller" testimonies, and many alcoholics sought the penitents' bench. The initiative was so successful that other cities duplicated New York's effort and continually expanded the Boozer's Day outreach until the passage of the Eighteenth Amendment.[69]

The Art of Advertising

Even as the Booth-Tuckers launched new social initiatives, they needed to find funds for their ambitious program of institution-building. Officers and soldiers still contributed during Self-Denial week, auxiliaries and supporters added pennies to the Mercy Boxes that the Consul suggested placing in every home, and worshipers at services were routinely asked for donations. During the Harvest Festival, first held in 1896, Salvationists collected food, clothing, and household items to sell at auction. At Christmas the kettle and tripod appeared on city streets. And in 1902 Booth-Tucker even asked the City of New York for money. Noting that the Army had never received an appropriation before, he explained that the $6,500 it spent caring for fallen women had saved the city from maintaining them as public charges. Booth-Tucker asked for $7,000 to continue the work, and he received $5,000.[70]

Booth-Tucker's success at incorporating the Army also helped with fundraising. After the Moore schism there had been no further attempts to incorporate the Army under American law. In fact, when the Booth-Tuckers took command, Ballington Booth held the title to all Army property and funds, and for a short time his successors worried that he might not hand it over. Although that transition was accomplished without incident, the gravity of the situation became clear to International Headquarters, and Booth-Tucker was allowed to pursue a legal change of status. The process took two years, complex political machinations, and a great deal of patience. In 1899 the Army was incorporated by the State of New York under a special act which differed from the general provision covering other religions and charities. The Army's special act of incorporation was modeled after similar legislation passed for the Roman Catholic church, which permitted the Pope to appoint trustees for the American church. Likewise, the Army's International Headquarters retained the authority to appoint and supervise the American effort.[71]

Booth-Tucker also led the American Army into several entrepreneurial ventures that paralleled Salvationist marketing and sales operations in London. The International Trade Headquarters in London was a seven-story building that exported household goods, furniture, musical instruments, bicycles, stationery, coal, and clothes around the world. The American Trade Department began as a modest operation. Initially, in the 1880s, it sold only uniforms, books, and musical instruments, but by the late 1890s its offerings included flags, mottoes, badges, watches, magic lanterns, stereopticons, stoves, and three varieties of tea. Under the leadership of Major Ransom Caygill, the department also expanded its clothing stock from caps and uniforms to shoes, mackintoshes, and outer wear. The Army shoe store, with an eye-catching show-window, enticed strollers passing by the 14th Street Headquarters. The twenty-man tailoring shop accepted outside work, as did the printing office. Together the departments brought in about $1,000 a week, which helped subsidize spiritual activities.[72]

Emma Booth-Tucker made certain that the women the Army assisted also contributed their share. When her plan to teach bookbinding to residents at Salvationist rescue homes succeeded, the Consul turned next to millinery work. Augmenting the Army's dressmaking capacity, she put reformed women to work making uniforms and bonnets as well as doing plain sewing for Army supporters and friends. At the heart of New York's shopping district, the Army factory produced 2,000 uniforms and 3,000 bonnets annually. Some 13,000 Salvationist women per year ordered clothing by mail order from New York. Delivery took just three weeks.[73]

Uniforms and bonnets, along with other Army products, were peddled in the back pages of the *War Cry*. The Army followed the standard advertising conventions of the day. A profusion of ornamental typefaces covered the page accompanied by short descriptive paragraphs and illustrations. Although these advertisements lacked the ornamentation that many secular advertisers used in the 1890s, they were similar to display ads that appeared in newspapers and magazines. In 1897, in a statement of its advertising credo, the Trade Department pledged to be honest and never to offer anything but the best possible products. Salvationists produced excellent facsimiles of secular ads, but they were wary lest they slip into deceptive practices or promote false values. Accordingly, they specified that their trade was conducted under different assumptions from those of the world: employees were saved, neither worldly nor sweated goods were sold, negotiations were truthful, and every penny went to save mankind.[74] In short, the Army was reliable:

[The advertiser] should always bear in mind one or two principles, the most important perhaps being: First: To say nothing in advertisements that he is not positive and absolutely sure of. Second: He should advertise nothing as being beneficial to another that he would not use himself. We can conscientiously say that we fill out those two important particulars to the very letter. Our word can be relied upon! When we say we have an article cheap our friends can rely upon it that we are not simply using the word "cheap" as a catch stock trade word, but the article mentioned is really a bona fide bargain.[75]

Until the Army incorporated, its financial state was difficult to gauge because there was no full or coordinated reporting on its nationwide activities. Typically, its annual reports included only funds handled at National Headquarters, showing revenue streams from the Trade Department, shelters, salvage sales, street collections, and special offerings. Contributions to and disbursements from the 700 local corps and social programs outside New York City were not tallied in the reports, although balance sheets were supposed to be available locally. When, as part of the incorporation process, the Army filed its first official Annual Report (covering May 31 to September 20, 1899) with New York's Secretary of State, it declared nationwide totals of $600,835 in property, $67,738 from shelters, $9,970 from salvage sales, and $12,549 from children's homes.[76]

The Booth-Tuckers' emphasis on providing social services multiplied the Army's property holdings and financial growth. Between 1896 and 1904, Army accommodations for the poor rose from 600 to 10,000 and the number of social service institutions increased from 30 to 209. In 1897 the Army's property holdings totaled about $650,000; seven years later, they amounted to $2,000,000.[77] Not surprisingly, financing Army work was a continuing concern. In the early twentieth century Salvationist leaders established two for-profit companies: the Reliance Trading Company in 1902 and the Salvation Army Industrial Homes Company in 1903.

The Trading Company, capitalized by $300,000 worth of stock, would "carry on and extend" the Army's American trade. The Industrial Homes Company, offering $500,000 in stock, sought to acquire property and extend the work of the Army's industrial homes, shelters, hotels, and restaurants. In both cases the Army retained the common stock and a small portion of the preferred stock. The remainder of the preferred stock was sold to the public. Shares were $10 apiece with a 6 percent annual dividend. Although both schemes generated money, their administration proved onerous. The corporate officers who were legally responsible for the ventures also belonged to Headquarters staff. Careful supervision of the companies' financial management proved to be a time-consuming task. Moreover, outsiders criticized the Army for setting up profitmaking businesses that generated significant dividends for investors. Internal demands and external criticism doomed the companies. The Industrial Homes Company was dissolved in 1912, a year after the demise of the Reliance Trading Company.[78]

The trade and industrial home schemes also seemed to generate problems among the Salvationist leadership. Few details can be found in Army sources, suggesting that leaders did not wish to advertise the dangers inherent in pursuing what critics called a worldly path. According to Edward H. McKinley, "something seemed to have gone seriously wrong between several high-ranking officers and The Salvation Army after the stock scheme was started." This was not the only time troublesome business transactions roiled Headquarters during the Booth-Tuckers' tenure. In November 1900 the Commander discovered that several of his top officers, "infected with the commercial spirit," were speculating in a Colorado mining company. Colonel William Brewer, the editor of the *War Cry,* was the group's ringleader and served secretly as the local manager of the Great Republic Gold Mining Company. When Booth-Tucker reminded Brewer and the others that Salvationists believed in laying up treasure for heaven, not in the here-and-now, the men promised to stop. Brewer turned over his interest in the mining company to Albert Hall, a compositor in the printing department who was not an Army officer.[79]

Two years later Booth-Tucker found out that Brewer was still speculating, now through the Albert E. Hall Company. Engaged in selling highly speculative and unlisted stocks, Brewer had even convinced some Army members to invest their own meager savings. Since Army officers signed an agreement stipulating that they would not be involved in moneymaking ventures or get-rich-quick schemes, Brewer was doubly culpable—not only had he himself sinned but he had enticed others to join him. Forced to resign from the Army, Brewer leveled his own charges at Booth-Tucker. Echoing accusations that others had made before (though none were ever proven), Brewer accused the Commander of misappropriating funds, indulging in extravagant conduct, and creating a two-tier system that benefited the National Staff at the expense of the field officers. As in the past, Booth-Tucker denied the charges by impugning the integrity of the one who made them.[80]

In october 1903 Emma Booth-Tucker was killed in a train wreck while traveling from the Army's farm colony in Colorado to meet her husband in Chicago. The *War Cry* eulogized her as "the incarnation of true womanhood."[81] The secular press seemed to agree:

The subject in which Mrs. Booth-Tucker took the least interest was, perhaps, the great feminist movements of her generation. For all practical purposes, the movement for equal suffrage, the women's club movement, and the higher education of women did not so much exist for her. She never voted, and no one can ever remember ever hearing her express a wish to vote. Women's clubs did not interest her. She herself was the president of a woman's club which included thousands of members in Europe, Asia, Africa, and America. She never talked women's rights. She took them. She was accustomed to the respect, the admiration, and obedience of the men she met, and she seems to have been as little given to theorizing about the political or social relations of men and women as she was over the training of children. With a temperament emphatically masterful and militant, she did the things, says Ensign Carr, "that other women talk about."[82]

Emma Booth-Tucker both built on and ignored Maud Booth's ideas about gender. By embodying the womanly woman, one who saw her work in the world as a form of enlarged moral housekeeping, Emma provided a safe vision of Salvationist womanhood which bridged the Victorian and Progressive eras. Moreover, her privacy, piety, and devotion to family reinforced the image of respectability that Maud and other female officers had projected. But Emma had no interest in promoting "Women Warriors," Maud Booth's term for independent, self-reliant Salvationist women. Neither did the Consul advise male Salvationists on domestic self-reliance. Yet during Emma's tenure the public vision of the lassies (not just the top officers) improved. Army women gained a new respectability along with a sincere admiration for their self-sacrificing work.

After his wife's death Booth-Tucker's grief made it difficult for him to continue leading the American army. Within a year he returned to England and went to work at the Army's Foreign Desk. Several years later he remarried and returned to India with his third wife and children. There he spent a dozen years until he was recalled home, where he served out the rest of his career at International Headquarters.

The years of the Booth-Tuckers' tenure, from 1896 to 1904, were a time of transition for The Salvation Army in America. Building on the Ballington Booths' legacy, Frederick and Emma further enhanced the Army's image with the public. They also refashioned that image, casting the Army's philanthropic work alongside its religious mission. Their success was reflected in the praise of Christian social activists who, preaching a message of individual and social salvation, cited the Army as a model for balancing these dual goals. No doubt Salvationists seemed to combine the best of both worlds. Their religious impulse provided a flexible and humane dimension to philanthropic ventures that more secular efforts, such as the Charity Organization Society, lacked. Likewise, the Army's humanitarian emphasis gave its religious work an immediacy that most churches sorely needed. Given the temper of the times—an era fraught with social problems, rapid industrial change, and a pervasive, if fragmented, religious sensibility—The Salvation Army offered an appealing vision that penetrated all aspects of life. In keeping with its earlier attempts to saturate public space, the industrial homes and farm colonies now filled moral discursive space. At the same time, Salvationist leaders had become aware of the need to project their movement into physical space. The cathedral of the open air was still important, but buildings—concrete embodiments of mission inscribed on the city landscape—were a growing priority.

Even greater changes loomed on the horizon. Whereas the Booth-Tuckers operated within a world view consistent with nineteenth-century evangelical values, their successor, Evangeline Booth, encountered a changing cultural consensus accelerated by the new century. The Army's signature performance, as staged by its leaders and acted out by its officers, would shift again. In "Love and Sorrow," Emma Booth-Tucker illustrated the Army's commitment to the poor by describing its work with society's most needy. In "The Commander in Rags," Evangeline Booth's best-known dramatic monologue, the Army leader embodied a new synthesis of religion and service, making more explicit the Army's role in serving middle- and upper-class interests by assuaging the needs of the poor.

4

THE COMMANDER IN RAGS

1904–1918

THE OPENING of The Salvation Army's Annual Congress of 1906, advertised as a benefit for the victims of the San Francisco earthquake, drew a large crowd of curiosity-seekers. Seated in the audience at New York's 6,000-seat Hippodrome theater, uniformed Salvationists rubbed shoulders with the city's elite. As the orchestra warmed up, its mellifluous tones intimated that this was not going to be one of the Army's rollicking streetcorner services but rather a symphony-caliber performance. Promptly at 8 PM the curtain opened and singers clad in hooded robes of crimson and white mounted the illuminated stage to form a huge red-rimmed cross. The room darkened, and a single shaft of blue light picked out a woman dressed in rags. Slowly making her way to the center of the stage, the slender figure was flanked by fifty gingham-dressed slum sisters.

The costumed waif was none other than Evangeline Booth, Commander of the American branch of The Salvation Army and one of the few female denominational leaders in the early twentieth century. On this night Booth was using New York's largest stage to present one of her acclaimed pageant-sermons. Massed bands, songsters, and soloists were integral to the recitation along with lighting effects and props of all kinds—including live lambs, sheep and, on at least one occasion, a horse.[1] This evening's presentation, "The Commander in Rags" (alternatively referred to as "The Four Keys" and "The Tale of a Broken Heart"), was the story of service and salvation. Like the Booth-Tuckers' illustrated

Evangeline Booth as the Commander in Rags. AWC, Feb. 3, 1906, 1,
SAA

lecture "Love and Sorrow," it was a dramatic performance staged in a
commercial theater. But Evangeline Booth's lecture was much more of an
extravaganza than her sister's had been; moreover, it put her, not the
Army, at the center of the narrative. "The Commander in Rags" combined the expository quality of "Love and Sorrow" with the revival em-

phasis of "The Red Crusade." But contemporary accounts indicate that it was more successful at inspiring audiences to support the Army than at securing their conversions.

In the lecture Booth recalled her experience as a teenager in London's East End, where, working among the poor, she was dubbed "The White Angel of the Slums." When she performed the lecture on stages across the country, promotional materials announced that the "Commander Miss Booth" would "tell the tale of a broken heart and sing the song of love." But her real message was the need for action. Love was vital, sacrifice necessary, but action was preeminent. As the *War Cry* declared: "It is not even enough that we sacrifice. We must do—do with our hands, do with our lives, do with our money, do with our influence. Action, action! Religion in action, this is what the world needs—religion alive, religion living among the people, religion going about doing good as well as singing hymns."[2]

In the midst of the Progressive Era, an action-oriented age, The Salvation Army was known first and foremost as an action-oriented religion. It was hailed by members of the press, from the pulpit, and in the political arena for its shelters, employment bureaus, and rescue homes as well as its quick response to urgent needs. Whether providing free breakfasts to New York's poorest schoolchildren or finding jobs for the casualties of an economic depression, Evangeline Booth made certain that the Army took the lead. Theodore Roosevelt, the era's quintessential action hero, summed up the sentiments of Army supporters: "There are few serious thinkers nowadays who do not recognize in the Salvation Army an invaluable social asset, a force for good which works effectively in those dark regions where, save for this force, only evil is powerful."[3]

In "The Commander in Rags," Evangeline Booth's skillful mixing of elements from pageants, sermons, and public lectures captivated audiences who might not have responded to a religious service. And even as her performances inspired some listeners to commit to Christ and others to support the Army, Booth's presentations were also instrumental in reshaping public discussion about the organization she headed. Between the mid-1880s and World War I the American image of The Salvation Army changed from a vulgar, ragtag religious mission to a respected provider of social services. Several factors predating Evangeline Booth's tenure expedited this transformation, including the astute public relations as well as the accomplishments of her predecessors and the warm critical reception garnered by William Booth's *In Darkest England and the Way Out*. But most significantly, Booth, whose service as the American Army's commander lasted thirty years, stamped the organization in her own image. Even as she facilitated the Army's institutionalization by overseeing the acquisition of property, the systematization of fundraising, and the creation of a strong, centralized bureaucracy, Booth gave the Army a human face—her own. Through performances such as "The Commander in Rags" and a steady barrage of coverage in Army publications and the secular press, Evangeline Booth conflated her identity with that of the movement she led.

"The Commander in Rags" was Booth's tour de force, elaborating on her work in the London slums as a trope for the Army. In the dramatic light cast by her role as tattered angel, Booth hoped to make audiences see The Salvation Army with new eyes—as an exemplar of love, sympathy, sacrifice, and action. Although the first three were fundamental Christian virtues, action was the Army's special contribution. Through repeated performances around the nation, Booth's emphasis on an action-oriented Christianity became the hallmark of the Army's identity in an age when Americans sought active solutions for society's ills. Her performances, augmented by the public relations savvy learned from her father and honed by experts including Bruce Barton and John Wanamaker, helped consolidate the Army's reputation while propelling Booth to celebrity-hood. Charles L. Ponce de Leon has described "celebrity discourse" as the product of media professionals' transforming individuals into "symbols of larger developments and trends" that also bridge the distance between the "masses" and the "classes."[4] Evangeline's performances demonstrated both. Her performed persona symbolized the animating religious spirit of the Progressive era while also encompassing differences in class, gender, and ideology.

The Founder's Daughter

Evangeline Cory Booth was born in London on December 25, 1865. Catherine Booth chose the name Eva after the heroine of *Uncle Tom's Cabin,* but William Booth registered the newborn as Eveline. Called Eva by her family, she adopted the name Evangeline in later life after the temperance crusader Frances Willard suggested that it sounded more distinguished for a leader. The seventh of eight children, Evangeline grew up in a home where religious work was central. By age five she was preaching to her dolls, and several years later William Booth discovered his young daughter propped on a chair, exhorting the kitchen staff.[5]

Historians have tended to be dismissive or patronizing in their estimations of Evangeline Booth's character. Interviews for Margaret Troutt's biography *The General Was a Lady* (1980) portray her as quirky and demanding, but negative characterizations of Booth's personality reveal as much about cultural attitudes toward women in power as about Booth herself. Evangeline Booth was a complex individual who often used her public platform to explore her own conflicting feelings about class and gender identity. While noting her kindness, her administrative ability, and her platform skills, biographers routinely describe her as imperious, vain, and histrionic.[6] Difficult to categorize, she comfortably wielded culturally defined masculine traits of leadership and command while also engaging in small acts of kindness and the attention to details that seemed more characteristically feminine. Unlike Maud or Emma Booth, Evangeline did not project a strong maternal image. Neither did she defer to a husband or share her power. In short, Evangeline Booth eluded conventional classifications. She was a "womanly woman" who led a religious movement defined by the rhetoric of war. She enjoyed life's luxuries while portraying herself as one who had lived among the poor. She was a shrewd politician, fundraiser, and institution builder who also professed the primacy of spiritual salvation.

Booth said she had been called by God at an early age. In an anecdote recorded in P. W. Wilson's authorized biography she described a childhood incident that spurred a religious awakening. As with many of the recollections in Wilson's account, Booth herself provided the dramatic details. (She said she never wrote an autobiography because she was too busy living her life.) The family's cook took her to an exhibition of religious paintings, where a scene of Jesus on the cross reduced her to tears. Turning to another picture, Booth was struck by a sinner calling out to Christ.

"Why doesn't he throw those evil things away from himself," I asked.

"You can't throw evil things away from yourself without the help of Jesus Christ," said my companion.

"Do they cling too hard?"

"Yes."

In this picture my child's logic saw the reason for the cruelty to Christ on the cross, and my own future spread out before me. My life should be lived for the poor, the wicked, the helpless—they should have my life—have it all.[7]

Evangeline Booth's public ministry began when she was still a teenager, and she quickly established herself as a compelling speaker gifted at subduing hostile crowds. At eighteen she was stationed in the impoverished Marylebone section of London, where she won the hearts of local children by opening a shop to repair broken toys. To reach the adults she conceived a more dramatic plan. Dressed as a flower girl, she "worked" Piccadilly Circus to gain first-hand knowledge about how the poor lived. Years later, as "The Commander in Rags," Booth recalled this period with evocative stories of the people she befriended. At the age of twenty-three Booth became the principal of the Army's International Training College in London, and her next assignment was Army Field Commissioner for Great Britain.

While working in the London slums, Booth met Major Thomas McKie, a dynamic young officer who was smitten by her. By the time she became Field Commissioner, Booth reciprocated his love. McKie asked William Booth for his daughter's hand in marriage, but the General refused, saying it was an unsuitable match because both had similar high-strung temperaments. (According to some accounts, brother Bramwell was behind the refusal.) Although she could have married without her father's approval, Evangeline accepted his advice. In later life, when asked if she had considered marriage, Evangeline responded that she had, and quipped, "That's why I am single."[8]

During these years the young Miss Booth blossomed into the woman whose potent presence would stir crowds for the next six decades. At five feet, eight inches, she was an attractive woman with flowing auburn hair, dark luminous eyes, and a strong, aquiline nose. Colleagues described her as handsome and meticulous about her grooming. As the Army's American Commander, Booth had silk-lined uniforms handmade by a French seamstress. She enjoyed athletics and music, composing hymns and playing harp, guitar, and concertina. But her favorite activity was her role as Salvationist leader. Contemporaries said the stage lost a great actress when Booth made the Army her vocation, and the Commander hinted she had been tempted otherwise: "My parents didn't know how much their work, and devotion had stirred me. They were always afraid I might leave the Army, and as I grew older they even suspected I might go on stage because—well, I had a bit of good looks, and a gift for speaking. Besides, I was no cold, prudish creature. But I was never tempted into the world—at least, not too much. It's interesting to be tempted a little."[9]

Booth's flair also found expression in her personal courage. Her disregard for her own safety induced William Booth to deploy his daughter as a troubleshooter wherever Army activities were impeded by unfriendly mobs. The perceived wisdom of the decision to "Send Eva!" was the reason for her trip to New York in 1896 during the Ballington Booth crisis. Although her presence irritated Maud and Ballington, the strategy proved effective when Evangeline held public meetings before audiences unsettled by the couple's defection. Waving an American flag at hostile crowds, Evangeline challenged, "Hiss this if you dare." Once quieted, listeners were captivated by her dramatic oratory. By the time the Booth-Tuckers arrived, Evangeline had reasserted the International Army's control.

Later that same year William Booth chose Evangeline as Territorial Commissioner for Canada and Newfoundland. The Canadian Army was at a low point when she arrived, and, by garnering support from people of means while also reaching out to the masses, she bolstered its reputation. Booth's popularity grew as she traveled around the country. Her accomplishments included organizing and accompanying a mission and a nursing corps to the Klondike.[10] Among the Canadian Army's loyal ranks was one Minnie Kennedy, the mother of Aimee Semple McPherson. Young Aimee grew up in the Army, and her own ministry reflected the drama and theatrics that marked Evangeline's performances. During Booth's Canadian tenure her household came to resemble an extended family. After informally adopting three children in England, she took in a fourth when she settled in Canada.[11] Also in her entourage were Major Mary Welch and Lieutenant Richard Griffiths. Welch, nicknamed "Gipsy" because of her dark hair and bright eyes, had lived with the Booth family in London and remained with Evangeline for the next sixty years. Griffiths joined the staff in Canada. As Welch took care of Evangeline's household, Griffiths—her personal secretary for more than forty years—presided over her professional life.

Booth stayed in Canada for eight years. In 1904, when Frederick Booth-Tucker returned to England, William Booth transferred her to the United States. By that time the Army's street parades were a familiar sight and its delivery of social services was growing, but the organization's assets and properties were limited. Seeking to place the Army on firmer financial ground and to bolster its image, Booth made it a priority to acquire impressive buildings rather than continue renting rundown premises for local corps and social services. Her campaign was facilitated by her ability to move in elite circles. William and Catherine Booth had grown up in artisan and working-class homes, but the Army's success had enabled them to live a middle-class life. Moreover, Army fundraising efforts and William Booth's social reform policies had thrust him and his family into upper-class circles. Raised in this fluid environment, Evangeline Booth had complex class sympathies. Although her speeches dwelt on her great love for the poor, she lived among the rich. Acadia, her home in Hartsdale, New York, abutted the estate of the banker Felix Warburg, where she daily rode her horse Golden. Camp Cory, her summer retreat at Lake George, was close to the property of another friend, the owner of the *New York Times,* Adolph Ochs. Booth enjoyed beautiful things and decorated Acadia with care. Among her prized possessions was a four-poster French mahogany bed, a gift from the Army's longtime supporter John Wanamaker.[12]

Booth's reputation grew as she involved the Army in the issues of the day. Her vocal support for Prohibition, a movement whose grassroots popularity did not preclude political controversy, was criticized by some as religious meddling in politics. But her swift responses to emergencies and disasters, including the San Francisco earthquake of 1906, raised the Army's status in American eyes: Salvationists were on the scene when and where they were needed. Booth was also a good steward. When she arrived in New York, Army property was valued at $1.5 million; when she left thirty years later, that figure had risen to $48 million plus a capital account of $35 million. But she was less successful at attracting new soldiers. The Army's early growth stalled as the novelty wore off and National Headquarters could not regularly provide adequate subsidies for field officers.

During the 1910s Booth expanded the Army's social programs and spotlighted its campaigns against white slavery, alcohol, and cigarettes— all issues of the day. But the Army's public image received its biggest boost when General John Pershing granted permission for it to provide social and welfare work to American troops during World War I. Instructing her officers to find out what soldiers needed, Booth surmised from their reports that a woman's touch would be welcome at the front lines. Accordingly, she sought young women to "mother" the troops and stationed them close to battle. No more than 250 Salvationists actually served in France, but the accolades they received far outstripped their numbers. Setting up "huts" near the soldiers' camps, Salvation Army lassies—nicknamed Sallies—sewed clothes, banked paychecks, and prayed with the men going off to fight. The strategy's success catapulted the Army into national prominence. Evangeline Booth achieved a place equal to her father's in the public eye.

Booth's biographers and Salvation Army historians have noted the strong affinity between Evangeline and William Booth. They had similar physical characteristics and similar temperaments. Both were gifted with a raw, spellbinding energy which commanded the loyalty of subordinates and captured the hearts of the masses. Evangeline understood from an early age how much her father loved her, and even his decision to discourage her marriage to McKie failed to affect the bond, which she poignantly described after his death: "The loss of my precious father has almost shattered me. I can't yet realize it. As I think you know he was everything to me. After God, I lived for him, thought for him, worked for him and as yet I cannot realize he is not more with me here."[13]

Seen from another angle, this bond defined Evangeline, as one of her colleagues told Margaret Troutt: "And her way of identifying herself. She used to take about five minutes to do this. When speaking about her relationship to the Founder, she would say, 'The Founder of The Salvation Army—William Booth. William Booth was my father. Now I am not a niece; mind you, I am not the daughter of the sister of the Founder. You must understand very clearly that the Founder of the Salvation Army had this daughter, Evangeline Booth. And I am Evangeline Booth.'"[14]

The Founder's daughter patterned her life after his. While most women learn gender differences from their cultural milieu, including its social institutions and discourses, Evangeline's early acquisition of power and authority mitigated against her wholesale acceptance of a feminine role. She also had access to models of behavior and to vocational opportunities that were denied to most women. She never attended school; she and her siblings were tutored at home. She was not a member of a traditional church, nor did she participate in social activities that reinforced notions of women's subordination or promoted marriage as the only appropriate goal for women. Given this freedom of self-definition, Evangeline began to "perform" herself, creating a public narrative on her own terms. Much of her identity was constructed through relationships which she later dramatized, such as her experiences with the poor in "The Commander in Rags."

In "Rags" Booth used herself, her body, as a bridge between the classes. By embodying the Cockney flower girl, she defused class antagonism and gave poverty a human face. Booth's performance provided a valuable service: it drew attention to suffering and offered an appealing religious gloss to the Army's philanthropic work. But the performance also served Evangeline by allowing her to enact conflicting impulses: her attraction to leadership, wealth, and power versus her identification with the suffering poor. Just as "The Commander in Rags" expressed Booth's divided class sympathies, "My Father" bound together her conflicting notions of gender. A dramatic recitation with slides and motion pictures, "My Father" was among her most popular lectures. While celebrating William Booth's accomplishments, it reinforced Evangeline's link to him. Dramatizing her appropriation of her father's identity, the performance enabled her to create a self made up of both male and female traits. In addition, it provided an acceptable framework of daughterly devotion to bolster the dynastic authority of her own leadership.

Taught since childhood to command, Booth was forthright and decisive. The Salvation Army was a family business; moreover, it was a public arena in which strength and power were paramount. Its inspiration may have been religious, but maintaining the organization—supplying bricks and mortar, recruiting soldiers and sponsors—required the secular skills of institution-building. These Booth mastered: among her greatest accomplishments were raising money and acquiring real estate. Yet, while her command reflected an ease with masculine notions of leadership style and authority, Evangeline's rhetoric reflected a feminine sensibility. Her speeches drew on images of love, nature, and family. Even when she adopted the masculine discourse of social progress, she inflected her message with the female language of reform. In "The Salvation Army Appraises Prohibition" she noted that the best argument for the liquor ban was "the vital statistics of insurance companies." But she concluded with reasons that would have resonated with Frances Willard: "The women of America do not tolerate an inebriated manhood. It is no mere coincidence that the Eighteenth Amendment, prohibiting liquor, should have been historically simultaneous with the Nineteenth Amendment, giving the vote to women, and should have preceded by a few years only the proposed Twentieth Amendment, drafted to abolish child labor. These legislative enactments and proposals are, all of them, parts of a general movement toward the defense of domestic life against the destroying menace of selfishness in the environment."[15]

A supporter of women's suffrage, Booth extolled new opportunities for women, yet she also advocated traditional notions of female moral and religious superiority. In a pamphlet entitled "Woman" she acknowledged the spread of the women's movement around the world and celebrated the possibilities it offered, including the right to choose a fulfilling career over a feckless marriage. But the Commander also urged women not to abandon their most precious legacy: fostering and safeguarding religious faith. In language updating Maud Booth's argument that the real New Woman was one reborn through Jesus Christ, Evangeline Booth offered her description of Christian feminism:

> For what we call the women's movement is not social merely, not political merely, not economic merely. It is the direct fulfillment of the gospel of the Redeemer. It was Jesus who taught the world the full lesson of what is meant by chivalry to women. It was He Who, at the well of Samaria, talked with the oft-divorced woman and told her of a God Whom she could worship in spirit and in truth . . .
>
> Happy, then, is the woman who realizes, even in these days of enfranchisement, that her life, however abundant it may be, is still hidden in the Christ of God.[16]

In many ways Booth enacted masculine behavior while espousing feminine ideals. Like many of her contemporaries, including Frances Willard and Jane Addams, Booth paid homage to women's traditional homemaking role while casting it in a broader context: "We women have made many homes in the world. But we have now the task of changing the world into a home."[17] Even so, Booth never bound herself to that role in exactly the same way she proposed for others. As the Founder's daughter, she played by a different set of rules.

Mothers and Sisters

Evangeline Booth was not alone in her efforts, intentional or otherwise, to negotiate and transcend the limits of gender expectations for women during this era. The growth of cities and subsequent employment opportunities for women complicated Victorian notions about women's sphere and role in society. Kathy Peiss has argued that young working-class women in turn-of-the-century New York "experimented with new cultural forms that articulated gender in terms of sexual expressiveness and social interaction with men, linking heterosocial culture to a sense of modernity, individuality, and personal style."[18] Such women were drawn to "cheap amusements"—dancing, excursions, amusement parks, and movies—which embodied independence and autonomy while also offering opportunities for pleasure and romance. Peiss points out that "cheap amusements" had a double edge: while providing a sense of autonomy, they also tied women to the consumer market. This new market culture, vaunting fashion, freedom, style, and fun, stood in direct opposition to older notions of womanhood.

Throughout the nineteenth century the dominant gender discourse had delineated a "woman's sphere," which considered women's responsibility to home, family, and religion to be her paramount duty. By the end of the century, however, that traditional definition of womanhood was increasingly contested. Many middle-class club women, reformers, and religious workers used the older rhetoric of domesticity to justify "moral housekeeping" in the civic arena. Seeking to inscribe the bonds of home and family onto the society at large, they touted women's ability to transform their poor and working-class sisters into religious paragons and proper homemakers through the power of "motherly" love and "sisterly" compassion. At the same time, they aimed to instill in the recipients of their benevolence the belief that women's moral superiority was grounded in feminine virtues such as modesty, chastity, and piety.

But reformers were hard-pressed to appeal to young women giddy with new possibilities. They tried offering entertaining alternatives to commercial amusements. The Army sponsored a ten-day summer vacation for working girls; other religious organizations provided reading rooms and social clubs. But these held limited appeal. More exciting was the frisson of social and financial independence that accompanied expanded opportunities for employment. In 1900 nearly one-third of New York's 343,000 female wage earners were between sixteen and twenty years old; four-fifths of these women were single, and a majority were either immigrants themselves or the daughters of foreign-born parents.[19] It seemed to many women of this generation that money could buy a new and better identity. Status was sold in the marketplace; department stores peddled cheap copies of *haute couture* clothes and convincing knockoffs of Fifth Avenue furniture. Adventure could be purchased as well—entertainments ranging from Coney Island excursions to evenings at a nickelodeon offered chances for sociability and courting. The working-class embodiment of the New Woman intuited that the future was hers—even as surrounding voices grew shrill with concern and criticism. In particular, that criticism centered on the alleged demise of home and family, the presumed result of a decline in spiritual values spurred by young women's increasing independence.

Among the voices of concern and criticism was Evangeline Booth's. Despite the equality of ministerial opportunity offered to Salvationist lassies, the Army still upheld Victorian notions of womanhood. Twenty years earlier Maud Booth had evoked the image of women warriors as militant fighters who nevertheless, like Jesus, retained their modesty. But Evangeline promoted a softer model for her female troops. Although she supported suffrage and women's rights, she maintained the home-centered discourse of mothers and sisters when describing the role of female Salvationists. Such descriptions were not new in the Army, but the historical context had changed. In the 1880s critics had routinely described lassies as coarse and unrefined, casting aspersions on their sexual morality. By the 1910s a slew of popular movies used female Salvationists to represent a wholesome, religious impulse that could transform even the most wayward man.[20]

Booth's concern about changing gender roles was expressed in myriad ways. Even as the type of service provided by Salvationist slum sisters and rescue workers was being professionalized by growing numbers of social workers, she expanded Army relief programs. In 1906 she dedicated the Cherry Street Settlement House, a five-story brick building that Salvationists erected near the site of their first slum post in lower Manhattan. Borrowing techniques from the secular settlement house movement, the Army set up a neighborhood center with laundry room, public meeting hall, kindergarten, day nursery, and clubs for working girls. Eventually sewing classes, Bible study, and children's clubs were added. A close reading of the *War Cry* suggests a contested framework for social welfare activities of this period. An article in 1911 indicated that Salvationists used the same procedures as social workers: slum officers investigated each of the 16,000 cases they had materially aided. Likewise, the slum settlement did not coddle: there were no breadlines, soup tickets, or give-aways. However, a piece in 1913 described the free distribution of bread, vegetables, meat, and fish four times each week. Although most recipients were known to settlement officers, even those who were unfamiliar were "ask[ed] no great questions: they [the officers] are not professional investigators: their passion is to help." Actual Salvationist practice seems to have varied between these two poles of scientific social work and indiscriminate religious charity, as workers tried to define their place in changing circumstances and also to serve the poor.[21]

Yet, whether motivated by the tough-mindedness of a social worker or the boundless compassion of a saint, the slum sisters' ministrations were defined by the female roles of domestic, nurse, and mother: "She is that much-vaunted individual, an all-round woman is the slum sister. She can wash, iron, evolve a dinner from a few pennies and cook it appetizingly; she can scrub a room and give a lecture on hygiene at the same time. She is an admirable nurse and can render 'first aid to the injured.' The newborn babies are laid in her tender arms and she performs the last sad rites for the dead."[22]

Of greater scope and the site for even more explicit representations of gender was the Army's rescue work. Salvationist outreach to "fallen women," that is, prostitutes and unmarried mothers, began in 1884 when Florence Booth, Bramwell's wife, opened a Rescue Home in London. Plans for a home in New York were announced the following year, and Morris Cottage, an Army haven for "fallen women," opened in 1886. Before long the *War Cry* reported that Morris Cottage had attracted enough residents to warrant expansion. Rescue work faded from view sometime after the Army's initial success, but the outreach resumed under the Ballington Booths.[23]

Maud Booth stressed the work's familial dimensions. The door of the rescue home was always open; residents were free to leave if they wanted. *War Cry* narratives, whether fictional or depicting "real life," usually presented "fallen women" as innocent victims "more sinned against than sinning."[24] Many were betrayed by unscrupulous men, who either abandoned them or sold them to brothels. Others were led astray by commercialized entertainments; the dance hall and the theater were particularly dangerous places. Lassies, convinced that most fallen women would choose an alternative if it was sympathetically presented, trolled brothels, saloons, and the midnight streets to plead with their lost sisters. In an early report on the Army's midnight campaigns, Commissioner Frank Smith noted that one lassie, storming "a den of infamy," was informed by the proprietor "that this is no place for a lady." She replied, "'I know that. That is why I am here. I want that girl,' pointing her finger to a fine, pale-faced form, shrinking into a corner." In the 1890s the outreach became more systematized when a training garrison opened in upper Manhattan to prepare female officers for rescue work.[25]

When the Booth-Tuckers assumed command they tripled the number of rescue homes in six years, from seven to twenty-one. In addition to opening a New York home at the site of Phoebe Palmer's former house, Emma Booth-Tucker oversaw the creation of a women's industrial home where residents learned skills such as bookbinding, fancy needlework, and expert dressmaking. Whereas Maud Booth had sought to place reformed prostitutes as servants in Christian homes, Emma Booth-Tucker recognized the need for other options. Fallen women from the middle and upper classes looked down on domestic service, and their best hope lay in finding meaningful work: "If a girl turns away from a life of vice . . . she must have something more attractive than that life to hold her. She isn't always in the grip of strong religious conviction. She is human. She wants work she can love and take pride in. Put her at work she loathes and in an environment she hates and you are likely to make virtue so unattractive that she will go back to vice."[26]

When Evangeline Booth took charge of the American forces in 1904, the problem of vice in New York City was a public concern. Several municipal commissions had documented the extent of prostitution and proposed various solutions. Timothy Gilfoyle argues that interest in prostitution was widespread because it signified a range of urban problems including municipal corruption, housing reform, health reform, and liquor reform.[27] The interest in prostitution also reflected growing apprehension about women's changing roles. Economic self-sufficiency, political autonomy, and heterosocial expressiveness threatened to make all women, like prostitutes, independent from men and from the home. Both the prostitute and the New Woman challenged the pervasive construction of woman's place as helpmeet and moral arbiter. Both also threatened assumptions about gender that, underlying social roles, defined women's "true nature" as physically delicate, intellectually limited and sexually uninterested.

Seeking to combat the threat to religion and domesticity posed by this alternate view of womanhood, The Salvation Army subtly conflated images of the prostitute and the independent working girl. Both needed the restorative influence of motherly guidance and sisterly compassion. That influence could be found in Army-sponsored hotels for working girls and rescue homes for fallen women. Both sets of institutions were intended to protect residents from the siren song of pleasure, a new social value legitimating the self-oriented enjoyment obtained from participation in the commercial culture. Pleasure contravened duty, and in an interview in 1911 Evangeline Booth warned that its pursuit led to a dangerous loss of women's spiritual authority. Citing the rising numbers of women who smoked, drank, gambled, and attended motion pictures, Booth decried their eagerness to be "smart" and "up-to-date." As an antidote she proposed opening more Army-sponsored homes to instill the kind of "character education" that would enable women to find contentment as "model housewives and good mothers."[28]

The same explicitly formative goal motivated other evangelical rescue groups, which like the Army, switched their focus from prostitutes to unmarried mothers during the early decades of the twentieth century. The Army had always defined "fallen women" broadly, including drunks, drug addicts, and homeless women as well as prostitutes in the category.

But as Regina Kunzel notes, neither the Army's nightly outreach to street-walkers nor its standing offer to rehabilitate first-time offenders filled enough of its beds.[29] Moreover, as the image of prostitute shifted from victim to criminal, a change spurred by social and economic changes in the Progressive era, the unmarried mother better suited the melo-dramatic role of the "fallen woman." Victimized by her own expecta-tions—whether of sexual autonomy, gender equality, or economic independence—the unmarried mother demonstrated that the social order had not really changed. Men still betrayed women and women still suf-fered the consequences.

Building on the familiar Victorian construction of sisterhood, women taking care of one another and delineating a sphere that they could over-see, Salvationists used the rhetoric of home to define optimal social rela-tionships. To explain why an Army rescue home succeeded when other attempts failed, Evangeline Booth quoted an unnamed philanthropist who turned over the operation of his rescue home to the Army: "The tone of that place was uplifted from one of patronage to sisterliness. Our matron and her assistants were good and pious women, but had looked on the inmates as beings apart. They were 'fallen women' that was the conscious spirit. The Army sisters came and all that changed. Nothing more was heard of 'fallen women'; it was sister to sister."[30]

At the head of the rescue work was the formidable Brigadier Emma Bown. When approached by a reporter who, without identifying herself, appealed for help, Bown grasped the woman's hands: "You are in trouble, my child? Don't hesitate to tell me. Let me be your mother for the mo-ment." Disarmed by such sincerity, the reporter confessed that her curios-ity had brought her to the home. Although the Brigadier disliked "her girls" being the object of journalistic scrutiny, she gave the reporter a tour. Residents included "every condition" of womanhood—a mix of un-spoiled country girls, deserted wives, unemployed working women, the homeless, and those escaping a life of vice. There was a "beautiful young Italian, a negress, a refined-looking older woman, and an emaciated, young mother." The door was open to all. No questions were asked.[31]

Employing the gendered rhetoric of reform to win new supporters for the rescue work, Evangeline Booth appealed to the Federation of Women's Clubs for assistance. Mrs. Priscilla D. Hackstaff, the Federa-tion's treasurer, was enthusiastic: "If I had not been preaching another gospel for the past twenty years, that of woman suffrage, I should have been out on the street working for The Salvation Army." Mrs. William Grant Brown, a past president of the Federation, explained the appeal:

the Army made it possible for "delicately nurtured" women to "uplift" the "unfortunate members of their sex." With that aim in mind, more than 400 women organized the Women's Auxiliary of The Salvation Army Rescue Work. Their first project was remodeling the two brownstones that served as the Army's rescue home. Chief among their accomplishments was installing a new operating room with modern surgical equipment supplemented by medical supplies donated by the Johnson and Johnson Company. The club women's success at refurbishing the home—including decorating the living quarters and a playroom for the children—inspired one to comment, "I like the whole thing—the spirit of the place, especially; I'm almost tempted to do something to be sent here!"[32]

That spirit was rooted in the Army's understanding of love. Christian love, like a mother's love, was forgiving. In practical terms, rescue workers treated each resident as an individual rather than as a "case." Many of the women under their care suffered from what Salvationists described as a lack of mothering: no one had taught them how to discern right from wrong. Army literature suggests that this was a problem for members of all classes. Wealthy families often contributed to their daughters' ruin by introducing them to drink; poor families seemed oblivious to their daughters' choice of clothes, friends, and entertainment. Salvationists attempted to rectify the lack of moral education through a mixture of love, work, discipline, and spiritual guidance.

Girls stayed in the homes for several months. They worked, studied, and attended religious services. Good conduct was routinely rewarded. Some girls joined the Army, but recruits were few in number. Salvationists had better luck reforming their wards. Evangeline Booth boasted that rescue workers succeeded 85 percent of the time. According to the New York Rescue Home, 126 girls passed through its doors between September 30, 1913, and October 1, 1914. Of these, 42 were "in situations," 36 were "with friends," 2 were in the hospital, 5 were "unsatisfactory, and 41 remained at the home. But such statistics—challenged by contemporaries including the charity official and Army critic Edwin Solenberger— are impossible to substantiate. Salvationists also understood that their work was not completed even when a resident left the home with a job in hand: "The ultimate aim is not reformation, but regeneration; of a change in character rather than social status."[33]

To continue and safeguard the process of regeneration, rescue workers organized the Out-of-Love Brigade, a social club for former residents. Each month members of the brigade spent a day and a night at the rescue home to participate in social and religious activities. Members also held reunions and made financial contributions to the work. When residents went back into the world they were encouraged to take their babies with them; Salvationists and their supporters believed that mothering had a transformative effect. Expressing the assumptions about class and gender that underlay Salvationists' ideas about womanhood, Mrs. William Grant Brown, the President of the Women's Auxiliary of the New York Rescue Home, said, "While a woman never fully forgets the shame of her fall, as time goes by and the holy ties which bind her to her irregular offspring become stronger, a sense of security returns, and happiness and peace follow. In other words, the child becomes the redeemer of the mother."[34]

In these ways, Evangeline Booth's skillful use of gendered rhetoric—specifically nineteenth-century assumptions of women's moral superiority and greater sensitivity to family and religion—helped build and strengthen the Army. Gendered rhetoric underlined the Army's self-understanding as a reformist movement with an evangelical Protestant world view, and it bolstered the Army's position as a conservative force for traditional values at a time when many Americans worried that ideals such as God, home, and country were being undermined by changes in women's roles.

The Age of Demonstration

In 1907, after a local appearance by Evangeline Booth, the *Chicago Record-Herald* noted: "Whatever may have been said (of the Army) in the days of its first struggles, it is now generally recognized that its labors are of unquestionable value to the world."[35] This transformation in the public perception of the Army owes much to Booth herself. In an action-oriented age, Booth's performances revisioned her Army in compelling form: dramatic, noble, and active. Yet performances such as "The Commander in Rags" and "My Father" employed an artifice that had been absent from either the illustrated lectures of the Booth-Tuckers or the speeches of the Ballington Booths. That artifice was a result of Evangeline's theatrical bent as much as of her aim to design and promote a product that would win public support.

From the time she arrived in New York in 1904 Booth sought to strengthen and institutionalize the Army. Working on two fronts, she built up the Army internally while bolstering its external image. To accomplish the former she utilized the regnant business principles of organization, efficiency, and systemization in a process parallel to what Ben Primer has called denominational rationalization.[36] But Booth went one · step further than leaders of other Protestant groups. Rather than raise up a faceless bureaucracy, she gave the Army a persona—her own.

Thus an understanding of the Army's institutionalization is inextricably tied to language and performances which cast both the Commander and her movement as active and action-oriented. Since these characteristics were central to the Progressive temper of the times, the Army garnered popular and financial support, which fed expanding social programs, new building projects, a growing bureaucracy, and a vigorous public relations campaign. In this light, Army descriptions of Booth's lectures as "representations" rather than theatrical performances is significant. Protestants had long been wary of the thin line between artifice and authenticity. Jackson Lears has observed that the tension between the two "was at the heart of Anglo-American Protestant culture."[37] Salvationists prized plain speech, but they also were heirs to the theatrical techniques of antebellum revivalists. Their desire to spiritualize the secular world, as well as their need to finance their work, entangled the sacred and the profane in a complex web of images, entertainment, and market relations.

The Trade Department's approach to marketing and advertising was a case in point. The Army sold a variety of goods—from food to clothes to fountain pens—to help subsidize its work. Attempting to imbue their products with religious value, Salvationists gave their teas names such as "purity blend" and "triumph blend." Similarly, when selling wall mottoes, Army agents assumed that the mottoes' religious message hallowed their decorative function. A notice soliciting sales agents for the wall mottoes appealed simultaneously to aesthetic, spiritual, and entrepreneurial impulses: "Help us to get these beautiful Bible truths into the homes of the people, and at the same time you can make money. The profits go to help the work of The Salvation Army."[38]

But it wasn't just the perceived spiritual worth of their products that · distinguished Salvationists from run-of-the-mill marketers; the Army also differentiated itself by the intentionality of its advertisements. A disclaimer on "The Art of Advertising" promised readers in 1897 that Army ads were truthful and its products were "bona fide bargains." Nevertheless: "We want to write our advertisements in such a style as to make them interesting, and compel people to read them whether they want to or not." By the late 1910s the most effective way of capturing attention and remaining truthful was to print testimonials from satisfied customers.

"My uniform arrived in good shape and according to promise," wrote one happy buyer. "It is a perfect fit, and the officers who have seen it are in high praise of it altogether. The material and workmanship are all that I could desire."[39]

The tension between artifice and authenticity also permeated the Army's view of its "performances." As R. Laurence Moore notes, the similarities between theater and religious revivals had dogged evangelists ever since George Whitefield turned "preaching into a performance"[40] Although Whitefield eschewed references to the theater when discussing his work, later revivalists made the connection explicit. The "practiced spontaneity" advocated by Charles Finney was modeled on stage acting, although the great revivalist did distinguish between acting and evangelizing. In his view, actors perverted their nature by assuming a variety of roles and corrupted their audiences by presenting fictions that aroused base passions. Evangelists were different: they projected only themselves, and they presented truths aimed at inspiring listeners to seek salvation.

While liberal Protestants in the postbellum era accepted secular theater as long as it offered wholesome entertainment, many evangelical Christians remained opposed to it. As an evangelical group seeking to provide alternatives to commercial entertainments, The Salvation Army employed the idioms and instruments of popular culture. Thus the Ballington Booths gave Chautauqua-style lectures, the Booth-Tuckers presented religious vaudeville, and Evangeline Booth designed spectacular pageants and theatricals. That she succeeded in entertaining secular audiences on their own terms can be inferred from the defensiveness in *War Cry* reports of her performances. For example, since Booth's recitations stirred audience emotions just as a satisfying drama would, and since the Army did not approve of commercial theater, one correspondent felt compelled to differentiate between a theatrical performance and Booth's "representation," which derived its power from reality: "The audience applauded and wept, laughed and cried as they beheld that child of God in tatters before them, as delicate almost as the flowers she carried in the basket on her arm; and this was not a performance, it was a representation of real life—of a life lived by the one who was portraying it."[41]

That this "representation" was a performance of an earlier performance did not trouble Salvationists familiar with the idea of masquerading to gain access to the lower classes. Yet the distance from Evangeline's initial impersonation of a flower seller in Piccadilly Circus to her performance in "The Commander in Rags" encompassed significant changes for both the actor and the organization. Evangeline was no longer a teenager seeking to repair dolls in the East End slums. As the head of a large religious and philanthropic organization, she was trying, by sentimentalizing poverty, to win over wealthy audiences. Similarly, the Army itself had evolved from a local evangelical mission to a worldwide movement requiring millions of dollars to fund its operations.

Although Salvationists chose to ignore the implications of such changes, they were not entirely lost on their contemporaries. An early admirer of the Army's band music, George Bernard Shaw, wrote several anonymous reviews praising the music's "precision and snap." When he learned that William Booth had cited these reviews publicly, Shaw approached Army leaders and suggested that they develop their dramatic skills. Offering to write a play for their use, Shaw was told that unless every incident had actually occurred the play would be a lie—and therefore objectionable. (He was asked, instead, for a donation.) Shaw noted: "To my mind, of course, this was a very curious misapprehension of the difference between truth and mere actuality."[42]

Initially supportive of Booth's attempts at social reform, Shaw grew critical because he believed such efforts were undermined by acceptance of money from the very people—capitalists, liquor interests, and entrepreneurs—responsible for poverty. While William Booth insisted he would take money from the devil if it could be used for good purposes, Shaw wondered whether such money was simply fuel for maintaining the Army bureaucracy. Shaw's speculations about the effect of "tainted money" took dramatic form in his play *Major Barbara* (1905), the story of a wealthy girl who joins the Army and the subsequent offers by her father, a munitions dealer, to fund the Salvationists' work. The British *War Cry* noted the play's opening with a brief summary of the plot and a quote from the (unnamed) playwright noting that he "greatly admire(d)" the Army's rescue work.[43]

Major Barbara, which opened on Broadway in 1915, was not the only play to use the Army to discuss larger themes. As early as the 1880s the satirists Harrigan and Hart tweaked religious enthusiasms by parodying Salvationists in their musical revues: "Away, away with the rum and gum! / Sound the drum! Here we come! / The regular, popular hum, tum, tum, / Is to join the Army oh!"[44] But by the end of the next decade the blue-uniformed soldiers were no longer stand-ins for comic excess. Now viewed as paragons of virtue, Salvationists were redemptive figures whose example and whose love, represented by a beautiful and virtuous lassie, triumphed over evil. In the musical *The Belle of Broadway* (1897) a young wastrel is transformed when he falls for a Salvationist lass. The play, which did moderately well on Broadway, was a popular hit in London, where it ran for almost 700 performances. Although one critic dismissed *The Belle of Broadway* for having neither "a fertile or suggestive topic," it enjoyed several more incarnations on stage and film. A new version of the movie in 1919 provided a vehicle for Marion Davies, and in 1952 yet another adaptation starred Vera-Ellen and Fred Astaire.[45]

A decade after *Belle*'s debut, Broadway audiences embraced *Salvation Nell*. A melodrama by a Edward Sheldon, a fledgling playwright who went on to achieve critical and commercial success, *Salvation Nell* thrived despite mixed reviews. A scrubwoman whose lover is sent to jail for murder, Nell considers prostitution to support herself. At the last moment she decides instead to join The Salvation Army. When her sweetheart is freed, he wants her to return to their old, immoral ways. Refusing, she prays for his conversion. He reforms, becomes a Salvationist, and they wed. While some critics loved *Nell,* others were unimpressed. The *New York Times* opined: "Such an exhibition of sordid and vulgar depravity as Mr. Sheldon presents in *Salvation Nell* will accomplish no good purpose." Like several other plays that season, *Nell* offered audiences a vivid picture of slum life, in this case typified by a Cherry Hill street scene complete with tenements, colorful crowds, and The Salvation Army slum post.[46]

The conceit behind *The Belle of Broadway* and *Salvation Nell* presupposes that turn-of-the-century audiences found it believable that rich playboys and poor scoundrels could be redeemed by Army lassies. In an age when cultural elites, religious leaders, and social reformers expressed anxiety over the mores and morals of working-class women as well as the growing numbers of middle- and upper-class women choosing careers instead of marriage, the Salvationist lassie represented traditional feminine values. A generation earlier the lassie had been considered a sexually questionable figure. Now, in a remarkable turnaround, she set the standard for "true womanhood." Her vindication made sense in the context of the shift from Victorian to Progressive values. Army women represented a bridge between the two eras. They upheld the primacy of religion and family, yet they toiled in the public sphere—marching boldly into dives, brothels, and the darkest tenements. Moreover, they were eminently suitable love objects. Unlike Catholic nuns, another group of religiously committed and traditional women, Army lassies embraced marriage and motherhood. Feminine without being sexual (the uniform guaranteed that), lassies inspired the type of wholesome and redemptive love more commonly associated with mothers and sisters.

Poster for the Broadway show *Salvation Nell*. SAA

That redemptive love was depicted in an early D. W. Griffith movie, *The Salvation Army Lass* (1908), the tale of a moll-turned-lassie who saves her gangster boyfriend from a life of crime. The theme proved popular. Of fifteen movies made between 1911 and 1920 that feature Salvationists as main characters, eleven depict lassies whose goodness conquers recalcitrant men.[47] (In a few cases wayward women found salvation in the Army.) It seemed as if the Army could help anybody. Socialites *(Salvation Joan)*, country girls *(A Gutter Magdalene)*, and artists *(Shifting Sands)* find new life when they don the uniform. Most find adventure, too. The former socialite falls for a member of a slum gang who is really a Secret Service agent pursuing war spies. The artist-cum-Salvationist marries an American spy and helps him unmask her former boyfriend, a German operative. Orphaned girls and fallen women join the Army, gain salvation, and ship out to serve American troops in France in *The Blue Bonnet* and *Fires of Faith*.[48] Even in the lighthearted *How Could You, Jean?* the heroine's life becomes much more interesting when she pretends to be a Salvationist. In this comedy of errors, Mary Pickford dresses in an Army uniform to get a job as a cook and goes on to beguile (and marry) a millionaire's son.

An exception to the virtuous celluloid lassie is *Soubrettes in a Bachelor's Flat* (1900), a short that Kathy Peiss cites as an example of a film using "the salacious sexual imagery and risqué humor" prevalent in working-class theater. *Soubrettes* shows three chorus girls carousing with a young bachelor. When the police raid their apartment, the nearly nude women jump into Salvation Army uniforms.[49] *Soubrettes* commingled the older, more sexually ambiguous image of Salvationist women with their more recent, straitlaced incarnation for comic effect. The viewer laughed either way—at the Army's hypocrisy or at the chorines' cunning.

While Hollywood was busy projecting its image of the Army, Evangeline Booth and her strategists were spinning their own. Whereas Hollywood used the Salvationist lass to signify purity, religiosity, and wholesome traditional values, the Army used Booth to embody love, sacrifice, sympathy, and action. These themes were trumpeted in the *War Cry*, where reports on the Commander's lectures appeared more regularly than had comparable stories about her predecessors. Articles emphasized her success and talent—as well as her fragility. Frequently described as "frail" or "slender," Evangeline's figure, well into her fifties, was deemed "girlish." The *War Cry*'s columns also included reports on the Commander's health, which was usually described as precarious. Booth was often incapacitated by nerves, exhaustion, and other ailments. That such a fragile figure symbolized both action and sacrifice was among the most potent messages expressed through Booth's performances and her *War Cry* persona. Underscoring the Commander's womanliness, the metaphor of female illness emphasized Booth's dependence on the public for support.

The Army's skill at deploying imagery was not evident only in Booth's performances and public relations. Her tenure also saw a rise in Army pageantry and filmmaking. Beginning in the late 1880s the Army mounted pageants to celebrate its ethnic diversity and widespread activities. Staged primarily as in-house events for annual congresses and special rallies, these productions featured Salvationists in the native dress of their homelands and performing scenes of their work to aid the needy. Under Evangeline Booth's leadership these pageants became spectacles designed not only to inform fellow Salvationists of current activities but also to amaze and delight the public. Salvationist pageants borrowed from an • already eclectic tradition of public amusements which drew on church rituals, carnival parades, and theatrical tableaux. David Glassberg has argued that during the Progressive era pageantry served as a public ritual whose sponsors hoped to spark political and social change.[50] Army pageants had a similar rationale and aim. They too were public rituals that drew a community together as spectator/participants in the Army's transformative activities.

The "Spiritual Wonderland" mounted at the Carnegie Music Hall in 1909 to celebrate General William Booth's eightieth birthday was illustrative. To create a festive mood, Salvationists trimmed the auditorium with flags, electric lights, and decorations. For more than four hours a succession of living tableaux and musical performances occupied center stage. From a throng of white-garbed children whose presence launched the evening to appearances by choruses, veteran officers, and soldiers in foreign dress, the flurry never faltered. Living tableaux depicted programs in prisons, slums, and shelters (among other activities), and the Commander elaborated on each one. Toward midnight a squad of parading youngsters were joined by representatives of various groups and brigades to form "a bewildering but fascinating sea of color and motion."[51]

Two years later a similarly titled "Salvation Wonderland" was presented at the same venue, Carnegie Music Hall. This time the pageant included six homeless men, "as they were," who told their stories and then reappeared, rehabilitated, in a subsequent scene of the Army's industrial homes, as welders, painters, and furniture movers. In another enactment of Army work, white-gowned nurses with babies marched around a semicircle of swinging cradles. If anyone in the audience doubted whether the blanketed bundles were the real thing, piercing squalls assured them that they were indeed.[52]

While the Army's pageants were intended to impress spectators with the scope and vibrancy of its activities, they also used entertainment for • uplift and education. Much like the organizers of historical pageants, Salvationists "plac[ed] their faith in new techniques of mass persuasion to

inform public opinion, evoke public sentiment, and spur public action on a variety of issues."[53] By using pageantry to dramatize the Army's civic contributions, Evangeline Booth projected her organization into the public arena. Yet to attract as broad a public as possible Salvationists played down their particularities, especially their brand of revivalist evangelicalism, and emphasized that their service was rooted in a nonsectarian humanitarianism. Their success was predicated on their familiarity with
· worldly trends and techniques—and their skill at subverting them:

> Why it is an age of demonstration! Merchant princes demonstrate their goods: musicians demonstrate their harmonies: druggists demonstrate their remedies: Not a "copper" pounding the pavement, a pill mixer in the apothecary's shop, a broker's clerk at the tape, a jockey on the courts, an actor on the stage, a ball-player at the bat, an artist with his brush or a writer with his pencil, but what is anxious to show rightly or wrongly that he is prepared to "deliver the goods." Good men demonstrate their goodness and alas! bad men their badness. Yea, and even the devil himself is a great demonstrator—the greatest of all, in many ways.
>
> Why then to change the nature of the question, should we not be at the forefront with a demonstration of God's miraculous power in the regeneration of humanity?[54]

Sharing Evangeline Booth's penchant for demonstration and spectacle was Lieutenant Colonel Edward Parker, who in the 1910s headed the Army's division for social programs, stage-managed its pageants, and directed much of its media work. Parker's enthusiasm for technology dated back to the early 1890s. As a corps commander in Hartford, Connecticut, he had stretched a twelve-foot muslin sheet from the second-story window of his office to a building across the street. With the aid of a magic lantern Parker had projected both announcements and biblical texts on the giant outdoor screen. On a smaller scale, he organized "Limelight Services" similar to the popular "Limelight Lectures" that used a magic lantern to project stereopticon slides. Parker showed illustrations while his wife sang familiar Army hymns.[55]

The Limelight Services led to his own Limelight Lectures, at which Parker charged admission for illustrated talks on topics such as "The Rise and Progress of The Salvation Army." In addition to creating illustrated lectures for his own use, Parker assisted Emma Booth-Tucker in developing slides for "Love and Sorrow," her presentation on the Army's social work. Parker was not alone in finding religious uses for the magic lantern: city missions, Sunday schools, and temperance societies had been engaged in similar projects since the 1880s. But Salvationists around the world · were leaders in advancing the evangelical potential of visual media.[56]

In the late 1890s Australian Salvationists, directed by Commandant Herbert Booth, began using magic lantern slides with motion picture film. Among the earliest of these endeavors was an illustrated lecture, with 200 slides and 2,000 feet of film, entitled "Our Social Triumphs." To the middle and upper classes in Australia, as in the United States and Britain, moviegoing initially was considered a working-class pastime. But Herbert, William and Catherine Booth's fifth child, recognized movies as a significant tool for spiritual conversion and moral reform. Under his aegis the Australian Army's Limelight Department became a leader in the country's burgeoning film industry. Perceiving that "story" films were more successful than documentaries—and sex the best story of all—the new department produced several shorts on its rescue work, which depicted lassies saving unwed mothers or delivering innocent girls from wicked seducers. The department's next effort was a series of short films about the life of Jesus culminating in a full-length movie entitled *The Soldiers of the Cross*. A saga of the early Christian martyrs, *Soldiers* was first shown in 1900 and ran for more than two hours. Hymns, classical music, and the resonant voice of the Commandant told tales of martyrdom while audiences watched graphic scenes of Christians being crucified, stoned, speared, beheaded, torched, and devoured by lions.[57]

In 1901 Parker became head of the American Army's Trade Department. Aware of the Australian Army's success, he added cameras, photographic slides, lantern slides, stereopticons, and motion picture equipment to the product list. He also set up a darkroom at Headquarters and directed several officers to prepare photographs to meet the increased demand for lantern slides.[58] His enthusiasm was boundless: Parker designed and manufactured photographic equipment, including a stereopticon called the "Optic Lantern" and a camera called the "Warrior." His *nom de plume* in the *War Cry* was "Optic," and he penned a monograph explaining the workings of the magic lantern. During World War I he took hundreds of photographs illustrating Army work at the front lines.

Unlike his Australian counterparts, however, Parker did not begin using the motion picture camera until the 1900s. His first film was of Emma Booth-Tucker's funeral in 1903. A subsequent project, "Problems of the Poor," integrated lantern slides and motion pictures. Disguised as a tramp, Parker rented rooms in lower Manhattan, where he lived among the poor and photographed their suffering. He presented the resulting multi-media chronicle to churches, YMCAs, and fellowship clubs across the nation. He also helped Evangeline Booth design "My Father," her recitation that integrated slides, film, and music for dramatic effect.[59]

The Army's spectacles, pageants, films, and slide shows were vehicles for explaining its brand of religion and social service both to spiritual seekers and to donors. The efforts succeeded—especially with the latter group, members of the middle and upper classes who saw the Army as performing a vital public service. But the Army's success at commodifying itself through performances began to blunt the efficacy of its evangelical work. In other words, the representation began to overshadow the reality. The resulting confusion between what Army missionaries thought they were doing and what the public perceived can be glimpsed in a *New York Times* story of 1914. When Salvationists "invaded" several Broadway dance palaces, they asked "tango enthusiasts" to reflect on life's serious side. To the soldiers' surprise, the crowds listened respectfully, "apparently enjoying the novelty." At one club the maître d' himself led the "picturesque little group" to the center of the dance floor, where they sang and prayed. Afterward the crowd applauded loudly and threw coins. The Salvationists accepted the money and were invited to call again.[60]

To nightclubbers in the mid-1910s, aware of the Army's penchant for pageantry, the invasion of the dance hall looked like another form of entertainment. The evangelical thrust was blunted by the familiarity of the image and the novelty of the actual encounter. The Army's power to shock and offend had ebbed as its performances moved from evangelical street theater to philanthropic fundraising. In 1880 the Army's exhortations actively annoyed patrons at Harry Hill's; thirty-four years later they merely amused members of the city's demimonde.

Why the Capitalist Should Help The Salvation Army

A reporter who expressed surprise when Salvationists accepted coins from the dance hall patrons may not have appreciated the Army's persistent need for funds. During Evangeline Booth's tenure social programs begun by the Booth-Tuckers continued to grow. At the same time, Booth and her key advisors were extending Army real estate holdings. As Edward H. McKinley has noted, in its early days the American Army had little interest in owning property. Salvationists preferred to remain unencumbered so they could move quickly when ordered to start new corps. The Army owned only twenty-seven properties in 1890 and bought few others during the remainder of the Ballington Booths' administration. The new National Headquarters, dedicated in 1895, was the only significant Army building purchased or erected in the period. The Booth-Tuckers, however, encouraged real estate acquisitions. Within ten years the Army owned 159 pieces of property whose value was eighty-three times the 1890 valuation.[61]

Evangeline Booth was eager not only to buy more properties but also to build better ones. She was convinced that the Army would attract larger audiences if meetings were held in comfortable auditoriums rather than in shabby halls. Evaluating the Army's accomplishments for 1907, Booth articulated these goals, noting, "Rapid strides have been taken in the acquisition of properties, and for style, equipment, and location, our new buildings surpass almost everything that has been attained heretofore."[62]

In addition to purchasing properties, Evangeline Booth's Army continued to broaden its social programs. Under the aegis of the ubiquitous Edward Parker, the Army's social arm opened new facilities while establishing national guidelines for its work. Between 1904 and 1913 the number of relief institutions grew from 195 to 413. The Army's seven-story industrial home in New York was the largest in the world, and the Booth Memorial Hotel, opened on the Bowery in 1913, had 610 rooms.[63] To help publicize these strides among Salvationists and their supporters, Parker oversaw the launch of a new publication, the *Social News*, in 1911. Funding for social projects was a priority; the old, familiar channels—Self-Denial week, kettles, corps contributions, and auxiliary support—were no longer sufficient. The Reliance Trade Company and the Industrial Homes Company continued to seek investors until they disbanded in 1911 and 1912, respectively, and Evangeline continued to apply for municipal support. Such avid fundraising did not go unnoticed by the public.

Critics like Edwin Solenberger in the United States and John Manson in England charged that funds collected for social work actually funded spiritual outreach. S. B. Williams, a former officer, accused the Army of an "unholy and unethical condition of affairs," including a despotic leadership, graft among the officers, and spending only 10 percent of its collections on social services. In its defense the Army maintained that it was doing God's work. As George Scott Railton observed when British critics made similar charges, The Salvation Army would never be self-supporting because its mandate was always to do more. It was up to the public to help.[64]

Evangeline Booth agreed that public support was crucial for sustaining significant growth. According to her biographer P. W. Wilson, from the beginning of her American tenure Booth planned to reorganize fundraising—elevating it from a "shoestring operation" conducted on streetcorners to a system in which the method of collecting revenues reflected the importance of the services provided. The sums Booth sought and the tactics she employed grew more extravagant over time. In a letter to "comrades and friends" in 1906 she asked for $20,000 made up of quarters, half-dollars, and dollars so there would be "no great tax upon anyone individually." Several years later the week-long "Commander's Sale" at National Headquarters used department store techniques to entice shoppers. Targeted to women, the event raised $25,000, which was earmarked for rescue work, nurseries, and children's homes. The sale's tastefully decorated stalls displayed merchandise ranging from linen and china to clothing, furniture, groceries, and live birds. Special attractions included a zoo, a restaurant, and a mail-order service. Unlike the run-of-the-mill church bazaar, the Commander's Sale offered "none of the usual mixture of pin cushions and preserves, handkerchiefs, and books; the departmental idea was immensely a success." It is likely that the event profited from the advice and assistance of Booth's good friend John Wanamaker. Wanamaker, who opened the Commander's Sale, was a recognized leader in department store marketing and advertising as well as a devout Christian.[65]

Booth's next project was a national campaign to create a "University of Humanity." William Booth had proposed the idea for an officers' college years earlier, and Emma Booth-Tucker had even solicited support from Mrs. Leland Stanford, the California philanthropist—until the General insisted on locating the school in London. Intent on reviving the plan, Evangeline announced that the University, along with two new social institutions, would be located in New York following a $500,000 funding campaign.[66] Despite a strong start, the fundraising effort was sidelined by World War I. Once the United States entered the war Booth offered her troops to the American government. But to fund Salvationist relief work at home and abroad she was forced to borrow money. When the Army's efforts began winning praise, Booth turned to the public for help. In 1917 she organized the War Service League; supporters donated fifty cents each month to support the Army's war relief efforts. But more revenue was needed, and in 1918 she launched a drive for an unprecedented one million dollars. To her delight, the Army took in more than double that amount.

In tandem with the Commander's efforts to raise ever larger sums for the Army was her effort to reshape its image from subversive to accommodationist. While part of that reshaping was achieved by Evangeline's stage performances, articles in the *War Cry* were also important. The subversive aspect of the Army's message had been its drive to spiritualize everyday life: to saturate all forms of public discourse with its religious message and to bring an end to the secular commercial culture. While Salvationists had targeted all the world for redemption, they began by converting individuals. Army leaders were explicit: political or social efforts alone would not bring about reform; only a changed heart could do that. But winning hearts entailed an all-out battle, which the Army fought with the devil's own tools.

When polite society deemed such tactics vulgar and sensational, Salvationists initially ignored the criticism, but by the 1890s they had begun to listen. The Army blunted its subversive edge, repeatedly contrasting its version of peaceful spiritual warfare with the bloody systemic change sought by anarchists and socialists. Army policy required that Salvationists remain aloof from political and social issues, but sometimes soldiers and officers could not resist getting involved. In 1896 the Army aided striking Pullman workers, and throughout the 1890s Salvationists denounced and tried to stop lynchings. After 1890, the year in which *In Darkest England* and *How the Other Half Lives* were published, the *War Cry* routinely printed exposés on slums and sweatshops, decrying the economic system that resulted in such inhumane conditions.

During Evangeline Booth's tenure these articles continued but others, of a different nature, appeared. As earlier stories had assumed an implicit identification with the poor, the new pieces underscored the Army's ties to business and capital. In the past members of the Booth family had exhibited conflicting views toward class. While William Booth reached out to the masses, his wife Catherine told businessmen that their support would keep slum dwellers in line. American leaders like the Ballington Booths and the Booth-Tuckers—all advocates for the poor—similarly appealed to the upper classes, though they may not have made the case quite so baldly. Rank-and-file Salvationists, in contrast, had more allegiance to and more in common with working people than the well-to-do. Thus in the guise of a reminder to *War Cry* readers of the need to spiritualize the profane, "Materialism in the Temple" a front-page story of 1913, signaled sympathy for business practices provided they were conducted from a religious perspective:

> Jesus had no quarrel with merchants as such nor with money-lenders as such. He sanctified the necessary occupations by working at one of them until the beginning of his public ministry. We could scarcely get along without merchants and money-lenders—theirs are among the necessary occupations in the current construction of society. Nor did He condemn the mixing of trade and religion . . . Jesus wished to bring in conditions in which religion would sanctify trade, but here trade was profaning religion . . . Instead of religion spiritualizing business, business was materializing religion. Religion is not a matter of another world; it is in this world, but it loses its character when it begins to imbibe of the spirit of this present world.

Noting that the "cold, withering hand of materialism" touched religion, too, the writer called on the Army to resist the danger. But because Salvationists worked in the material world—raising money, constructing buildings, organizing relief work—they found that "the materialism in [it] transfuses itself to our spirit. This is the conflict everywhere and we cannot be free of it."[67]

Such frank confessions were rare. Increasingly, the entrepreneurial spirit of the times found expression in Army publications. In a widely reprinted article Evangeline Booth explained "Why the Capitalist Should Help The Salvation Army." Declaring that the basic conflict between labor and capital was of a "moral character," Booth said that "Capital" should support the Army because it sought to rectify labor's moral shortcomings. The Army was "making tens of thousands the whole world over of honest, sober, consistent, to-be-depended-upon working-men, and because of this great contributive feature to Capital's interest, if for nothing higher, the capitalist should support the movement."[68] Booth was echoing a theme sounded earlier by her mother and her siblings, but she stated it more boldly. Speaking in economic terms rather than religious or moral language, she called waste (that is, the wasted labor found in workhouses, prisons, and breadlines) "wrong" because "a vast crowd of non-producers have been, and are, consuming much that the army of labor secures by its toil." She argued that the Army took society's dregs—beggars, prisoners, and paupers—and rehabilitated them to "carry their share of the community's burden." Driving her point home, Booth noted that the religious conversion wrought by the Army turned wicked men into honest workers who did not need constant monitoring. In this way the spiritual benefit of salvation enriched the community at large. Supporting the Army, she concluded, was a civic and patriotic duty.

Booth's, and by extension the Army's, class sympathies were further revealed in 1915 when an economic depression, fueled by the war in Europe, swelled the ranks of the city's poor. That winter the Army organized "Bundle Day." After collecting old clothes from other agencies and organizations, the Army hired temporary workers to clean, mend, and repair the garments. Bundles were then distributed to the needy who, explained the *War Cry,* were "not the men who use dynamite to express their discontent with the existing social order. They are simply down-and-out." The success of this twofold strategy, hiring temporary workers to help provide needed resources, spurred New York's civic leaders to consult with the Army on additional ways to aid the unemployed. The result was the establishment of temporary workshops throughout the city where women prepared bandages for the war effort and men repaired used household materials for future sale. Viewing subsequent efforts at National Headquarters, former U.S. President Theodore Roosevelt praised the Army as both disinterested and efficient—the two prerequisites for successful work with the poor. John Wanamaker stopped by, too, and complimented the "efficiency in relief work" provided by hiring the unemployed.[69]

But what Wanamaker and Roosevelt deemed efficient others called exploitation. The Salvation Army hired 300 destitute women, in two shifts of six hours each, to make bandages and other first aid supplies. The women's salaries, fifteen cents an hour, were paid by "several Wall Street men." Soon after the workshops opened, the Industrial Workers of the World denounced the small stipend the women received and urged them to strike. Yet every time a woman walked off the job the Army immediately found another to take her place. It was after one of the I.W.W. protests that Wanamaker praised the Army's efficiency.[70]

A changing sensibility toward the poor can also be inferred from the Army's decision to shut down one of its free food stations. The cessation occurred after a city official visited the breadline to hire men for out-of-town jobs which paid $1 to $3 daily. When only 5 of the 200 men in the line expressed interest in working, the official investigated and found that many of them were regulars at other food giveaways around the city. This discovery led Army leaders to conclude that "there had grown up a distinct breadline class, living in ease if not luxury." Appalled by its part in encouraging pauperism, the Army stopped the handouts in a move praised by local opinionmakers. Wrote one editorialist: "This somewhat belated decision of The Salvation Army encourages the hope that in time the tiresome clatter about the 'coldness' of scientific charity . . . will come to an end."[71]

This shift, aligning Army policy with the comfortable classes rather than the suffering masses, was part of a process of institutionalization that Army leaders perceived as necessary to ensure organizational growth. As early as 1904, when Evangeline Booth began her American command, the institutionalization—the creation of a bureaucracy, a funding strategy, and an organizational ethos capable of sustaining a religious movement after its initial enthusiasm waned—had begun. Aware that the size of the United States and the scope of Army activities made it increasingly difficult for one office to administer and coordinate efforts, International Headquarters divided the country into Eastern and Western Divisions with the latter based in Chicago. The head of the Western Division, whose title was deputy commander, reported to Booth, who administered the Eastern Division as well as serving as American Commander.

In addition to the deputy commander, Booth was supported by an informal cabinet of officers whose leadership, loyalty, and skill helped place Army programs and finances on firm ground. These men (Evangeline's inner circle was all male) oversaw the acquisition of properties, the expansion of social programs, and the administration of local territories. Whether it was a function of the Army's growth, Booth's thirty-year tenure, or her skill at identifying and empowering talented subordinates, the Army flourished as these savvy administrators steered its transformation from a struggling social and evangelical mission to a multimillion-dollar philanthropy. Army leaders understood that a great change was taking place. "The Army was becoming more staid and less effervescent and emotional," Colonel William McIntyre, the Army's head in New York and New Jersey, told a reporter. He added that this was a good sign: "We are educating our children so that they can take up the burden of the life and have a fair chance to win."[72]

The growth of the Army's social programs and its increasing institutionalization fueled the criticism that hounded Salvationists on either side of the Atlantic in the early 1900s. Unlike earlier detractors who had disapproved of the Army's "sensational" forms of religious outreach, these later critics found fault with the Army's work as a social institution. Both John Manson and Edwin Solenberger charged the Army with keeping inaccurate records, misdirecting funds, and refusing to cooperate with other charitable organizations. Manson argued that the Army's main interest was in safeguarding its bloated bureaucracy, while Solenberger raised questions about the propriety of the Army's for-profit sister corporations, the Reliance Trading Company and the Industrial Homes Trading Company.

Similar charges surfaced throughout the remainder of the decade. In 1907 C. C. Carstens, the secretary of the Massachusetts Society for the Prevention of Cruelty to Children, castigated the Army's penchant for secrecy and wondered "Shall the Salvation Army Take the Public Into Its Confidence?" In his doctoral dissertation of 1909, Edwin Lamb stated that funds collected for social work were routinely diverted into evangelical programs. That same year I. N. Nascher published "a sociological study of the Bowery" in which he found The Salvation Army not entirely free from "mercenary motives." As an example Nascher noted that several of the Army's hotels for workingmen were no better than any other lodging houses and probably made more money. Nascher called the Army's Christmas and Thanksgiving banquets "repellent" and an excuse to foster pauperism. But the feature of Army life he found most troublesome was the sale of the *War Cry* in dives, saloons, and concert halls: "The women of The Salvation Army enter these places not to do evangelical work by the distribution of *War Crys* as tracts, but they come as news vendors to sell their wares. Their religious garments save them from abuse. They are engaged in a purely business enterprise."[73]

Most of the time the Army did not respond to its critics. Ignoring them seemed the most effective strategy. But Booth answered Solenberger's charges in a statement that was reprinted across the nation. Rebutting his allegations point by point, she declared that Army programs held to high standards and that the organization's financial matters were part of the public record. While the Commander took the high road, limiting herself to a straightforward rebuttal, local officers were not always so circumspect. A Salvationist officer in Solenberger's hometown of Minneapolis suggested that the charity official's criticism had arisen because he was "jealous" of the Army's successful social work.[74]

The Doughnut Girl

Only a few years later the kinds of accusations made by Solenberger and Manson would be almost unimaginable. Cresting on a wave of public popularity, the Army was almost impervious to critical attacks. The change began in 1917. When the United States joined the Allied side in World War I, Evangeline Booth also swung into action. Deciding that the best way to distinguish the Army from other welfare agencies would be to provide unique services in wartime, she sent lassies abroad to "mother" the troops. Setting up huts—temporary recreational centers—as close to the front as possible, the lassies brought a little bit of home to the American boys stationed in France. If the ploy appeared reckless, quixotic, and even doomed, it nevertheless succeeded. Evangeline's decision to choose lassies of impeccable virtue who would be "neither tourists nor butterflies" won the doughboys' hearts.[75] Their subsequent praise of Salvationist activities in letters and testimonials catapulted the Army into the front ranks of American social service organizations. Salvationist work in World War I wove together themes of action, gender, and patriotism—already markers of Booth's tenure. Fashioned into a shining tapestry of God, country, and motherhood, these themes hallowed The Salvation Army as America's own nonsectarian faith, a religion of action.

Even before America joined the Allies, Booth had organized support for the war effort. Launching the "Commander's Old Linen Campaign" in 1914, she appeared at National Headquarters in the immaculate white costume of a nurse. Calling on Americans to donate linen and cotton to the Army, Booth announced that used cloth would be turned into fresh bandages to be sent abroad.[76] Two and one-half years later, when President Woodrow Wilson declared America's entrance into the war, the Commander offered him her troops. Initially neither the United States government nor Booth's Army was clear about the role Salvationists could play either at home or with the American Expeditionary Force (AEF) in France. The Red Cross was in charge of relief work while the YMCA supervised welfare work; other agencies coordinated their services with these two. Military officials knew of The Salvation Army, but few envisioned what it could add to the work of those already designated to provide medical as well as social, recreational, educational, and religious services. Moreover, the Army had no money to pay for war relief work. Booth needed to find $125,000 to fund the endeavor.[77]

Stateside, the Army cooperated with other welfare agencies in setting up recreational huts near military training camps. Overseas was a different matter. When the Commander sent an emissary, Lieutenant Colonel William Barker, to ascertain how Salvationists could best serve the troops in France, he was received graciously by the head of the AEF, General John J. Pershing. Pershing recalled that the Army had helped him when a

The Spirit of 1918

FOR GOD AND COUNTRY

The Salvation Army began its war work assisting the Red Cross and the YMCA, but, as this *War Cry* cover of 1918 suggests, its status soon changed. Here the Sallie is out in front of her Red Cross and YMCA colleagues, who look to her for direction. The headline "The Spirit of 1918" echoes the classic "Spirit of 1776," while the caption "For God and Country" underscores the interwoven patriotic and religious message. AWC, Aug. 27, 1918, 1, SAA

With her tin hat and her tub of doughnuts, this Sallie served as the *War Cry* cover girl for the United War Work Campaign. Her direct gaze is reminiscent of the era's military recruitment posters, one of the many contemporary styles the Army appropriated for its publications. SAA

fire swept through his San Francisco home and killed his family. Despite the fact that the Army would perform tasks similar to those of the YMCA, Pershing gave permission for Salvationists to open their own huts in part of the militarized area. To finance the work Booth borrowed $25,000, which Barker spent on a large tent and a car. Accompanied by eleven Salvationists—four women and seven men—he toured the front lines, assessing what contribution the Army could make.

Barker quickly realized that homesickness was the scourge of the troops and that the presence of upstanding American women would be a real boost to morale. He cabled Booth to send more women, and she put out a call for young, single female officers and soldier-volunteers whose moral rectitude and Christian commitment were unshakable. (Several married and widowed Salvationists also served abroad.) Of the approximately 250 Salvationists who served in France, only a small minority were women. Male Salvationists served the American troops as faithfully as did their female counterparts, even following the soldiers into battle—something the women were not permitted to do. Yet it was the women, nicknamed "Sallies," who made the deepest impression on the doughboys and whose presence distinguished the Army from other welfare agencies (even those who also deployed women). The Sallies represented home for the American boys stationed abroad. Celebrated in poetry and song, the women embodied the purity and goodness the soldiers believed they were fighting to preserve. In one soldier's words, "These good women create an atmosphere that reminds us of home, and out of the millions of men over there not one ever dreams of offering the slightest sign of disrespect or lack of consideration to these wonderful women."[78] In a lighter but no less reverential vein, the United States Army newspaper, *Stars and Stripes,* printed a paean to the Sallies:

> Tin hat for a halo!
> Ah! She wears it well
> Making pies for homesick lads
> Sure is 'beating hell!'
> In a region blasted
> By fire and flame and sword
> This Salvation Army lass
> Battles for the Lord![79]

After receiving Pershing's go-ahead, Salvationist groups of two and three began setting up huts as close to the front as possible. Sometimes a hut was a tent staked to the ground; sometimes it was a deserted, ramshackle building. Ensign Margaret Sheldon worked in a hut constructed on the foundation of a house that had burned down years before. Twenty-seven feet wide and 150 feet long, the space was lit with 8 large oil lamps and had room for 24 tables and 48 benches. There were writing tables as well as games, magazines, books, a piano, and a gramophone.[80]

Not all the huts were equally commodious, but the prevailing spirit of love and warmth made them the closest thing the soldiers had to home. The Sallies, always pleased to see the "boys," darned socks and mended uniforms. Once the women mastered cooking under wartime conditions, hot drinks and baked goods were always available. Whenever possible Salvationists even delivered coffee and doughnuts to the front. While men in combat were given goodies for free, those who came to the hut paid only a small amount. The Army was not concerned about collecting money. If a soldier was short of cash he was extended credit and asked to repay the next group of Salvationists he met.

In the evenings Salvationists held religious meetings. Sometimes using a cracker box for a pulpit, they led simple services made up of gospel songs and short talks. The religious meetings started small, but the crowd grew as men joined in the singing of the old, familiar tunes. By the end of a meeting several often raised their hands for prayer; some even converted. Salvationists found it easy to share their faith on the battlefield: faced with death on a daily basis, many soldiers were predisposed to hear what they had to say. Even atheists and members of other religious traditions appreciated the Salvationists' hospitality, which included allowing members of other groups to use the huts. Fraternal orders held meetings there, Jews and Catholics conducted services, and divisional bands gathered for practice. The Army's popularity sprang not only from what it did but · from what it was. Salvationists made it clear that they served the enlisted men, not the officers. Accepting no favors from the brass, Salvationists slept, ate, and worked under the same conditions as the doughboys. Not surprisingly, infantrymen considered the Salvationists their own.

The zeal for service that inspired Sallies to persist under enemy fire was expressed in their diaries as a placid acceptance of danger and discomfort. The monumental difficulties of everyday life at the battlefront were recounted in matter-of-fact tones. It rained incessantly, the mud was knee deep, and living conditions ranged from stark to primitive. The bitter cold often forced the women to sleep in their clothes, and opportunities to bathe were rare. Then, too, there was the horror of war itself: the constant shelling and bombing, the ever-present gas masks, the dead and mutilated bodies. Ensign Sheldon described the conditions at a U.S. Army station under attack during the summer of 1917:

> Some of us made lemonade and s'wiches and others attended the boys. Then we would charge about. It was terrible and no one could imagen it. Our boys were bro't in on trucks loaded like logs and the blood would be running through the floor of the truck. Through it all the boys would wave their hands and call, "Hello there Sister Sallie, how proud we are of our Sallies, their always on the job." We had to leave the place many times because of the raids, the planes came over most all the time. One night I remember better than any other was when a plane dropped a GI can on the dressing station kitchen smashing up five trucks and killing the men and boys; it knocked all of us down. I was only a few yards from it. It was quite awhile before we knew what hit us.[81]

Several months later Sheldon was still following the advancing troops. She and her Army companions slept in a room that had six inches of water on the floor and no roof or walls. There were frequent gas attacks, severe casualties, and many unburied bodies. When a U.S. officer suggested that the women leave the area, Sheldon assured him that they were unafraid and, more to the point, that they wanted to stay and take care of the troops. Taking care of the boys was the topic the Sallies described most effusively in their diaries.[82] In particular, they enjoyed recording the numbers of doughnuts and pies they baked daily. To the boys on the front line, the Sallies' offer of fresh baked goods, especially doughnuts, was central to their success: the fried doughnut came to symbolize home.

The idea for making doughnuts originated with Sheldon and Helen Purviance. Arriving at a camp in Montiers, the two women wanted to give the boys stationed there a little mothering. After playing records on a phonograph and conducting a short meeting, they decided to bake something. Pies and cakes were impossible as they had neither the supplies nor the appropriate equipment. But doughnuts could be done. The first night Sheldon and Purviance fried 150 crullers on the small canteen stove. The following day they jerry-rigged a cutter from a can of condensed milk and a tube of shaving cream so they could make a hole in the crullers and serve the real thing. Simple to make and satisfying to eat, the doughnuts caught on among Salvationists and soldiers. As their proficiency grew, Sallies turned out as many as 9,000 a day—along with pies, biscuits, flapjacks, cookies, and cakes. In a letter home Sheldon described the daily

Working near the front, the Sallies made pies, doughnuts, cookies, and cakes.
SAA

drill: "Well, I must tell you how the days are spent. We open the hut at 7: it is cleaned by some of the boys: then at 8 we commence to serve cocoa and coffee and make pies and doughnuts, cup cakes and fry eggs and make all kinds of eats until it is all you see. Well can you think of two women cooking in one day 2,500 doughnuts, eight dozen cup cakes, fifty pies, 800 pan cakes and 225 gallons of cocoa, and one other girl serving it. That is a day's work in my last hut. Then meeting at night, and it lasts for two hours."[83]

The diaries shed little light on the Sallies' ideas about religion. They rarely described their actions in religious terms or ruminated about their spiritual direction. Instead they noted when a meeting was especially good and if a large number of boys requested prayer. Occasionally a diarist asked God for strength or recounted a religious exchange with a soldier. The writing is equally silent about the women's relationships with the soldiers themselves. No one hinted at the possibility of romance or even a minor flirtation. Rather, the Sallies described how they took care

Sallies serving coffee and doughnuts to troops near the front. SAA

of the boys and how the boys treated them as surrogate mothers. Although most of the women were not much older than the soldiers, they distanced themselves by their quiet self-sufficiency and their dedication to service. Indeed, the Sallies saw the soldiers as "boys" to care for. Twenty-four-year-old Mary Bishop was surprised but pleased when soldiers called her "little Mother." Mary Robinson Young noted that when the "boys" wanted a favor, they called her "mother, too." Set apart by their uniforms (the Sallies had traded in their blue serge for military khaki and their bonnets for tin hats) and distinguished by their upright behavior, the Salvationist women must have seemed to the young American soldiers to be as sexually remote as their own mothers.

Writing to families and friends, soldiers praised the Sallies' baked goods as "just like mother used to make" and described the Army huts as the closest thing to home. War correspondents, observing the rapport between the Sallies and the doughboys, filed stories that reinforced the women's image as maternal surrogates. On Mother's Day of 1918 report-

Sallies were honored in poems, stories, and even sheet music. SAA

ers described Sallies, at the request of American mothers, decorating 1,000 graves with flowers and flags. Afterward the lassies wrote letters stateside, telling mothers about the sites where their sons were buried.[84] Evangeline Booth, aware of the impact the women had, helped publicize their work. Writing in secular publications, she stressed two points: Army

Blending religious and patriotic themes, this *War Cry* cover places the Sallie at the center of an encounter between human and divine. "The Consoler" may refer to the young woman as well as to the spectral figure of Christ. AWC, July 7, 1917, 1, SAA

war workers served without pay, and they never forced religion on anyone. She also made sure that the Army's work was noted by the mass media. Salvationists played a large part in a U.S. Public Information film, *America's Answer: Following the Fleet to France* (1918). The following year two commercial films, *The Blue Bonnet* and *Fires of Faith*, dramatized the Sallies' role. Tin Pan Alley, too, commemorated their work in several popular tunes, one of which—"My Doughnut Girl"—Booth even endorsed.[85]

War Cry covers reinforced the image of the Sallies' war service. Adopting a range of popular styles to present the women's work to the public, editors borrowed the hallmarks of contemporaneous advertising and commercial art. Since designers had to repeatedly spotlight a continuing story, creativity became the byword. Some covers resembled commercial photography; Sallies posed in front of their baking equipment in setups reminiscent of display advertisements for household products. Another technique was the rotogravure style of contemporary magazines, which included a liberal use of photographs, fanciful "frames," and captions. Further underscoring the illustrations' motif were design elements that represented the war work, such as pitchers and rolling pins, needles and thread.

Evangeline Booth was able to use the Sallies, even as she used herself, to embody the Army's message. Early in her tenure she had singled out action as the aspect of Christian living most likely to resonate with the American character:

> The American, when you come to religion, is not a theorizer, an Oriental dreamer or a philosophical speculator. He has little use for a religion which is sedate, or ornate, or ceremonial. He needs a religion that *does* something for him and *in* him, and provides something for him to do in the way of helping others. And it must be simple—something that he understands and can catch on to as he passes by, so to speak. Push, go, hustle is the spirit of the country.
>
> As tacticians, we of The Salvation Army take note of this. We have something alive to offer America—an active, energetic, hustling religion.[86]

That hustling religion found full expression in war service. Represented by lassies' wholesome womanhood and expressed as reverence for God, home, and country, the Salvationist form of religion appealed to a nation in which undertones of Protestant evangelicalism intertwined with the secular themes of Progressivism. Booth found an appropriate formulation to express these notions when she called for a religion of action. But she herself could only take the message so far. Her performances and public relations efforts reached many, but they lacked urgency. The Sallies made the religious commitment vital. Even though their numbers were few, the authenticity of their work made a deep impression on the public.

The Army's success in World War I was riddled with ironies. Never again did Salvationists have to worry about financial survival; their war service moved them to the front ranks of American philanthropies. The institutionalization that Evangeline Booth had spearheaded was finally complete: the public perception of the Army had been transformed. As one soldier wrote: "We always thought of The S.A. as an organization made up of well-meaning people who collected money on the streets with a tambourine for the purpose of feeding the poor at Thanksgiving or Christmas . . . We were wrong, dead wrong."[87] Rather, the new view was that the Army was a religiously inspired organization providing services that reflected Americans' most cherished ideals: God, family, and country.

The Army's success sprang from its acceptance of this secular trinity—a credo for living that hallowed the society's core values but that differed significantly from the key Christian message of salvation through Jesus Christ. Rather than spiritualizing the profane, the Army's message had become diffuse, able to be absorbed by a religiously diverse society. In *Piety and Poverty* Hugh McLeod argues that pluralism rather than secularization defined New York's religious life in this era.[88] Though the Army had promoted a nonsectarian stance in its delivery of social services before the war, its activities in France furthered its adjustment to—and acceptance in—the modern, urban(e) city. Lassies, kettles, and doughnuts were part of the cityscape, but they did not sacralize it and, perhaps, no longer expected to. Commercial culture had proved stronger, more resilient, than anticipated. The Salvationists' appropriation of worldly strategies, in the hope of subverting their meaning, had instead changed the Army, rendering it less sectarian and better adapted to the cultural hallmarks of the new millennium.

The Sallies represented that transformation. Unlike their counterparts a generation earlier, they did not see themselves sacralizing secular space— they claimed neither France nor the AEF's front lines for God. Likewise, the Sallies did not define their mission as saving souls. Their agenda was more modest. Gazing at the graves of the soldiers she had known, Margaret Sheldon vowed "to live better and be braver in the struggle of life." Condoning this shift, a change in perspective that enabled a sectarian, evangelical movement to thrive in a diverse and modern city, the *War Cry* affirmed purity of intention over the explicit efficacy of activity. In other words, a silent witness for God might be more effective than an overt act of proselytization. "It is not what you do—that may seem very important or may be very trivial; but it is the manner of doing it and the motive behind it which is the main thing."[89]

As the new century progressed, the challenges the commercial culture posed to The Salvation Army increased. The issue of intentionality became central as Broadway and Hollywood sought to use the Army's image for their own ends—ends that did not always coincide with Salvationist goals. At the same time, the Army had to consider the proper deployment of its image for publicity and fundraising campaigns. Since the figure of the Sallie had become the dominant representation of the Army, issues of gender and sexuality came to the fore. Salvationist women were used to signify the sexual ambiguity that lay between the spiritual and the secular. The uniform, once symbolizing the integrity between motive and action, now signaled a more provocative notion—the ability to put on or cast off an identity as easily as a new suit of clothes.

5

FIRES OF FAITH

1919–1950

ON MAY 5, 1919, *Fires of Faith,* a Paramount picture about The Salvation Army's war work, premiered at the Harris Theatre in New York City. Even before the feature began, the audience saw the Army in action. A filmed travelogue documented Salvationist work with the American Expeditionary Forces in Toul and Orleans. Set designers re-created the Old Rheims Cathedral as the backdrop for a dramatic tableau on the theater stage. Spotlights projected a stained-glass window on the back curtain, and in the foreground a Red Cross nurse tended wounded soldiers in a makeshift hospital. When the nurse finished her rounds, a Sallie strode onstage with a pan of doughnuts. After offering them to the bedridden men, she stepped into the spotlight to sing the eponymous song dedicated to the movie.[1]

That same evening Colonel William McIntyre, the Salvation Army officer overseeing New York and New Jersey, thanked the audience for their support. While other films depicted Salvationist efforts, *Fires of Faith* was the only one to have full Army cooperation; Evangeline Booth even played herself in several scenes. In appreciation of the Army's war efforts, Adolph Zukor and Jessie Lasky, the men who ran Paramount and its in-house acting company Famous Players-Lasky, had agreed to donate the evening's receipts to the organization. A grateful Colonel McIntyre said the moguls' assistance underscored a new appreciation for the once-mocked mission: "Salvationists are coming into their own, particularly

The Army's participation in the making of the film *Fire of Faith* helped ensure verisimilitude. This movie set of a wartime Army hut included a pan of doughnuts, wall mottoes, and the simple furnishings typical of actual Salvationist outposts. MOMA Film Stills Archive

among theatrical folk who once found [us] always reliable material for vaudeville laughs."[2]

Between 1919 and 1950 the Army evolved from an urban religion to one of the nation's most respected charities. In a period when political and social upheavals, notably the Great Depression and World War II, provided favorable settings for the Army's brand of active religiosity, Salvationists' work was represented in theater, film, and the popular press. But even the most sympathetic of these representations did not always match Salvationists' self-perception. In the media, for example, lassies were vibrant and appealing while their religion was less so, inverting the emphasis the Army would have chosen. The process of cultural negotiation, as the Army sought media attention while trying to maintain control over its image, illuminates problems faced by religious groups who must balance their understanding of a divinely inspired mission with their dependence on the public's goodwill. In the Army's case, representations of its female followers became a symbolic site where the movement's very identity was contested. The culture at large liked a lassie who was pretty and good-hearted, while a real Salvationist was a militant soul-saver—her entire life organized around service to God. Forced to mediate between reality and an image the public would support, the Army minimized the lassie's evangelical commitments while focusing on her womanly appeal. As a result, the movement appeared more concerned with helping those in need than with redeeming society.

The Army's transformation from evangelical outsider to philanthropic insider can be seen as intentional, a strategy for suffusing urban space with religious imagery and making evangelicalism compatible with commercial culture. Or, from another angle, the Army's story can be read as a cautionary tale about the fate of sectarian religious enthusiasm in a pluralist, market-driven society. Indeed it is both and more—but above all it is an account of a religious group struggling to maintain its spiritual commitment in the midst of substantial cultural change.

The *Fires of Faith* premiere, occurring at the height of The Salvation Army's prestige, set the stage for the Army's role as one of the new century's most popular expressions of public religion. It also illustrates the cultural negotiation between a spiritual mission and a commercial venture—that is, the Army's aims and Hollywood's bottom line. While there are no extant prints of the film, the surviving publicity stills, reviews, and studio press book suggest that *Fires of Faith* was, by Salvationist standards, the best representation they could expect from outsiders interested in reaching a mass audience. The collaboration required compromise—from Paramount's perspective the movie was to be a commercial melodrama, not a religious tract. Thus in *Fires of Faith* the Army's strategy of explicit spiritual warfare to Christianize society gives way to new tactics of stealth and diffusion. After World War I the Army modified its militant evangelism to a silent model of service and sacrifice, entering peacetime in the guise of "the doughboy's goddess," a fresh Hollywood face.

Stealth and diffusion meant representing religious ideas in easily identifiable symbols: lassies, of course, but also coffee and doughnuts, kettles and Christmas baskets. After the war, in a period of flux and uncertainty, these homespun images captured the country's imagination and provided

Edward Sheldon's play *Salvation Nell* was adapted for film three times. This still is from the 1921 version, with Pauline Starke as Nell. MOMA Film Stills Archive

a common vision even as many religious alternatives flourished. Some Americans dabbled in nontraditional faiths, while others flocked to the Fundamentalists' ranks. Still others were becoming more comfortable publicly expressing their Jewish or Catholic beliefs. As the public evangelicalism that once had united the nation became increasingly attenuated, The Salvation Army offered an appealing option: deeds (as opposed to creeds) that celebrated the pillars of American life—family, home, God, and country. Though the Army's message relied on the icons of American evangelical Christianity, its modes of presentation were more subtle and up-to-date. Having previously appropriated aspects of commercial culture—evidenced in Army advertising, pageants, "vaudeville," and *tableaux vivants*—Salvationists now turned to the movies. When Paramount approached Evangeline Booth for help in telling the Army's story, she readily assented.[3]

The heroine of *The Angel of Broadway* (1927), played by Leatrice Joy, is a cabaret performer with a flair for the scandalous. As part of her act she masquerades as a Salvation Army lass. MOMA Film Stills Archive

The very simplicity of the Army's religion combined with the potency of its symbols made it an ideal vehicle for Hollywood. In years past Salvationists had borrowed from commercial culture to attract new audiences to the gospel message. Now commercial culture was ready to borrow back. The lassie, renowned for her war service, made a thoroughly modern and highly marketable heroine. She was courageous, virtuous, and immediately identifiable. Most crucial for Hollywood's purposes, she could also have a romantic life (unlike the similarly recognizable nun). From D. W. Griffith's *The Salvation Army Lass* (1908) to postwar movies like *Salvation Nell* (1919) and *Hell's Oasis* (1920), the Sallie saved (and got) her man.[4]

The Army benefited from its new status: its ability to raise funds and to command media attention was unprecedented. But increasingly it was forced to share the power to define itself with the very cultural forces it hoped to reform. And the real struggles of an Army lass at a local mission were superseded by the fictional travails of the Hollywood version. In the past Salvationists had simply ignored or dismissed portrayals they

The heroine of *The Angel of Broadway* appearing, in her act, as the temptress Eve. This image, contrasting with her pose as a Salvation Army lass, represents the conflict in the young woman's soul. Virtue ultimately wins out. MOMA Film Stills Archive

deemed insincere, unflattering, or hostile. Compromising images generated by alleged friends and sympathizers were a trickier matter, harder to contain, much less name. When Broadway showgirls donned the uniform to raise money, did their dressing-up subvert Army notions of spirituality? Or was it just a clever fundraising scheme? This ambiguity signaled a new

Jean Simmons (Sister Sarah Brown) and Marlon Brando (Sky Masterson) in a still from the film *Guys and Dolls* (1955). MOMA Film Stills Archive

relationship between the religious group and the culture it hoped to redeem. Spiritual warfare cannot continue when the opposing sides decide to work together.

If well-intentioned attempts to help the Army had such mixed results, representations fueled by less noble motivations were even more problematic. The Army's very success at embodying a faith for the new commercial culture became its Achilles' heel. The lassies in *Fires of Faith* epitomized virtue, but in later movies, such as *The Angel of Broadway* (1927) and *Laughing Sinners* (1931), Salvationist women were ambiguous figures. The heroine of the former is a cabaret dancer who burlesques the Army in her act. In *Laughing Sinners* a showgirl joins the Army when her lover deserts her; but she mocks her newfound faith when trying to win him back.

Over time the Hollywood lassie evolved into a stock figure. At best she was a religious do-gooder; at worst her religiosity left her naive, even exploitable. Sister Sarah Brown, the zealous heroine of *Guys and Dolls*, exemplified this caricature. Brown was based on the real-life "Angel of Broadway," Captain Rheba Crawford. Although Crawford was known for her street smarts, Brown is reduced to a dupe in the Broadway show. Her innocence may help her win the heart of the gangster Sky Masterson, but the character has little dramatic potential or staying power. After the movie *Guys and Dolls* (1955), few beautiful, bright, and capable lassies lit up the screen. The image had reached a dead end.

IN THE early years of moving pictures more than a dozen films had featured Salvationist characters. But *Fires of Faith* marked the first time the Army participated in making and promoting a movie. Paramount publicists said Jesse Lasky made the picture as a "tribute" to the Army rather than a commercial feature, but the film's marketing campaign belied that premise.[5] For the Army the movie provided a way to expand its audiences and to raise money for its Home Service Appeal fundraising campaign of 1919. But the Army's participation in the making of the film was rarely publicized among the Salvationist rank and file. The *War Cry* did not report on the movie itself, the Army's role in making it, or the money raised by the preview.

Evangeline Booth probably did not want to draw the attention of her brother, General Bramwell Booth, to her involvement in such a worldly activity. The Army often used forms of popular entertainment for its own purposes, but it opposed patronizing the secular versions. As a disclaimer in the movie's publicity kit makes clear, Salvationists differentiated between their own representations of reality and the fictional sort. The press kit took pains to point out that the Salvationists' American leader was being, as opposed to playing, herself: "Miss Booth does not appear as an actress in the development of the story but incidentally as the executive head of The Salvation Army, in the performance of her usual duties."[6]

As a theatrical production, *Fires of Faith* was standard melodramatic fare. The complicated story revolves around Elizabeth Blake, a beautiful young woman who is seduced by a cad and saved by the Army. Following her rescue she becomes a Salvationist and sails off to serve American troops fighting in France, where she encounters several former friends. Agnes Traverse, the daughter of Elizabeth's wealthy patron, has also become a Sallie. Agnes's fiancé, Harry Hammond, who was shanghaied and taken to France, has escaped and joined the Air Service. When Harry's plane is shot down, he ends up in Elizabeth's care. Half-blinded in battle, he does not recognize her. Meanwhile, Luke Barlow, a farm boy who loves Elizabeth, enlists in the U.S. Army because he knows his sweetheart is in France. After many twists and turns, the two couples celebrate a double wedding. In the course of the story the film recounts Salvation Army history and depicts the organization's religious and humanitarian efforts. Publicists, aware that such potentially didactic material could doom the film, stressed its drama, star power, and authenticity.

Reviewers praised the movie's dramatic and "heart appeal," as well as casting, plot, and direction. According to the *New York Tribune*, "one need have no trepidation in attending this new film . . . there is no 'holier than thou' atmosphere in it." The *Moving Picture World* noted that "it interests and entertains regardless of creed." *Exhibitors Trade Review* was even more explicit: "No exhibitor need have any fear of *Fires of Faith*. It is not a preachment. It is an absorbing drama with a tinge of the war about it."[7] That both commercial reviews and trade publications explicitly addressed the film's entertainment value suggests that the Army, for all its popularity, was not seen as an organization that easily fit within the parameters of commercial entertainment.

Fires of Faith was the first and last attempt to find a mutually profitable meeting ground between the movie moguls and the Army's commanders. As the reviews suggested, representing the Army strictly in its own image held little commercial appeal. Virtue and more virtue was not a box-office draw; backsliding and sin were more interesting. Even *Fires of Faith* had to supply some sparks: an old-fashioned cad ruins Elizabeth Blake, and even as a Salvationist she falls (however briefly) for her best friend's intended.

The movie's press kit indicated that neither a smidgen of sin nor a raft of reviews would be enough to entice the public. The twenty-four-page booklet included illustrations of posters, photographs, and lobby displays available to exhibitors as well as advertising copy, advance press stories, and publicity tips. One article described the "novel exploitation" that accompanied the movie's three-week run in New York. The publishers of the *Fires of Faith* song cooperated in a tie-in with Woolworth's: several of the stores featured a display of the sheet music and song posters. The novel *Fires of Faith* was arrayed in the windows of local department stores, and clerks at Wanamaker's, Lord and Taylor, and Franklin Simon stuffed movie flyers into every package they wrapped. Smaller stores helped too, distributing calling cards printed with the name "Miss S. A. Lassie" and a handwritten message: "I would like to see you at the Harris Theatre tonight." At the theater itself, ushers wore Army uniforms.

When the movie played at the Stratford Theatre in Poughkeepsie, New York, the local exhibitor was equally inventive. Bakery windows touting the film offered a discount on doughnuts. One local drugstore served up a

Jesse L. Lasky Presents

"FIRES of FAITH"

WITH

Catherine Calvert, Eugene O'Brien and Ruby de Remer

Produced by
FAMOUS PLAYERS-LASKY CORPORATION

She'd Have Pulled Her Skirts Away—

ONLY a few yesterdays away she'd have pulled her silken gown away from "this terrible creature"—

But now she clutched her in the arms of loving sisterhood, with a feeling of real companionship in her heart!

They met on an equal plane for the first time in the lives of each—and each felt no surprise.

In the seething melting pot of war were brought together the Belle of Society and the Belle of the Bowery, sisters in one cause—the cause of humanity under the banner of the army of the soul—the Salvation Army.

It's just one of the many thrills with which "Fires of Faith" abounds but it is, perhaps, the thrill which will most surely stir your heart.

If you miss "Fires of Faith" you will later blame yourself for missing one of the very greatest pictures of all time.

All Week Beginning Monday

STRAND

Broadway at Main Street

An advertisement for *Fires of Faith* emphasized the film's melodramatic plot line by focusing on the differences between the two female leads. USC Cinema-Television Library

Fires of Faith sundae, while another offered a drink-and-doughnut combination named for one of the film's stars. Taxicabs mounted placards for the movie, and private cars followed suit. The newspapers featured endorsements from ministers and women's clubs, and local merchants sold *Fires of Faith* sheet music and books.[8]

The Army did its part, too. Salvationists participated in the production of the movie and, to ensure verisimilitude, allowed the filmmakers to shoot religious services and officers' meetings. Stills of Evangeline Booth were made available for advertising and display, and local corps were encouraged to help exhibitors with promotional strategies. But the Army's most significant contribution was its tacit acceptance of the celluloid lassie. Ruined but redeemed, Elizabeth Blake is beautiful and courageous. Agnes Traverse is both of these and virtuous, too. Standard melodramatic types, as opposed to the real-life Margaret Sheldon or Helen Purviance, Traverse and Blake were "the Belle of Society and the Belle of the Bowery, sisters in one cause—the cause of humanity under the banner of the army of the soul—the Salvation Army."[9] Hollywood's version of lassies was the lure and, in this case, the Army hastened to provide the bait.

The Angel of Broadway

Fires of Faith was not the only time the media glamorized the Sallies. A khaki-uniformed cutie adorned a war-era cover of *Cosmopolitan,* and *Literary Digest* described her as the "doughboy's goddess." Broadway audiences and impresarios also took notice. The Ziegfeld Follies revue of 1919 presented "a sort of apotheosis of The Salvation Army lassie, and [was] received with entire respect and admiration by the ultra-sophisticated audience of this frivolous theatrical representation."[10] Chorines in uniform had appeal; the obvious frivolity played off their drab suits, and the urbane setting diluted the Army's religious bent. Commercial performances of an earlier era had also featured showgirls in Salvationist blue, but those masquerades had skewered the organization. Now the Great White Way celebrated the group.

If Salvationists objected to the entertainment industry's appropriation of the lassie, there was no mention of it in the *War Cry.* Likewise, uses of the uniform for prurient entertainment went unremarked, even though the newspaper had formerly deemed worldly use of the garb blasphemous.[11] The Army's silence on the issue suggests that it either had acqui-

May

25 Cents

Cosmopolitan

THE SALVATION ARMY

I Helped. Will You?
Buy Victory Bonds

The Army lass appeared on many magazine covers in the wartime era, but the *Cosmopolitan* image was among the most fetching. The patriotic motif, emphasized by the flag in the background, overshadowed the figure's religious identity. SAA

esced to the commercialization of its image or was not yet prepared to make distinctions between acceptable and unacceptable use of it. Broadway's chorines exemplified the latter, but *Cosmopolitan*'s cover girl was more difficult to criticize. Looking straight into the camera, the doe-eyed brunette looked similar to Sallies in *War Cry* illustrations. But was it her bobbed hair or just the secular context that made her seem suspiciously like a pinup?

Still, since William Booth had declared that any publicity was good publicity, the postwar exposure must have seemed very good indeed to many Salvationists. But there was a price to pay. In an age of flappers and sexual freedom, the lassies' hint of sexuality would eventually come to flower. Army leaders could root it out within the ranks, but they could not stop the moviemakers from speculating whether bad girls became good by putting on the uniform and, conversely, whether good girls became bad when they took it off. The uniform's use by outsiders—whether waitresses, society women, or showgirls—had already demystified the garb. Ending the connection between the internal (soul) and the external (suit) had theological ramifications: surrendering the uniform was tantamount to secularizing a spiritual object. Donning it no longer had to entail a spiritual commitment. Rather, it was more like an actor's costume: meaning inhered to the clothes but not to those who wore them.

While there was no explicit discussion of these developments in official Salvationist sources, a sense of the leadership's thinking can be glimpsed in the case of Captain Rheba Crawford. Crawford's brief Army career demonstrated the way the Army sought to control its image by enforcing conformity and decorum within its ranks. Crawford's ministry violated both; as Edward H. McKinley explains, she was placed on rest furlough in 1922 because of her "unorthodox theology and dress."[12] But it was arguably her independence, popularity, and sexual charisma that most disturbed Salvationist leaders.

Celebrated in the popular press as "The Angel of Broadway," Crawford was indeed unorthodox. Feisty, attractive, and articulate, she lived in Greenwich Village, liked pretty clothes, and plainly spoke her mind. ("I'd take a bunch of chorus girls and put them against a bunch of school teachers or nurses any day, as far as morality is concerned," she once opined).[13] In her own person she linked the Army lassie to the media's "doughboy's goddess." The connection could not have been more explicit: she requested assignment to the Army's Broadway mission and preached weekly on the steps of a commercial theater. Her friends included the Schuberts and the Barrymores, and her own newspaper background—a short stint reporting for the Atlanta Constitution—made her a favorite with the press. Crawford developed a new image for the lassie which, ultimately, did not pass muster with the Army's top officers. But it was an understandable outcome of the Army's *pas de deux* with popular culture.

Crawford's contemporaries made the connection between the Broadway lassies and the Army's own, referring to her as the best example of Salvationist womanhood. One account linked her with two secular beauties: the actress Edna May, who had played a lassie in the play *The Belle of Broadway,* and the socialite Frances Fairchild: "The stage gave Broadway an alluring conception of the Salvation Army lassie in Edna May. Art and society gave Broadway another in the Salvation Army poster for which Frances Fairchild, a beautiful society girl, posed. But the Salvation Army itself, in Rheba Crawford, has given Broadway a lassie with the magnetism of Edna May, the beauty of Frances Fairchild, and something else which is all her own."[14]

A "cradle" Salvationist, Crawford grew up in an Army family in Atlanta; as a youngster she marched in open-airs and sang of Jesus' saving power. Smart and talented, she initially resisted the worldly temptations posed by wealthy friends, but after high school she asked her father if she could leave the Army. She worked briefly as a reporter, but soon decided to resume the religious life. After first studying at the Army's Training College in New York, then serving in St. Petersburg, Florida, Crawford alighted at National Headquarters to edit *The Young Soldier,* the junior version of the *War Cry.* But working at a desk job did not suit her. She yearned for active duty and requested permission to revive the moribund Broadway corps. At her first open-air meeting Crawford was rattled by hecklers clamoring for a date. But she held her ground and quickly gained local prominence.[15]

Sobriquets soon followed: Crawford was dubbed "The Angel of Broadway," "The Beauty in the Blue Bonnet," "The Prettiest Girl in The Salvation Army." Caught up in the media spotlight, Crawford even took a screen test before realizing she was about to succumb to the very sins she had pledged to fight. Chastened, she renewed her crusade to save Times Square's most hardened habitués, its gangsters, chorines, and boozers. Her Sunday evening open-airs, held on the steps of the Gaiety Theatre, attracted 1,000 listeners every week. Then, in the autumn of 1922, a policeman tried to break up one of her meetings, saying the crowd obstructed traffic. He asked Crawford to stop preaching and, when she refused, arrested her.

Rheba Crawford soon after her arrest in 1922 for obstructing traffic in Times Square. UPI/Corbis-Bettman

The crowd booed and hissed as the police officer escorted the young woman to jail. Many followed them to the station house, stirring fears of a riot. Released on bail, Crawford received permission from the city's Police Commissioner to resume her meetings. But she disappointed supporters on two subsequent Sundays when, according to press reports, she suffered from nervous exhaustion and was unable to appear. A reporter who visited Crawford's Greenwich Village apartment during this "rest period" duly noted the lassie's off-duty wear—"dainty slippers" and an "attractive black satin gown."[16] Over afternoon tea the two women chatted about Crawford's mission to Broadway, her show business friends, and her desire to return to work. But less than two weeks later Crawford resigned her commission in The Salvation Army.

She later explained that the Army had ordered her to stop preaching and she could not obey:

> My superiors said they sought no conflict with the police. They wanted me to fight my fight—silently.
>
> And I couldn't! I couldn't! I had come to Broadway a young girl bred in the serene South, wondering if this roaring whirlwind had a soul. I think I found Broadway's soul. I tried to win it. My only weapons were the voice and the spirit God gave me. I was asked to surrender them, to lay down the only weapons God gave me . . .
>
> So I resigned from The Salvation Army . . . I do not blame the Army. It is the Army's standing policy to avoid dispute and to frown on personal publicity.[17]

In February 1923 some 1,000 of Crawford's friends and admirers held a "Farewell to Broadway" fete for her at the Selwyn Theatre. Will Rogers, one of the celebrities on hand, underscored, probably unintentionally, the ambiguity that made Crawford's ministry untenable for the Army. When bootleggers heard her preaching, Rogers said, "They go away and cut $5 off a case."[18] Rumors were rife about Crawford's departure. Some said Evangeline Booth was irritated by the young woman's popularity. Others claimed Crawford was conducting an illicit romance that would have scandalized the Army's supporters. But it was also her success at transforming "the doughboy's goddess" into a real live girl that caused her undoing.

Crawford's charisma and sexuality could not be contained or controlled by Army officials.[19] As Hollywood sentimentalized and Broadway sensationalized the Army's image, Salvationist leaders allowed socialites to pose as models and showgirls to raise funds in uniform. But the Army drew the line between reality and representation. Representations could transgress Army notions of propriety if they served a good cause. But the reality, the lassies themselves, had to hew to a proper image. In but not of this world, they were faceless soldiers in a spiritual Army. Their task was not to seek attention for themselves but to serve and sacrifice for others.

Of course, one lassie was exempt from all such expectations. Evangeline Booth, still the Army's public face, attracted personal attention even as she represented her organization. While Booth enjoyed a little temptation, she managed to project a (mostly) pristine image. In fact her formality and fussiness might have seemed a bit dry had she not indulged in some un-Armylike extravagances. Her flowing red capes and high-heeled shoes always stood out. Likewise her penchant for costumes. But while her enthusiasm for dress fit the times, other aspects of her style were less up-to-date. Her speeches—full of rolling, flowery phrases—sounded stodgy in the postwar period. And her abiding passions—prohibition and soul-saving—seemed increasingly old-fashioned.

Booth was moving into old age. Ill-health and hard work had taken their toll as she neared her sixth decade. The once-girlish profile had thickened, and her face was etched with lines. More and more the media image of the Army lassie contrasted with Booth's increasingly matronly figure. Even the Army's own choice of representations, such as the use of Frances Fairchild as a model, tended to favor svelte and striking beauties. Elmore Leffingwell, the Army's publicity director, promoted this image in the yearly fundraising campaigns, asking famous illustrators to contribute campaign posters featuring the lassie at work. The trend continued through the 1930s and 1940s: comely blondes and brunettes gazed wistfully at donors while also tending small children or passing the tambourine.

As the nation settled into peacetime, the preeminent image of the Army shifted from the Sallie to the "Angel of the Slums."[20] The change in identity was crucial: the Army now needed support for its work at home. Less glamorous than dodging bullets and delivering doughnuts to the front lines, home missions focused on the downtrodden—a population at a literal and figurative distance from the soldiers who had benefited from Salvationist war work. Confronted by societal changes in women's roles, Salvationists portrayed their female followers as exemplars of freedom and equality who eschewed the excesses associated with the New Woman or the flapper. While decrying women who embraced materialism, scorned motherhood, and succumbed to sexual immorality, *War Cry* writers regularly penned profiles of female officers who were active and obedient.[21] Yet a both accurate and appropriate image—a lassie who was religious, capable, and attractive—proved elusive. If *War Cry* photographs can be trusted, model officers were more stolid figures than the idealized winsome lass.

Popular illustrators like Howard Chandler Christy contributed their work to aid Salvation Army fundraising efforts. While the woman in this illustration of 1938 does not appear to be wearing a Salvationist uniform, the tambourine signals her Army identity. SAA

At the height of the Depression the Army reached out to white-collar professionals who were unaccustomed to needing help. This handsome "victim" hardly looks like a typical "down-and-outer." AWC, Oct. 24, 1931, 1, SAA

Clark Gable, playing a kindly Salvation Army officer, tries to save the erring Joan Crawford in *Laughing Sinners* (1931). MOMA Film Stills Archive

Laughing Sinners

During the Great Depression Army iconography acquired a masculine cast. The lissome lassies who had previously dominated *War Cry* covers and Army appeals were supplanted by handsome, broad-shouldered men. It was as if the lassie's slender frame could not shoulder the burdens caused by the nation's economic collapse. In the war against poverty, robust men were needed at the front. Since the Army's military language and imagery presupposed an aggressive approach to the world, the emphasis on masculinity was not a new direction. Rather, it was a redeployment of an old motif. *War Cry* covers showed Salvationist soldiers hard at work; even men not in the Army were portrayed as busy with masculine pursuits. Similarly, victims of the economic crash were sturdy men whose inner strength belied their straitened circumstances. On one *War Cry* cover a dignified-looking man, sporting an elegant topcoat, stared out past the reader. While his chiseled features recalled the sophisticated ease of an Arrow Shirt model, his hands, clutching a fedora, betrayed a certain tentativeness. A caption in the lower right corner identified him as "The Victim," but boldface letters in the upper left read, "Mr. Citizen, Temporarily Embarrassed, The Salvation Army understands—and is your friend."[22]

The remasculinization of the Army's image is also reflected in Hollywood portrayals of the period.[23] Lassies became more ambiguous figures as strong and sexy male officers occupied the screen. The film *Laughing Sinners* (1931) illustrated both trends. Based on the Broadway play *Torch Song* by Kenyon Nicholson (1930), *Laughing Sinners* is the story of a cabaret dancer who, jilted by her lover, joins The Salvation Army. Following a chance encounter with her old beau, she tries—and fails—to convert him. Instead, they spend the night together. The next morning a fellow Salvationist finds her and begs her to return to the corps. She initially refuses, convinced of her own damnation, but when he declares his undying love she returns to the fold—and to him. With Clark Gable cast as the Salvationist swain, it is difficult to understand why she, the young Joan Crawford, hesitated.

Laughing Sinners had difficulty getting past Hollywood censors. After a preliminary screening *Variety* said "extensive repairs" were needed "to tame down the religious angle." The play stressed the relationship (and the similarities) between religion and sex, but when the film followed suit, studio executives worried that women's committees would protest. Several scenes were reshot, including one in which Joan Crawford performs a seductive burlesque of "Onward Christian Soldiers" atop a hotel table. Even so, one trade publication deemed the final cut "demoralizing" and predicted that civic and religious organizations would be offended by the sight of a straying lassie. The film received mixed reviews. Joan Crawford was praised, but little notice went to her co-star Gable.[24]

Mae West's *She Done Him Wrong* (1933) had another attractive actor

As a wily detective pretending to be a Salvation Army officer in *She Done Him Wrong* (1931), Cary Grant initially fends off Mae West's advances. But once his true identity is revealed he expresses interest in the sexy singer. MOMA Film Stills Archive

playing a strong Salvationist hero. In one of his first major roles, Cary Grant is an Army mission worker who catches the eye of Lady Lou, a sexy chanteuse involved with the underworld. When police raid the club where Lou sings, they charge her business associates with operating a white slavery ring. Their crime has been revealed by "The Hawk," a wily undercover detective who turns out to be the handsome Salvationist officer. After sending the hoodlums to jail, the Hawk turns his attention to Lou. He proposes marriage, declaring his intention to keep her on the right side of the law. While Grant portrayed an Army officer, he never wavered from his "mission" persona despite Lou's flirtations. But the revelation of his actual identity and his subsequent claim on her affections suggested that the character was too good to be true. As long as he wore the blue uniform, the Hawk did not respond to Lou's advances, but he ably joined in her salacious repartee as soon as he donned civilian clothes.

Frank Capra's film *The Miracle Woman* (1931) reprised the theme of the unstable female religious figure. Adapted from a Broadway play of 1927, *Bless You, Sister,* the film starred Barbara Stanwyck as a duplicitous faith healer. Inspired by Aimee Semple McPherson's career, the movie is the story of Florence Fallon, a true believer who is led astray by a sleazy manager. Drifting along in slinky silks and fur stoles, she tries to ignore his corrupt machinations—hiring shills, intimidating underlings, and skimming funds. Fallon believes she is doing God's work, but the crowds at her services are more intrigued by the spectacle—caged lions, perky choruses, dramatic healings—than by her religious teachings. When a trusting fan befriends her, the two gradually fall in love. Ashamed of her dishonesty, Fallon tries to go straight, but her manager will not allow it. After a host of modern-day plagues—including scandal, bankruptcy, and bad publicity—Fallon finds her true self. The film's last scene shows a Salvation Army street meeting with Fallon marching in uniform.

While the link between Florence Fallon and Aimee Semple McPherson was obvious to audiences, the ties that both had to Evangeline Booth went unremarked. Although many of Fallon's theatrical techniques were intended to remind viewers of the extravaganzas mounted at McPherson's Angelus Temple, they had been pioneered by Booth years before. Live animals, massed bands, swelling choruses, and artful costumes were longtime staples of Booth's repertoire. By the 1930s McPherson's relative youth and notoriety—as well as Booth's age and achievements—made the latter look the established leader and the former a religious rogue. Yet Booth had been an inspiration for McPherson, and the two shared a grand theatrical style in and out of the pulpit. Undoubtedly Salvationists preferred to be depicted as having the true religion, as they were in the movie. But the film's representations were more complex than they first seem. The good lassie replaced the false healer, but they were one and the same woman under the uniform.

God's Best Gift to America

During the 1920s Booth was one of the most respected female religious leaders in the nation. Others—such as Katherine Tingley, Alma White, Nannie Burroughs, Henrietta Szold, and Helen Barrett Montgomery—had religious vocations known only in limited circles. Booth alone commanded a nationwide following; her appeal spanned religious divisions and spilled over into the secular community. In 1919 the United States Government awarded her a Distinguished Service Medal for her war service. In 1921 Tufts University presented her with an honorary master's degree. General Pershing helped raise funds for her Army, and each succeeding U.S. First Lady helped out in the Army's annual Christmas drive. When *Success,* a popular national magazine, asked readers to name the living woman who had done the most for humanity, Booth ranked number one followed by Jane Addams. Almost twenty years later she was still a popular figure, selected by the General Federation of Women's Clubs as one of the nation's female exemplars. According to the *War Cry,* Booth was "one of God's best gifts to America."[25]

Despite an Army policy that mandated regular rotation of officers, Booth refused to leave the United States or, in Salvationist argot, to "farewell." When Bramwell Booth tried removing his sister, he was outflanked by her supporters. A group of well-known New Yorkers, including Ambassador to France Myron Herrick, Bishop William Manning, and the banker Felix Warburg, drafted a letter of protest to International Headquarters. Leaders in other American cities did likewise. Rather than alienate the Americans, Bramwell allowed the issue to fade away. In 1924 he reappointed his sister to another three-year term, although he tried again, unsuccessfully, to remove her two years later.[26]

By the 1930s Booth's secular talents were as admired as her spiritual gifts. Praising her financial acumen in a *New York Times* profile, S. J. Woolf noted that "the peculiar quality about her is the strange combination of hard-headed business ability coupled with a poetic sense of the beautiful, and a mystic love of music." Woolf was also struck by the Commander's histrionics. She seemed more like a stage character than the head of a large organization. In fact her self-conscious theatricality helped contribute to a shift in the Army's image from a youthful fighting force to an old-timey band of do-gooders. Booth's air of high drama appeared increasingly out of sync with the times. While her organizational power and personal fame enabled her image to withstand negative characterization, her followers had no such shield. Lacking individuality and institutional clout, they bore the brunt of her shortcomings.

In the meantime the success of Army programs kept Booth in public view. Throughout the early years of the Depression, Army fundraising campaigns placed her in the spotlight and broadcast her voice across fledgling radio networks. Similarly, as the national debate over the repeal of Prohibition grew heated, she spoke out forcefully for keeping the law in place. Even politicians who disagreed with her opinion paid her their due. She was asked to give the invocation at the 1932 Democratic National Convention, which nominated Franklin D. Roosevelt, a proponent

Evangeline Booth. SAA

of repeal, for President. Booth had been known to support the Republican party, but both she and the Democratic leaders appreciated the symbolism of the country's most renowned female religious figure blessing their convocation.[27]

Booth's last great wave of publicity peaked in the fall of 1934 when she was elected General of the International Salvation Army. On her return to New York after the election she was welcomed with a ticker-tape parade up Broadway. Two months later, at a "National Tribute of Farewell," 20,000 well-wishers thronged Madison Square Garden to hail "America's Gift to the World." Helen Keller made a rare public appearance, along with numerous civic, national, and religious leaders. A 1,000-person "March of Achievement" highlighted the Army's American successes, and a 700-member choir sang Beethoven, Handel, and one of the General-elect's recent compositions.

The novelty of an American, much less an American woman, heading a worldwide religious movement was not lost on the press. Reporters described Booth's physical appearance with detail and precision never used in profiles of male leaders. Before *Newsweek* explained her skill at making the American Army the movement's wealthiest outpost, it told readers that the General-elect wore "silk hose and moderately high heels" rather than the lassies' sensible shoes and cotton stockings. Likewise, even though she was in her sixty-ninth year, many articles mentioned her hair, her flowing capes, and her (alternately) girlish, stately, or womanly figure.[28] Her age and gravitas notwithstanding, Evangeline Booth was still, by her own design and the media's doing, the nation's first and foremost lassie.

Booth sailed for England in November 1934, but not before putting a final stamp on the American Army. Rather than name a successor, she appointed Commissioner Edward J. Parker to continue as National Secretary and to oversee the national organization. At the same time, she increased the autonomy of the territorial commanders, thus effectively diminishing Parker's powers. Although Booth had fought decentralization when she was National Commander, among her first acts as General was to strengthen local control, a step that in effect, buttressed her authority, and that of International Headquarters.

These decisions, as well as Booth's departure, began a change in the public perception of the Army. Parker and the other Salvationist leaders of his generation—men such as Alexander Damon, Donald McMillan, William McIntyre, and John Allan—were exemplary officers. Members of Booth's inner circle, they were dedicated, loyal, and resourceful. But while Army insiders were aware of their role in building up the organization, outsiders perceived them as an almost interchangeable group of graying, middle-aged men. Evangeline Booth's departure had removed the Army's most potent visible symbol, and Booth's own administrative changes had exacerbated the problem by ensuring that there was no identifiable leader. Even though the Army promoted a strong male image in its publications, there was no one man to publicly embody it. Without a clear face to define itself, the Army risked having others create a face for it.

From Doughnuts to Dollars

While Evangeline Booth was widely credited with securing the Army's financial health, she actually received inestimable assistance from those around her. It was Booth's idea to send female Salvationists to France, but it was the women themselves who decided to make doughnuts, and it was the publicist Elmore Leffingwell who seized on the fried cakes as a promising fundraising strategy. In Leffingwell's promotional materials, lassies and doughnuts went hand in hand. The image took hold; even *Fires of Faith,* according to one reviewer, was "a dramatization of the doughnut." The film's "fires" were not literal blazes but "the spirit of courage and service which enabled [the Army] during the war to bake itself into the hearts of the people."[29]

What was the magic of doughnuts? Existing in some form for centuries, they had received scant notice in the annals of American popular culture before the 1800s. Writers such as Washington Irving and Mark Twain had referred to them only in passing. But World War I catapulted the fried cakes into national popularity; returning doughboys wanted ones like the ones they had eaten in the trenches. Annual doughnut sales jumped from $5 million in 1920 to $57 million in 1938.[30] And Salvationist coffers filled up, too. The doughnut was more than fried dough for the men at the front and the Sallies who served them. For the Army it symbolized the secular expression of its Holiness theology and activist orientation. Finding a balance between its spiritual mission and its pragmatic philosophy had led the Army into a wide range of humanitarian activities. But few of these were as easy to grasp, as universally appreciated, and as evocatively rendered as the battlefield doughnut.

While many historians treat the turn-of-the-century Holiness movement as otherworldly and premillennial, the Army retained the spirit and mission of its antebellum forerunners by fashioning a faith that spoke and operated on a mundane level. As Timothy Smith demonstrated, evangelical postmillennial perfectionism was present in northern cities on the eve of the Civil War. But when charting the theology's subsequent history, most scholars assumed that its energies were redirected into either the premillennialism of conservative Protestants or the Social Gospel of their more moderate coreligionists. Yet The Salvation Army extended a specifically evangelical postmillennial vision well into the twentieth century through its creative use of symbols and its pragmatic approach to faith. The Army's strategy can be glimpsed in reports from soldiers and wartime observers of the Sallies' behavior. The women themselves rarely described their work in religious terms or contemplated their spiritual mission. Their faith was expressed by their actions, and the message was clear to those around them. One secular war correspondent wrote: "They apply their Christianity to whatever needs to be done at the moment." Another noted: "They seem to be just as religious when frying doughnuts or fixing the machinery of Fords . . . as when mounted on a cracker-box for a pulpit . . . They let the work of their hands do most of the preaching without ever for an instant forgetting that there's a big idea somewhere that inspires them."[31]

That big idea was evangelical Christianity and, more specifically, Holiness theology. As Salvationists understood Holiness, their duty was to transform the secular world into God's kingdom. Their initial attempts to create a vernacular religion—a religion that used contemporary forms and idioms to reach its audience as well as to redeem the forms themselves—had not been successful. Salvationists won members and attracted supporters, but the social order proved resistant to their vision of Christianization. Money was a problem. Unlike other religious groups, they did not have a wealthy or even middle-class constituency. Officers and soldiers gave what they could, but the Army's primary constituency, the poor, were unable to contribute much at all. As a result, local officers operated on a shoestring budget and National Headquarters was chronically underfunded. While it was difficult to raise large sums of money for soul-winning, it was easier to attract funds for nonsectarian social work: the government offered assistance, as did Catholics, Jews, and Protestants of many persuasions.

Shifting their strategy, Salvationists began augmenting soul-saving with social services during the late 1890s. The time was right—the problems of the urban poor were receiving attention from reformers, politicians, and religious leaders. The Army was a leader in the field; by the turn of the century it was known, especially to those involved in combating urban poverty, as an enlightened provider of rescue homes, salvage centers, shelters, and inexpensive hotels. Progressive era leaders hailed this dual focus on the social and the spiritual, and Evangeline Booth dramatized the double-edged strategy in her public performances. While Booth's performances projected a practical religion of love, sympathy, service, and action, the most effective expression of the Army's vision of Holiness was its World War I service.

As the Sallies modeled the Army's mission, the doughnut symbolized the faith. Incarnating notions of religion and service acceptable to the public, the doughnut held myriad meanings. A treat rather than a staple, it signified comfort and well-being to soldiers whose lives were otherwise marked by danger and privation. Since cooking was so difficult in wartime conditions, it also represented love and sacrifice. Evoking memories of home—a whiff of the family kitchen—the doughnuts were redolent of the ideals for which soldiers fought.[32]

Coming together for coffee and doughnuts created the appearance if not the reality of community. Religious meanings inhered to the doughnut's form and content. The simple circle was a traditional symbol for wholeness, while the bread itself held sacred and ritual meaning for Jews and Christians. Bread was the staff of life, the sustaining manna, and the vehicle for miracles. (Did not frying thousands of doughnuts per day suggest some comparison with the multiplying of loaves and fishes?) Breaking bread was at the heart of the Catholic Mass, the Protestant Communion, and the Jewish Sabbath.

Several of these meanings were evident in "The Salvation Army Doughnut" (1918), a paean to the cruller. In this ode the doughnut explicitly stands for motherhood, friendship, comfort, freedom, and divine love:

> A doughnut's just a doughnut, boys, til you are "over there"
> And day and night you're in a trench away in France somewhere;
> You get a fresh-made doughnut, seems it comes from heaven
>   above,
> That doughnut, boys, reminds you of a slice of mother's love.
>
> A doughnut's just a doughnut, boys, when times of peace prevail,
> But in the midst of worse than Hell where devil's powers assail,

>   Where rage and hate and murder strike their hellish deadly blows
>   The doughnut's a sweet-scented wreath which in God's garden
>   grows.[33]

The doughnut disguised the Army's sectarian strain with a generalized religiosity acceptable to people of any faith or none at all. It won public support for the Army's mission with a range of meanings that only partly reflected the Army's intentions. Holiness empowered the Sallies to fry up hundreds of doughnuts each day and enabled them to find peace even at the front lines. But most Americans simply saw a religion of good works. They were ignorant of the theological impulse that led the Sallies to the front, and they had no interest in learning about it. Hearing about the women's deeds was knowledge enough.

To reach the public and, more important, to win its support, the Army employed symbols that attenuated its religious specificity, allowing Americans to read their own meanings into the doughnut and the Salvationists' work. The most generalized reading suggested an inclusive, pluralist religiosity that preached through practice. For many the Army appeared to be the religious apotheosis of the Progressive movement. The Sallies cooked the doughnuts with heart and hands consecrated to God. The image caught the public eye while the message of Holiness, the Army's core doctrine, remained hidden in plain sight.

The first and most extensive use of the doughnut for fundraising purposes was the Army's 1919 Home Service Fund appeal. Booth hoped to capitalize on the Army's war effort by raising enough money to "revolutionize" its financial system. The goal was to collect $13 million, a small fortune by its past fundraising standards. Until this time Army funds had been provided primarily by individual benefactors (men like John D. Rockefeller Sr. and John Wanamaker made significant contributions), local government contracts for social services, and streetcorner solicitations. After the war Booth had wanted an end to "begging" on streetcorners and passing the tambourine. For the sake of "better efficiency," she launched the Home Service Appeal fund, asking the American people to contribute "a sum that will put into effective shape and condition all of the machinery which The Salvation Army has at its command and the new equipment that is necessary."

Booth explained that the $13 million dollars would extend the Army's work in the slums.[34] This appeal, by working on multiple levels, offered many reasons to support it. The Army would continue its dual focus, providing social services and sharing the gospel. In addition, Salvationist

Frederick Duncan's poster for the Home Service Fund Campaign (1919) became a classic Army image. With her arm upraised, the very feminine lassie signals her own strength while invoking God's assistance. SAA leaders promoted their work in pragmatic terms. They provided capitalists a hedge against the poor. Money spent on services would at least appease the masses. At best it might provide a way for some to improve their lot. As Booth explained it, she was not soliciting funds for charity. Rather, she was asking American businesses to invest in creating a better citizenry.

Many of her supporters linked the Army's goals to those of democracy. Cornelius Vanderbilt, chairman of the New York City Committee charged with raising $1.5 million of the campaign total, believed that the Army's nonsectarian services reinforced the nation's democratic ideal.[35] Thomas Marshall, the Vice-President of the United States, echoed this sentiment at a Salvation Army rally, explaining that the Army linked the principles of good government with God's rule:

> The American Republic does not rest upon the Declaration of Independence nor upon the Constitution of the United States, but its cornerstone is the Golden Rule. "Whatsoever you would that men should do unto you, do you even so also unto them" can be the only basis of a militant and triumphant democracy . . . I know of no so-important a factor in the rebuilding of human character, the remaking along lines of law and order of the nation, and the reforming of humankind toward greater democratic principles as is this consecrated band of men and women known as The Salvation Army.[36]

The artist Frederick Duncan made this idea explicit in a poster he created for the 1919 fundraising drive. A blue-bonneted lassie sheltered a child in the folds of her voluminous red cloak. At her feet clamored the faces of the needy, representatives of a wide spectrum of humanity. In the upper left-hand corner blazed the Army's new slogan, "A Man May Be Down, But He's Never Out." The advertising executive Bruce Barton, a longtime Army supporter, has been credited with coining the phrase, but it has also been attributed it to Elmore Leffingwell, the Army's publicity director. Leffingwell had proved himself in the successful campaign to publicize the Army's war work. Employing a similar strategy for the Home Service drive, he blanketed the nation's media. Army representatives organized grassroots support for the campaign while the New York office reached out to the country's opinionmakers. Government and society leaders were recruited; former New York Governor Charles S. Whitman agreed to be the national chairman as General Vanderbilt led New York City's effort.

Leffingwell's staff also circulated posters, photographs, and news stories. Local businessmen received advertisements for display and the new slogan appeared everywhere. Posters like Duncan's were widely distributed and fact-filled booklets were made available. Stories and photographs were forwarded to newspapers and magazines before the campaign began, and during the twelve-day drive articles were posted daily. The *New York Times* alone ran more than sixteen news stories as well as editorials and advertisements in less than two weeks. More than 100 magazines plugged the campaign, and business journals, church bulletins, and other closed-circulation publications did likewise. Readers of Chinese, Japanese, Syrian, Turkish, Polish, German, Italian, Swedish, French, Armenian, Greek, and Hungarian newspapers all received information in their native languages. The Jewish press, in particular, endorsed the appeal, noting that even though The Salvation Army *was* a Christian organization, its work on behalf of the poor deserved support.[37]

At the opening of the campaign Vice-President Marshall addressed a rally at Madison Square Garden and Evangeline Booth spoke on Wall Street. General Vanderbilt announced fundraising quotas from various industries and trades around the city (for example, $250 from dyers and cleaners, $50,000 from banks) and Junior Leaguers sold baked goods.[38] In preparation for the drive's Doughnut Day, Sallies worked alongside society women frying cakes in Mrs. Vincent Astor's Fifth Avenue kitchen. Down on Wall Street a squad of bakers made additional sweets for immediate consumption. The first doughnut, cooked by Evangeline Booth, was auctioned off for $550. When it was returned uneaten she promptly resold it for $5,000.

Doughnuts figured prominently in fundraising activities. Up at the Public Library Mrs. Astor supervised doughnut sales while the vaudevillian Fannie Brice entertained the crowd. Over at Pennsylvania Station the "Black Devil Band" of African-American musicians "jazz(ed) doughnuts into dollars," and throughout the city hotels and restaurant chains held their own "doughnut days" with proceeds earmarked for the Army.[39] Down in the financial district Broadway chorines joined Junior Leaguers hawking the fried cakes to brokers and bankers. While the society women sold their wares for up to $50 each, the showgirls asked for $5, then charged $45 for a kiss. The price discrepancy underscored the doughnut's mutability and the Army's acquiescence to commodified sex as a fundraising strategy. As George Bernard Shaw pointed out in *Major Barbara*, Salvationists never worried that the money they received was tainted. The good they did washed clean whatever stains had been incurred by the donor.

An eclectic array of activities continued through the drive. Policemen canvassed the city for contributions, and waitresses donned Army uniforms to pump up doughnut sales whose profits were sent to Salvationist coffers. The Army made use of celebrities to a greater extent than ever before. In the past politicians and society leaders had publicly supported Salvationist work. Now the Army received extensive help from the entertainment and the business worlds, too. This new synergy further blurred the line between the (religious) Army and the (secular) society. Actors and industrialists were not supporting a mission to Christianize the culture, they were assisting men and women who did good works. The title of the theatrical profession's testimonial to the lassies, "By Their Deeds We Know Them," summed it up. Among the evening's patrons were George M. Cohan, Victor Herbert, and Florenz Ziegfeld Jr., a Catholic, a Protestant, and a Jew.[40] Many of the same stars and producers also participated in a benefit at the Hippodrome theater at which the first rolling pin used to make doughnuts in France was auctioned off.

Business leaders were also active in the appeal. The banker Jacob Schiff joined high-ranking members of the American Infantry and Air Service at a midtown rally. August Belmont donated fourteen boxes at his raceway for auction. The Rockefeller family and R. H. Macy made very public contributions to the campaign, and a local entrepreneur donated money collected at the Biltmore, Commodore, Manhattan, and Belmont hotels. The year after the drive the Army extended this outreach with a new "Advisory Board System" that gave local civic and business leaders an institutional channel for assisting Salvationist work. Board members offered advice, bolstered community relations, and provided financial backing. By 1925 some 20,000 business and professional leaders nationwide participated.[41]

At the end of the 1919 Home Service Fund appeal, General Vanderbilt announced that New York had reached its mark, and Evangeline Booth released a statement of thanks for the public's aid in raising $13 million. The Army's victory was a harbinger both of its future success and of the looming changes in its status. Salvationists needed support from the widest possible public, which, in turn, wanted a nonsectarian vehicle for its collective goodwill. The Army's religious specificity was eclipsed by its concrete acts of compassion, and its de facto pluralist approach enabled it to claim a market previously served along primarily sectarian lines.

Among the most helpful strategists for claiming this market and aiding the Army's peacetime transformation was the writer Bruce Barton. In 1919 Barton helped start an advertising company that became BBDO

(Barton, Batten, Durstine, and Osborn), one of the most successful firms of its kind. Barton assisted with the publicity for the United War Work campaign, a joint fundraising appeal for the religious and welfare agencies serving the U.S. Army, and he continued to help The Salvation Army after the war ended. The son of a respected Congregationalist minister, Barton was raised in a home whose traditional Protestant values—service, hard work, and individual responsibility—meshed easily with those espoused by the Army. As a young man Barton had worked among the poor, and he appreciated the Army's innovative programs.

Although he was a preacher's son, Barton saw his own vocation in the world of business, and he believed Jesus, too, would have felt at home among American capitalists. His bestseller *The Man Nobody Knows* (1925) made this very case, portraying the Christian Savior with the traits of a successful Chief Executive Officer. Just as Jesus' example could sanctify business, Barton believed, "ethical advertising" could create a better world. His booklet "And They Shall Beat Their Swords into Electrotypes" (1918) elucidated this point. Sharing Salvationist ideas about truth and integrity in promoting products, Barton wanted to write copy that helped men and women make wise choices.[42]

Barton probably had such notions in mind when he wrote "Only One Thousand Dollars," a fundraising pamphlet which explained how the Army spent a $1,000 contribution over the course of a year. In short melodramatic sketches Barton evoked repentant convicts, unwed mothers, and homeless children whose lives were changed by Salvationist interventions. For $100 the Army rescued a woman from the streets. For $10 it helped a mother find her long-lost son. And for only $1 it saved a tradesman who drank too much. To those who wondered if the Army really did any good, Barton's booklet offered a compelling answer.[43] It also supported Booth's prewar formulation of the Army's utility for capitalists. A $1,000 donation was a sound investment: humanitarian aid at a reasonable price.

Around New York with The Salvation Army

Asking capitalists to invest in their work required Salvationists to make their social services, in the bywords of the age, efficient and effective. Gone were the Christmas spectacles at which the wealthy watched the poor consume their annual turkey dinner. During the 1922 Christmas season Army lassies commandeered a fleet of automobiles to distribute food baskets around the city. Noted a reporter: "Although it was hard work, the Army workers voted it much more satisfactory than their former system which compelled the poor to stand hours in line for the bags, a spectacle of anxious poverty." Likewise, as Prohibition took hold and fewer alcoholics needed help, the Army started drug treatment programs and expanded its outreach to women.[44]

The Army stressed its range of services and its awareness of changing needs in mass-distributed pamphlets. Evangeline Booth boasted that Army efforts were always "just around the corner." And *Around New York with The Salvation Army,* a promotional booklet of the 1920s, delineated the work of its many nurseries, hospitals, industrial homes, and maternity homes. Even the *War Cry* offered new and up-to-date information. Regular columns by the "family physician" and the "poor man's lawyer" tried to anticipate readers' concerns. A revamped women's page provided the latest tips on child care and homemaking even as the layout and headline changed—from "Women's Work, Ways and Warfare" to "The Ladies Forum" to "The Woman's Viewpoint."[45]

Efficacy was important to the Army, but so was efficiency. The old distinctions between the worthy and unworthy poor still held, and Salvationists continued to judge clients according to their willingness to work. The chairman of the New York Federation of Agencies for Homeless Men, Salvation Army Major Edward Underwood, urged the public to stop giving alms to beggars. Instead he recommended sending them to social service agencies that would help those who were willing to help themselves.[46]

Besides yearly fundraising drives and the continuing promotion of their social welfare activities, Salvationists still used public spectacles to educate outsiders about their work. From coast to coast—Aimee Semple McPherson's Angelus Temple to Christian F. Reisner's Broadway Temple—others also mixed religion with entertainment. But Salvationist galas often took on a more didactic tone than those of the competition. In years past Army pageants had focused primarily on Army work, but after World War I they increasingly included civic themes and milestones of American history. As David Glassberg has written, the era's secular pageants were "a way to make local residents look beyond their particular group identities to a common civic identity and thus a common interest in undertaking needed reforms.[47] The Army's pageants fulfilled a similar function: they provided a way for New Yorkers to link their common identity and shared concerns with the Army's mission. At the same time, the inverse also held true. By performing its own history alongside that of the United States, the Army furthered its own acculturation.

At the Army's "Historical and Industrial Presentation of Progress," a pageant staged at the Manhattan Opera House in 1924, Father Knicker-bocker—New York City's paternal symbol—served as master of ceremonies. In the course of the evening historical figures such as Betsy Ross, Peter Stuyvesant, and Abraham Lincoln shared the stage with the Men's and the Women's Social Service Divisions, the League of Mercy, and the doughnut girls. Further highlighting the Army's contribution to democracy and citizenship, the program booklet included statistics showing the growth in its evangelistic outreach and social services. Like the pageant itself, these statistics emphasized scale. For the Army, as for the nation, bigger meant better.[48]

New York's lead in Army fundraising was praised by outside sources. A fourteen-month investigation by the National Information Bureau, a Rockefeller-funded project, scrutinized Army finances, programs, and philosophy. In its recommendations, Salvationist officers nationwide were urged to adopt New York City's fundraising strategies. But ensuring the success of these yearly drives became harder as the 1920s progressed and the postwar urgency faded. It took the stock market crash and the Great Depression to reignite the Army's fire. In the autumn of 1930 Booth and her advisors hit on the idea of staging a postseason Army-Navy football game to benefit The Salvation Army. When the long-standing rivals finally met before a crowd of 70,000 at Yankee Stadium, Army beat Navy 6–0 and The Salvation Army took home more than $600,000.[49]

By spring, desperate for additional funds, the Army asked the banker E. F. Hutton for assistance with fundraising. The result was "Radioland," a gala benefit at Madison Square Garden that featured 1,100 performers of radio, stage, and screen. While Hutton sponsored the event, he also enlisted support from some of the city's wealthiest families, including the Biddles, the Chryslers, the Harrimans, the Hearsts, the Roosevelts, and the Vanderbilts. Politicians helped, too: Mayor Jimmy Walker and former Governor Al Smith served as masters of ceremony. To guarantee that the sound would carry throughout the arena, the National Broadcasting Company turned the evening's three stages into temporary broadcast studios. But the 300-piece orchestra, ballet troupe, and chorus line—not to mention Rudy Vallee, Al Jolson, Maurice Chevalier, Amos 'n' Andy, and many more entertainers—could only be heard by those 17,000 ticketholders who attended the event.[50]

The Depression-era appeals in New York succeeded because the Army enjoyed the support of local government, the press, and the public. Its campaign slogan of 1932, "Hunger knows no holiday," was printed on pamphlets sent to the city's civic, business, social, and charitable leaders. Thousands more copies were distributed at mass meetings and posted all over the city. After a series of radio spots, a small boy emptied his piggy bank and sent the contents to the Army. Another listener visited the Army's 14th Street Headquarters and, after inspecting the premises, handed $50 to an officer. "I haven't any more money with me," he said, "but I'll be back."[51]

The following year Salvationists aimed their drive at the "war on want." The opening of the campaign, a dinner for 4,000 at the Park Avenue Regiment Armory, featured Army "chow" prepared by cooks in motorized field kitchens. While Boy Scouts served the homely fare of beef stew and rice, lassies passed out doughnuts. In keeping with the military theme, invitations were "emergency orders," and George Dern, the U.S. Secretary of War, gave the evening's keynote address. The biggest coup of the campaign was a joint appearance by the former Presidential rivals Herbert Hoover and Alfred E. Smith.[52]

Try Religion!

Edward H. McKinley has called the 1920s a "bright" time for The Salvation Army, and, from a statistical standpoint, it was. Between 1916 and 1926 its membership more than doubled and the number of local corps grew as well. Social programs and evangelical activities thrived, fundraising ensured greater financial stability than ever before, and the Army's net assets, property, and buildings increased significantly. The Army was becoming more visible as a charitable presence in American life, and it was also succeeding in its own terms—"to win souls and make Soldiers."[53] Much of the Army's success in this era derived from its postwar popularity, but Salvationists enhanced their position by tailoring their humanitarian activities in response to social needs. But New York's Salvationists were less successful at spreading their evangelical message. Street meetings were barely tolerated unless, as in Rheba Crawford's case, they had novelty appeal. Once subversive, later amusing, the Army's streetcorner services appeared increasingly dated. The military motif no longer had the same cachet as the nation recoiled against the recent world war, and the evangelical message rang hollow for those who considered themselves part of a lost generation.

The Army's ranks were changing, too. Thoughtful deliberation replaced the gung-ho zeal that had sparked the conversion and enlistment of men like Edward J. Parker. One indicator was the rising age of cadets. In 1928 the average student at Army training colleges was twenty-two years old and many entered the program after working in the secular world. A majority were women, often from the helping professions: nurses, teachers, and domestics. Salesmen, farmers, and bookkeepers also matriculated; the graduating class of 1929 included a former Broadway dancer, a dressmaker, a chauffeur, a potter, and a supervisor for the telephone company. The age and diversity of officer candidates, suggestive of a broad-based search for meaning, may reflect on the upheavals that marked the period. A decade of transition and turbulence across the nation, the 1920s found full expression in the ethos of change, daring, and lacerating self-scrutiny that Ann Douglas calls the "terrible honesty" of Manhattan's artists and intellectuals. The avant-garde's contempt for what they perceived as Victorian hypocrisy and capitalist inequality did not lead to wholesale social change, but it did broaden public discussion of race, class, and gender. While members of The Salvation Army were neither participants nor agents in the social and cultural changes that Douglas describes, they were nonetheless affected by them. And, through their publications and evangelistic outreach, Salvationists tried to fight what they saw.[54]

Army leaders vigorously denounced repeal of Prohibition, flapperdom, and all aspects of modernism that challenged bedrock values of family, home, and religion. In 1928 they launched an aggressive evangelical campaign that also fought against the spirit of the times. A front-page story in the *New York Times* announced that Salvationists would begin the New Year by saving residents of Greenwich Village, the city's avant-garde enclave. Home of artists, intellectuals, and leftists, the Village was probably among the least religious neighborhoods in Manhattan. Accordingly, residents around Sheridan Square were unpleasantly surprised when at 9 A.M. on a cold Sunday morning they were awakened by band music and exhortations "to listen to the word of God." One elderly agnostic, already up and out, clubbed an Army major over the head with his umbrella. Unscathed, the major directed his soldiers to distribute summonses to passers-by, ordering them to appear at worship services. Salvationists also visited houses and restaurants, greeting residents and inviting them to a religious meeting.[55]

In the following weeks Salvationists took their crusade to more familiar haunts. They "invaded" the Bowery and the Lower East Side, conducted religious services at Tammany Hall, and mounted "a torch light parade on the Great White Way." During the "raid" on the Bowery some 200 "prisoners" were captured and marched uptown for a religious service. Of these, some 40 testified and were subsequently claimed as converts. In a newspaper interview Lieutenant-Commissioner Richard Holz, who oversaw the citywide campaign, explained that new tactics were needed for new times. The advent of speakeasies and police crackdowns on streetcorner prostitution made vice more difficult to root out; therefore the Army was canvassing neighborhoods, such as the Village, that it usually did not visit. But enthusiastic attempts to save souls in tearooms and cabarets notwithstanding, very few, other than the truly down-and-out, followed the Army band.[56]

Despite Army claims to use up-to-date methods for its soul saving, its activities appeared quaint and old-fashioned when reported in the daily newspaper. Unlike its social service work, which was seen in a positive light, the Army's religious outreach seemed dated. Lieutenant-Commissioner Holz had been a streetcorner evangelist for forty-four years. He looked and sounded like an aging soldier unwilling to surrender a long-lost fight. A savvier strategy was to use circumlocutions that masked the Army's actual intent. During a speech at Madison Square Garden Evangeline Booth urged the audience to "Try religion!" While devout Christians knew there was only one religion to try, unconverted ears heard an affirmation of all and any faith. As one editorial reported, Booth had spoken about "a deep appreciation of the permanent values of life" expressed as a "force in human society working to diminish human grief." A noble sentiment, yes, but not fully reflective of the Army's staunch evangelicalism.[57]

In a culture becoming ever less comfortable with public expressions of religious particularity, Salvationists were constantly challenged to find a balance between their spiritual work and their social commitment. Addressing Army delegates at a social work conference in 1933, Lieutenant-Commissioner Edward J. Parker asked, "Where Are We Taking the Army?" Warning that it could become a mere philanthropic organization or a "hobby" for socially minded millionaires, Parker emphasized the movement's core mission: "bring(ing) to the needy the ideals for which He stood." While Army leaders understood that a generalized faith enabled widespread support of Salvationist social services, Parker and oth-

The "Try Religion" campaign was aimed at a Depression-weary public that, despite hard times, had not turned to the churches. SAA

ers also tried to push an unadulterated evangelical platform into the public eye.[58]

"Try Religion," the Army's 1932 evangelistic campaign, was considered a message suited to the times. If men and women were willing to try almost anything, why not sample the Christian faith? "Why Go Round in Circles," asked a *War Cry* cover, depicting silhouettes of social dancing, gambling, and horse racing. Religious belief was a better alternative. Similarly, a humorous display advertisement in the Salvationist weekly touted a bottle of medicine labeled "Faith in God" as "good for what ails you." Such soul-winning attempts should have worked in the 1930s, since in previous eras hard times had helped spur religious revival. But the Army, like the churches, attracted few new followers despite its perseverance. In the summer Salvationists raised gospel tents around the city and dispatched automobile ministries to beaches and resorts. Its religious services were heard over the radio, and its seasonal celebrations welcomed all. Open-air work continued, too. More than a decade after Rheba Crawford had charmed the Great White Way, Lieutenant-Colonel Wallace Winchell held forth at Columbus Circle. Like Crawford, Winchell initially was met with hostility; police officers had to break up the ensuing scuffle. But Winchell kept returning, gradually winning acceptance for the sincerity of his ministry if not the truth of his message [59]

The High Council and the Jubilee

While the Army contended for souls on the streets, its second campaign was a defensive one. In the fight to control its image, in which battles were fought on the movie screen and in the press, Salvationists held their own throughout the 1920s. Even when they did not succeed in projecting the image they desired—for example, some coverage of the 1928 evangelistic campaign made them appear ineffectual—Salvationists retained public sympathy. But a struggle over the Army's leadership, which buffeted International Headquarters from 1928 to 1929, threatened to alienate its widespread support. The problems underlying the crisis had long simmered. As the Army grew larger, wealthier, and more global, commissioners around the world chafed under British and specifically Booth leadership.[60]

A group of reformers wanted a more democratic polity and greater local autonomy. As leader of the reform movement, Evangeline Booth had lobbied the General, her brother Bramwell, for change. But Bramwell refused, intent on keeping the Army exactly as his father had left it. Concerned that the opportunity for change would be lost if Bramwell were allowed to choose his successor (as Army policy mandated), the reformers decided to depose him. When Bramwell became seriously ill, Evangeline and her allies called for a High Council, a meeting of the Army's top officials from around the world. The subsequent intrigue, a veritable soap opera of betrayals, sickbed confessions, and desperate power plays, made front-page news for more than a month. Evangeline Booth's behind-the-scenes machinations notwithstanding, she struck a high-minded tone for American press coverage by defining her "onerous" task as democratizing an entrenched autocracy.

When Bramwell was finally removed from office, Evangeline hoped to replace him as General, but she was soundly defeated. Although complaining privately to her officers, she publicly professed her desire to return to the United States. Indeed, when Booth landed in New York her role as a reformer was lauded by civic leaders, and Salvationists hailed her as their own "Joan of Arc." On balance, secular coverage of the High Council was positive; newspapers mainly expressed worry that the struggle would affect the Army's work. Cautioning against a split in the organization, the *Chicago Daily News* noted: "With so much important work for the Army to do, friction and discord over matters of form and direction should not be tolerated." Likewise, the *Boston Post* lamented: "It would be nothing short of a world calamity to have [the Army's] work halted." When matters were resolved, the *New York World* spoke for many in opining that the Army's "more flexible and democratic government" was both good and necessary.[61]

With the High Council behind her, Booth focused on the American Army's Golden Jubilee. Held in May 1930, the Jubilee celebrated the Army's accomplishments in a half-century of work in the United States. A week's worth of events—including pageants, parades, open-airs, Holiness meetings, and music festivals—drew more than 35,000 spectators. Hewing to past patterns, the Army used anniversary events to underscore its role in America and its contributions to a democratic society. Booth and her officials, whose appreciation for scale had been demonstrated in previous pageants, went all out for the week's festivities. Each entertainment was grander than the next. Every promotional piece ballyhooed the Army's numerical growth, and the celebration's centerpiece was the dedication of a new Headquarters building. Booth had deemed Maud and Ballington's "skyscraping" citadel inadequate for the new century and was replacing it with an twelve-story Art Deco structure. The new building would be equipped with broadcast facilities; adjacent to it, The Evangeline, a residence hotel for working women, featured a gymnasium, a rooftop garden, and a swimming pool.[62]

The Jubilee's opening pageant, "The Rise and Progress of The Salvation Army in the United States," attracted a crowd of 8,000. An additional 4,000 Salvationists presented living tableaux that retold episodes from the Army's history as well as highlights from the nation's past. Opulent montages depicted a mix of religious, historical, and patriotic themes. The evening's finale spotlighted the Army's work abroad with lurid scenes of African witchcraft and "Hindoo" rites. The following night, at the "Great Musical Festival," 700 Army bandsmen and 1,000 Salvationist singers gathered on an oversized stage with the composer John Philip Sousa. Sousa had written "The Salvation Army March" for the occasion and dedicated it to Commander Booth. Not surprisingly, Booth claimed center stage throughout the Jubilee proceedings. She was lionized by friends, feted by followers, and honored with the bestowal of the Order of the Founder, the most prestigious award given to a Salvationist. [63]

The Great Depression

The Army's interwoven interests—preventing social unrest, providing a way for the public to help the poor, and saving lost souls—extended the link between Salvationist religion and American patriotism that was forged during World War I. But by the 1930s the Army's activist religion, based in a nineteenth-century evangelical world view, had been undermined by the new ideas and trends of the modern era. Still, core Protestant evangelical beliefs retained a hold on the popular imagination, and just as the Army projected a faith that united Americans during the war, it was able to rally the support of diverse groups during the Great Depression.

In the years between these two catastrophes the Army's charitable activities received more public attention than its missionary efforts. Although Salvationists tried to hold the two together—salvation led to service and service was predicated on salvation—many Americans preferred to separate them. Donors were more often interested in remedying social ills than in converting the heathen masses. Moreover, the Army had pledged to help all regardless of religion or creed, and heavy-handed proselytizing ran counter to its image. Most important, that kind of proselytizing rarely worked. Experience had shown that didactic preaching or requiring clients to attend religious services did not lead to conversions. Rather, modeling Christian behavior provided the best example for others to follow—and to fund.

In general Salvationists understood their strategy to be one of adaptation; they survived by finding a niche where their work was needed and infusing that work, as much as possible, with a religious dimension. Focus was all-important; they had no interest in the intellectual fads of the day. A Bowery officer cautioned against Freud and the new psychologists: "They are the intelligentsia—beware of them." Salvationists also steered clear of popular feuds. In the battle between religious liberals and fundamentalists the Army sympathized with the latter, but its leaders refused to become involved, noting only the inadequacy of the liberal position and the toll the fight took on both sides. One of the few occasions when the Army let its policy of neutrality lapse was the 1928 Presidential race. A passionate advocate of Prohibition, Evangeline Booth was known to favor Herbert Hoover. (Hoover was a churchgoing Protestant, while his opponent, Governor Al Smith of New York, was a Catholic who supported repeal.) Booth defended her anti-repeal stance as moral rather than political, but she drew the line when a New York officer announced a public lecture on "Hoover the Man." Booth ordered him to cancel the address until after the election lest the Army seem to violate its nonpartisan stance.[64]

While the Army was attentive to the outside world, it was slow to gauge the developing economic crisis. The Crash of 1929 came and went without much notice in the *War Cry*'s pages, but by the following spring the paper was reporting on the "almost unprecedented suffering" in the Bowery. Breadlines were at their longest since 1914, and all manner of men, from tradesmen to white-collar workers, stood in them. Still, the *War Cry* leavened bad news with an upbeat approach. Despite "hard times," noted one editorial, New Yorkers had deposited $50 million into savings banks during the first six weeks of the year. In May the paper reported that President Hoover had told the New York Chamber of Commerce that the economic news was good. Even a month later, when the American Federation of Labor informed Congress that 3.6 million workers (or one out of every four) were unemployed, Army editorialists predicted a turnaround.[65]

By the autumn of 1930 the paper's tone had changed. Articles focused on the Army's response to the growing problem. In New York, where 250,000 people were out of work, Salvationists set up free employment agencies for men and women. Pledging that no one need go without food and shelter during the winter, the Army opened eight new "feeding stations" in Manhattan and Brooklyn. Twice a week Army trucks visited city restaurants to pick up unsold food for distribution at its stations and shelters. By November Salvationists were feeding some 10,000 people daily and sheltering 1,700 people each night.

Their reputation as humanitarian social service providers enabled Salvationists to bridge the ever widening economic gap. Both the haves and the have-nots trusted them. When showgirls collected clothes for the poor, they donated them to the Army. When a wealthy donor wanted to provide shelter for homeless children, he leased his house to the Army. And when 600 of New York's most prominent club and professional women decided to raise money for the crisis, they formed an emergency aid committee to support the Army's work. The women's efforts, in particular, brought Salvationists massive amounts of free publicity. Campaign posters were plastered on buses, subways, and local trains. Radio stations broadcast fundraising appeals, and several department store windows displayed paintings by well-known artists that depicted the Army's work. When the drive ended the women's committee had exceeded its goal, raising a total of $600,000.[66]

As the Depression continued and more middle-class men lost their jobs, Salvationists targeted these newly unemployed white-collar workers. In one offer of help, a missive in the *New York Times*, Commissioner John McMillan wrote, "If this letter should reach the eye of any one in the circumstances described, we shall be glad if he or she will communicate with us," and promised to keep replies confidential. When economic prospects did not improve in the new year, the Army was deluged with requests from white-collar workers. Two days after opening an employment bureau for professional men, Salvationists were contacted by 1,000 job applicants. With little relief in sight, the Army opened new facilities: an emergency food depot in midtown Manhattan, a steamship fitted as a floating hotel for destitute seamen, and a shelter for "colored" men in Harlem.[67]

In the Army's promotional materials and in *War Cry* stories about its work, two ideological positions undergirded its extensive relief efforts: opposition to the dole and concern for public order. Evangeline Booth deplored the dole, or free governmental aid to the needy, as antithetical to Army principles. She believed that giving something for nothing stripped men of their dignity and self-respect. The dole was not only un-Christian, it was bad for society, rendering recipients more likely to riot and rebel.

For Salvationists, maintaining morale, along with providing basic necessities, was a political as much as a religious imperative. Secular leaders who supported Army work appreciated the latter but emphasized the former. According to New York's Police Commissioner and Commissioner of Public Welfare, "any break in the program of The Salvation Army would throw the city's welfare machinery seriously out of gear, and would entail an immediate menace of social disturbances by the destitute unemployed."[68]

Such concerns may have seemed realistic at the time. Large northern cities were the sites of repeated riots over food and rent. Often organized by the Socialist and Communist parties, these demonstrations began as peaceful marches but quickly erupted into violence and looting. Union Square, just down the street from Army Headquarters, was the rallying point for many Depression-era rallies and marches. In March 1930, when 35,000 unemployed workers and sympathizers prepared to march from the 14th Street park to City Hall, police broke up the demonstration, injuring some 100 people.

For its part, the Army tried to balance its social and religious goals. Addressing a conference of social workers, Army Commissioner William McIntyre explained that providing material relief was not their greatest challenge. Rather, building morale—or a sense of responsibility—was. When necessary the Army shifted emphasis; its 1932 fundraising appeal referred to one of its appropriations as "insurance against social unrest." Illustrating the point, a *New York Times* reporter described the "program of reconstruction" at the Cheer Lodge, an Army shelter for men on the Lower East Side. The ranking Salvationist in command, Adjutant T. Dickinson, noted that many clients, convinced that no one cared about them, assumed there was a "catch" to the Army's generosity. But their outlook soon improved: "Morale is better. The men feel that The Salvation Army and the public in general are interested in the welfare of the unemployed. Now, too, these men are making a determined effort to help themselves."[69]

Throughout the Depression the Army maintained a high profile in city life. By early 1933 the organization was providing 100,000 meals and 25,000 lodgings free of charge for needy New Yorkers each week. Whenever possible the Army tried to respect the clients' dignity. Officers sought to foster a sense of normality, either by keeping families together or by insisting that the unemployed remain active. An emergency food station for women and children, sponsored by Mrs. E. F. (Marjorie Post) Hutton, obviated the humiliating ritual of standing on a breadline by providing two spacious waiting rooms. In addition, the 200-seat dining room, decorated with comfortable chairs, new linen tablecloths, and sturdy crockery, lent a homey atmosphere to the midtown soup kitchen.[70]

Pledging "to keep the family intact," the Army's Family Welfare Department opened several shelters for women and children. One wealthy donor fixed up two homes on West 22nd Street as a residence for 100 women and children. But, even in the midst of the Depression, Salvationists remained vigilant for "scams and cheats." To separate the deserving poor from the undeserving, Army workers were trained to ask personal questions in a tactful manner. The same strategy was followed at the Gold Dust Lodge, a shelter and feeding station for unemployed men in lower Manhattan. The lodge, outfitted to house 3,500 men and feed 10,000 daily, was a six-story refurbished industrial building. During the day men worked around the house and looked for jobs. On evenings and weekends they could attend Army-sponsored lectures, recreational activities, or religious services. The lodge also conducted a part-time school with classes in art, economics, bookkeeping, and English.[71]

Up in Harlem The Salvation Army Colored Men's Hotel and Food Depot accommodated 120 residents and fed 1,000 each night. The hotel housed residents in two-week shifts, then sent them to the city's Welfare Council Central Registration Bureau in lower Manhattan. Men who plied a needed trade, such as barbering, were encouraged to offer their services at a reasonable price to other residents. Each day half the group stayed in the hotel to clean, cook, and do maintenance work on the facilities, while the other half went out looking for work.[72]

Even as the Army reached out to various constituencies, the city asked for more assistance. When the Municipal Lodging House ran out of beds in early 1932, the Army squeezed another 200 beds into its shelters. By the spring of 1932 the Army's $900,000 emergency relief fund was spent, and the demand for services was still growing. Desperate to save money, Evangeline Booth cut Army officers' salaries 10 percent and closed the four training colleges. At the same time, Army officials in New York launched a local fundraising campaign for $1 million. The *War Cry* reported that the Army helped some 33,000 New Yorkers each day, establishing, in effect, "a religion everyone can understand."[73]

Of course, not everyone did understand. In John Steinbeck's *The Grapes of Wrath* destitute farmers harbor bitter feelings toward the Army, and there were others, real men and women, not fictional characters, who resented what they perceived to be the Army's self-righteous attitude. Nevertheless, many others were glad for help. In New York

During the late 1930s Salvationists offered a hopeful message to a Depression-ravaged, war-weary world. AWC, April 15, 1939, 1, SAA

more than 6,000 white-collar professionals visited the Army's confidential employment service and millions took advantage of its free beds and free meals. Before large-scale federal relief began, the Army was a willing partner in local efforts. Mayor Fiorello La Guardia kicked off the Army's 1934 Citizens Appeal by citing the close relationship between the city and the religious group. When La Guardia asked the Army to administer feeding stations for free coffee and doughnuts, Salvationists sprang into action, setting up stations almost overnight. Later, when the federally sponsored WPA was organized, the Army supplemented its efforts, too.[74]

At the Copa

By the end of the 1930s, even as the nation was still struggling with the Depression, many Salvationists foresaw America's future participation in the European war. Readers of the *War Cry* were aware of the conflict's toll well before Pearl Harbor. In early 1941 German planes bombed the Army's International Headquarters in London, and that summer a series of airborne attacks destroyed the building. Throughout Europe and the Middle East Salvationists set up recreational huts and offered medical services, but each time the Axis powers occupied a nation they disbanded the Army and expelled local members. In early 1941 National Secretary Edward J. Parker, who had overseen war efforts in 1917, began preparations for America's inevitable involvement. After the United States instituted a peacetime draft, Parker invited six organizations to discuss a cooperative war effort. As a result The Salvation Army, the YMCA, the YWCA, the Jewish Welfare Board, the Catholic Community Service, and the Traveler's Aid Society agreed to provide joint welfare, recreational, and spiritual services. They launched a campaign for $10 million and raised $14 million.[75]

The joint effort was called the United Service Organization for National Defense or, more popularly, the USO. The largest interfaith program ever undertaken, the USO initially set up service centers near military bases around the country. As Salvation Army huts had been a home away from home during World War I, USO clubs strove to fulfill the same function by providing books, music, classes, recreational games, coffee, and doughnuts. There were variations in services: YMCA-sponsored clubs held dances, while those operated by The Salvation Army offered religious meetings. No one was required to attend these meetings, but those who did heard heartfelt testimonies and familiar hymns. Salva-

"A Home Away From Home"

Salvation Army work in World War II was channeled through the USO. This back cover for the *War Cry*'s Christmas issue of 1943 emphasizes Salvationist camaraderie while keeping the religious message to a minimum. AWC, Dec. 25, 1943, SAA

tionists also operated mobile canteens and opened Red Shield Clubs, providing showers and emergency lodgings, in the nation's larger cities.[76]

Salvation Army work in World War II had the same hallmarks as its efforts in World War I. Salvationists went directly to the troops, and Army "hostesses," as USO and Red Shield workers were called, darned socks, served food, and sewed buttons as the Sallies had done twenty-five years earlier.[77] But this time there was no overriding figure, like the doughnut girl, to catch the public eye. The joint USO effort obscured the Army's particular contribution, and the numbers of women serving in the clubs made the Sallies seem less unusual. It was also a different time; the nation was another generation removed from the old evangelical world view. The ideals that The Salvation Army represented—God, home, country—no longer required a religious frame. They were part of the popular culture, explicit in wartime movies such as *God Is My Co-Pilot* (1945) and *So Proudly We Hail* (1942).

When the war ended The Salvation Army was in a very different position than it had been in 1918. Although revered and respected as an American institution, it was no longer a vital symbol of the nation's religious and patriotic consensus. No movies celebrated the Army's war work. No showgirls glorified the lassies' service to the troops. No public relations bounce helped to fill its coffers. When the Army asked New Yorkers to contribute to its 1945 annual campaign; leaders sought only a third of their budget from donations. The rest came from its social services. Yet the war effort had strained the very social welfare work that was fundamental to the organization's survival. The number of cadets had fallen to an all-time low, and a scarcity of male officers—caused by mobilization for the war effort—forced the closing and consolidation of many local corps and service centers.[78] So the Army began anew—attracting recruits, designing new programs, soliciting old friends and, of course, frying up doughnuts.

Doughnuts notwithstanding, fundraising became even more difficult when the Army dropped out of the Greater New York Fund. Some Salvationist leaders felt that the Fund, which represented a range of social and welfare agencies, gave them too small a percentage of its annual collection. As a result of the Army's defection several business groups refused to support its 1947 drive for $1 million. But Salvationists retained some powerful friends. Support from the American Broadcast Company enabled them to promote their appeal on television, and assistance from the business executive Walter Hoving helped secure the Boston Symphony

Orchestra for a fundraising concert. The Army relied on old staples, too. In 1948 New York City Mayor William O'Dwyer kicked off the "Donuts for Donors" campaign, and during the 1949 campaign mobile canteens cruised the city passing out free coffee and doughnuts.[79]

The 1949 campaign was launched with a televised broadcast from the Rainbow Room in Rockefeller Center. Casting a wide net, the Army asked celebrities, including J. Edgar Hoover, Jackie Robinson, and Arthur Godfrey, to record promotional radio spots. But the most publicity garnered during the appeal was totally inadvertent. Perhaps presaging the commingling of mobsters and missionaries in *Guys and Dolls,* the Army unwittingly tapped the underworld leader Frank Costello as a vice-chairman for its annual drive. He was asked because he had donated generously the previous year, and although Costello was allegedly connected to illegal gambling, his name was unfamiliar to the Salvationists who requested his help.

Costello organized a $100-a-plate charity dinner at the Copacabana, a well-known Manhattan nightclub. His guests included Tammany Hall leaders, State Supreme Court judges, city officials, and several reputed gangsters. When word of the soiree was leaked to the press, it was hard to say who was most embarrassed. Most of the political figures refused to comment. Costello released a statement withdrawing from the Army campaign. And an Army official commented that no one had known that their Frank Costello was "THE Frank Costello." Not surprisingly, Army leaders kept the dinner's proceeds. Their legal department had deemed it permissible, and it was de facto Army policy not to worry about the source of its contributions.[80]

Hold Fast! Hold Fast!

From 1905 to 1934 Evangeline Booth was the single most important weapon in the Army's struggle to define itself. She had been a public figure and newsmaker as no other American Salvationist was before or since. Her long friendship with the publisher of the *New York Times,* Adolph Ochs, helped ensure coverage in his newspaper, but her own idiosyncratic charm contributed most to her popular appeal. Booth's eccentricities—her Victorian speech, her bright red flourishes—endeared her to readers and counterbalanced Hollywood's image of the lassie. By the mid-1930s, however, Booth began to fade from view. During her tenure as General she still received press coverage when she visited the States, but after retiring to her home in Hartsdale, New York, she was mentioned only infrequently.

Likewise, fewer stories about Army relief efforts appeared in newspapers; the economy had not fully recovered, but more people were working and the war would soon bring full employment. To the New York–based media, whose exposure to Salvationists was mostly on streetcorners, the missionaries seemed quaint: simple souls in old-fashioned uniforms who took care of the city's neediest. By the 1940s their once-radical qualities—women ministers, streetcorner bands, single-minded service—made the Army ripe for rediscovery as an urban religious artifact. Unlike stories written sixty years earlier, which depicted Salvationists as vulgar young rebels, this new crop of articles described staid but dedicated officers whose shortcomings ran more to naïveté and an excess of spiritual fervor. At a time when church attendance was in a lull and religion held little sway over the New York intelligentsia, a tone of sophisticated condescension was de rigueur.

Profiles in the *New Yorker*, for example, gently mocked the group's gung-ho evangelicalism. In "Hold Fast! Hold Fast!" (1940) Richard O. Boyer described a day with Brigadier Norman S. Marshall, the principal of the Eastern Training College in the Bronx. The school's curriculum included a mix of the practical and the theological, but Boyer focused less on the substance of what he observed than on its style. Male cadets were "scrawny and flat-chested" with thin necks and large collars. Their female classmates were deemed somewhat more attractive, but both sexes were prone to unseemly giggles and titters. Brigadier Marshall appeared most ludicrous of all. He barked like a "gym instructor" and ranted incoherently. His gestures were wild and his poses melodramatic. Conversing with cadets proved no more illuminating. Unable to follow their biblical allusions, Boyer could not understand how spiritual salvation led to public service.[81]

This ambivalence toward the Army, a discomfort with their religious dedication mingled with a curiosity about their humanitarian work, surfaced again in another profile by Boyer, this one of Captain Angelina Nawkins, published in the *New Yorker* in 1946. Shadowing Nawkins for several weeks, Boyer attended street meetings and services and even visited her home. But he saw little more than a caricature: a large, plain woman whose greatest skill was following orders. Nawkins regularly consulted the Army's *Orders and Regulations* on matters ranging from ventilating bedrooms to rescuing backsliders. Boyer was less interested in the source of her commitment than in its personal cost, dwelling on details he deemed revealing: Nawkins losing her temper with a disruptive drunk, gazing wistfully at a (forbidden) movie theater, brooding about the public's dismissal of her beliefs.[82]

Boyer explained Nawkins's internal contradictions and the Army's strictures by arguing that Salvationists were part of "an older and more rural America." The Captain's conflicts arose because urban realities were antithetical to antiquated rural values. Old-time religion could not compete in the modern metropolis; that was why the Army attracted only the elderly destitute and the delinquent young. Was it any wonder that Angelina Nawkins, too, was tempted by the freedom and autonomy implicit in the contemporary city? Was it surprising that she chafed under the dictates of a life planned and controlled by antedated religious notions? In Boyer's view, Nawkins's secret desire was to be like everyone else.

Boyer was not alone in seeking to understand—even explain away—a religious zeal that seemed out of place in the modern city. His analysis of the tensions between rural and urban life had merit but was not applicable in this instance. The Army had long been an urban presence in the United States. Even though many of its officers grew up in small towns and rural areas, their training and experience prepared them for battle on city streets. Thus while Salvationists may have been formed by the ideals and values of nineteenth-century rural America, the Army itself was designed for urban warfare. In this way the movement drew on both Populism and Progressivism in its religious mission. That link fueled the Army's success in the decades before and after World War I, but by the 1940s the social and political climate had changed. Progressivism had been overtaken by the New Deal, and populism was just an echo in the isolationist-interventionist debate. Appearing ever more out of step with the times, the Army's religious beliefs no longer seemed viable to writers and intellectuals like Boyer.

Not everyone agreed. "Shock Troops," an article in *Time* magazine in 1948, offered three examples of how the Army's mission served the modern world: a former alcoholic who now reached out to drunks; a prison worker who helped ex-convicts adjust to civilian life; and a young corps leader who spent his days visiting the sick, aiding the poor, and working with young people. This third officer was dubbed the "new type" of Salvationist. "An affable, well-fed Rotarian and 32nd degree Mason . . .

[he] could pass for a young banker," the news magazine noted, except for his uniform and his habitual "God bless you." Less than a month later the *New York Times Magazine* profiled one of the same men: Envoy J. Stanley Sheppard, the head of the Eastern Territory's Prison Bureau. The profile's author, S. J. Woolf, had met Sheppard's mother when he was a soldier and she was a Sallie in war-ravaged France. The young infantryman, impressed by the woman who brought doughnuts to the front lines, admired the Army's "religion in action." He found her son's ardor equally admirable. Unlike Boyer, Woolf was struck by his subject's intelligence and lack of sanctimoniousness. Envoy Sheppard balanced his faith with a solid understanding of social work and psychiatry.[83]

The officer corps was not the only facet of Army life that attracted media attention during the 1940s. Salvationist bands also made good copy. As important anniversaries provided news pegs for articles—1941 marked the fiftieth anniversary of the Eastern Territorial Staff Band and 1945 was the sixty-fifth anniversary of the Army's arrival—the once-maligned streetcorner band was now hailed as an urban institution. Times Square hosted more than four concerts each week, and across the country some 6,000 band members played regularly.[84]

The Salvationist band was another of William Booth's innovations. While religious harangues rarely assembled a crowd, lively music did. Brass music, in particular, was the popular favorite in late-nineteenth-century London, and Booth gladly accepted the services of saved musicians. As word spread that lively tunes helped build a crowd, local corps followed suit, and soon standardization became necessary: uniforms were mandated and musical selections were limited to what the Army published. Regulating instruments proved more difficult. Dependent on what members could play, local bands initially featured fiddles, guitars, violins, and flutes. William Booth was willing to allow most any instrument except organs or harmoniums. They sounded too much like church.

Salvationists believed that music captured the ear and conquered the soul. The *New Yorker*'s "Talk of the Town" did not disagree. Attending a noontime Army concert, the "Town's" anonymous correspondent noted that the band's music slowed the peripatetic flow of shoppers, bankers, and brokers. In an interview afterward, the bandleader, Captain Richard Holz, confessed to finding God in many musical incarnations, including bebop and swing. The magazine even portrayed the Captain slipping into Roseland, a well-known New York ballroom.[85]

The Era of Respectability

While the 1940s saw the demise of one long-standing outreach effort when the Cherry Street Settlement closed down to make way for a housing project, the decade also brought several innovations in Salvationist services. The Army opened its first psychiatric clinic to aid World War II veterans and to help families readjust to returning husbands and fathers. In this, as in other new ventures—adopting the Alcoholic Anonymous treatment program, for example—Salvationists demonstrated that, in less than two decades, their approach to social work had changed markedly. In the late 1920s the budding Salvationist Anita Phillipson Robb was cautioned (by her father, an Army officer) against seeking a graduate degree in social work because "the Army was not ready for professional people." Persevering nevertheless, she became the first professional social worker in the Army. Through the 1930s Robb noted a discrepancy between the Army's stated commitment to professional standards and the actual training and expertise of its social work staff. In this light—and within a group that only recently had considered Freud taboo—the acceptance of psychiatry was striking.[86]

The Army's pragmatic approach to the delivery of services did not change its commitment to evangelical theology, but it did modify its expression. The Cherry Street Settlement was torn down to build a new housing project, but the slum mission had already been doomed by changing times. Its model of outreach, providing a range of generalized services for mothers and families, was outmoded. Programs targeting specific populations were now in demand, and the modalities of treatment had changed as well. The motherly slum workers who ran Cherry Street lacked the training necessary for modern outreach work. Adjusting to the new paradigm, Army social workers designed a program to combat juvenile delinquency. Assisted by a New York State grant, Salvationists started an after-school intervention program for preselected problem youth.[87]

The one area of Army welfare work that consistently blended religious convictions and social work standards was its assistance to unwed mothers. According to the *Ladies' Home Journal,* the Army's maternity institutions set the standard for "newer and sounder methods of home and hospital care." Run by women officers with advanced degrees in social work, the homes provided love and support along with classes in sewing, cooking, and ceramics; guidance on education and employment, and information on childrearing versus adoption. The Army's long-standing policy toward these unwed mothers—finding alternatives for the future rather than casting blame for the past—seemed as progressive in the 1940s as it had fifty years earlier. As Colonel Florence Turkington, the secretary of the Women's Social Service department of the Eastern Territory, lamented, attitudes toward out-of-wedlock births had hardly changed since Nathaniel Hawthorne wrote *The Scarlet Letter*.[88]

The year 1950, the seventieth anniversary of The Salvation Army's arrival in America, began auspiciously. Bruce Barton agreed to oversee publicity for the anniversary-year appeal, and the head of IBM served as campaign chairman. When the drive began at a benefit held at the swank Hotel Astor, the troops were ready. Outside the hotel blue-bonneted lassies flanked a five-foot-high red kettle while a lighted blimp, trailing a banner for the appeal, flew overhead. In March the Bakery and Confectionery Workers Union celebrated the Army's anniversary by making a nine-foot-tall, half-ton cake. Installed in the lobby of National Headquarters with a hydraulic lift, the cake was decorated with 500 candied roses and 70 blue candles. At the top of the pink and white, five-tiered confection was a spun-sugar portrait of a lassie.[89]

That summer Evangeline Booth died. The eighty-four-year-old ex-General had been out of the public eye for several years, and the secular press reported her passing in a perfunctory manner.[90] Her direct influence on the American scene had ended more than a decade earlier, and although she was revered by an older generation, she represented a bygone era to anyone under thirty. The *War Cry*'s tribute, filling an entire issue, mourned the end of that era along with Booth's passing. Evangeline Booth was a direct link to the Army's founders, but the woman who engaged in flowery speeches and living tableaux, whose life spanned the contradictions of wealth and poverty, secular power and spiritual holiness, seemed far removed from the post–World War II world.[91]

What would Evangeline Booth have made of *Guys and Dolls*, the Broadway musical that opened several months after her death? One of the characters, a pompous and demanding superior officer, seemed to mock her, and the entire Save-A-Soul mission made the Army look a bit foolish. Yet in the tradition of wise fools, the missionaries ultimately triumph, and the play's resolution weds the secular to the spiritual in joint service to the city. Culturally constructed, then taken apart and put back together again, the Army's image, as *Guys and Dolls* suggested, ultimately depends on the eye, heart, and mind of the viewer.

In the years between 1919 and 1950 The Salvation Army's status changed from an outsider sect to an almost mainstream denomination. While its Holiness theology was alien to mainline Protestantism, its inclusive religious practice was recognizable, if not emulated, by practitioners of many faiths. While some articles, like those in the *New Yorker*, portrayed the movement in a less-than-flattering light, a majority of Americans appreciated the work Salvationists did. In fact *Time* magazine, in its Christmas cover story of 1949, wondered what William Booth would have made of the Army's current respectability. Booth had intended his Army to offend. Its preaching women, marching bands, and streetcorner testimonies were designed to shock the complacent and win the unchurched. Even "Blood and Fire," the Army's bold and colorful flag, served as a reminder of Christianity's startling claims. But what had once been transgressive now seemed tame, and even Commissioner Ernest Pugmire, the head of the American troops, had to agree: "We haven't got the opposition we once had . . . That kind of opposition bred the courage of lions."[92]

If Pugmire's Army lacked the courage of lions, it had gained many other things. Its war chest had funds to provide 300,000 Christmas dinners for the poor across the nation. Its annual campaign in 1949 raised $25 million. Its 115 low-cost hotels offered lodging for down-and-outers, and its 34 maternity homes looked after hundreds of unwed mothers. The Army was part of the American city, part of the American way of life. It had pioneered a vision of nonsectarian service and united a pluralistic nation during times of suffering and strife. As an urban religion, it blended into the city and spoke in many tongues. The *Time* magazine cover—a portrait of Pugmire framed by bells—was a final rite of passage. Hallowed by the media's high priests, The Salvation Army had indeed entered a new era of respectability.

EPILOGUE

FOR MUCH of the 1990s The Salvation Army has been the nation's largest charitable fundraiser, receiving more public support than the Red Cross, Catholic Charities, or the United Jewish Appeal. Such an achievement would have been unimaginable to William Booth and his fellow Salvationists, much less to their observers and critics, who no doubt would have been equally surprised by the Army's venerable but staid reputation. The Salvation Army entered an era of cultural respectability after World War II, but it has never lost sight of its longtime goals and strategies. Whether staging musicals based on the life of Evangeline Booth or performing rap concerts in lower Manhattan, Salvationists continue to use the vernacular culture in evangelical crusades—even if their image as street-savvy soul-savers has been eclipsed by their reputation as dependable providers of social services. Today emblems of that reputation are ubiquitous, as Army trucks, thrift shops, and collection boxes serve as silent reminders of a Christian mission that works across racial, religious, class, and ethnic divides.

Did The Salvation Army succeed in saturating the secular with the sacred? Did it, in its own words, "secularize religion" or "religionize secular things?" Certainly, as the iconic power of the red shields and Christmas kettles suggests, the Army made secular objects religious and made religion part of secular life. To be sure, the result was not the Kingdom of God that the Booths expected, but it was the development of a new dynamic between a sectarian religion and a pluralistic society, a dynamic defined by shared ideals, an emphasis on action, and a linguistic latitude that enabled listeners to assign their own signification to the category "religion."

The role played by religion in (and played upon it by) urbanization and commercialization remains largely unexplored. Historians have noted an intriguing confluence of politics, social movements, and cultural sensibilities at the turn of the century but only recently have woven ultimate beliefs and ritual behaviors into their tapestries. Even scholars who do consider religion are tempted to circumscribe its impact or truncate its appeal. While studies of religion and Progressivism have returned again and again to the (white Protestant liberal) Social Gospel, they are only beginning to explore the evangelical, African-American, Jewish, and Catholic aspects of the movement for social salvation. Likewise, research on the city has tended to cast the era as a time of religious declension or spreading secularism. While declension may help explain the downward trajectory of white Protestant hegemony, and while secularism may connote the concomitant sense of change, a more complex portrayal would include the growth of pluralism and the subsequent diffusion of white Protestant influence and values.

Case studies of institutions like The Salvation Army provide a corrective. The Social Gospelers were, in fact, inspired by Booth's Army and in many cases their theology was strikingly similar. Indeed, terms such as "moderate," "conservative," and "evangelical" have obscured the links between groups working for similar goals and reified theological distinctions that may not have seemed problematic to the parties involved. In a similar fashion, the focus on religious efforts to buttress traditional gender roles has overshadowed the ironies that inhered in many such attempts. Female religious leaders like Maud Booth embodied autonomy and independence even as they heartily denounced the New Woman. Likewise, the public's post–World War I embrace of the Army does not testify to the triumph of evangelical Protestantism, much less to the commercial culture's co-optation of religion. But it does suggest the adaptive capacity that has sustained Christianity through twenty centuries of change.

Re-visioning the years from 1880 to 1950 with The Salvation Army's New York experience as a starting point offers alternatives to previous efforts at mapping the urban landscape. Notwithstanding its reputation for sin and secularism, New York City provides a capacious stage for religious groups seeking an audience. But the extent of the competition and the size of the theater have made it easy to overlook the myriad of activities occurring on that stage. While concentrating on The Salvation Army, we have glimpsed John Kennion serving coffee, Jerry McAuley choreographing testimonies, and W. R. Rainsford experimenting with institutional capacity to help the poor. But, just as easily, we could have turned to innovators working outside the Protestant mainstream: Father Divine melding New Thought and Christianity to empower poor blacks; Rabbi Mordecai Kaplan striving for an authentic American Judaism; Anagarika Dharamapala teaching Gothamites intrigued with Buddhist practice. In each of these examples religious leaders seeking new publics created new rituals, staged new performances, and devised new linguistic strategies as expressions of the drive to integrate religion into a rapidly changing urban environment.

For its part, The Salvation Army eagerly engaged the larger culture, tailoring its message to redeem the religious, entertainment, and philanthropic establishments of the day. And that perhaps is the most significant lesson to be drawn from Army history. A militantly evangelical movement, it built its success by reading its particularistic experience into the wider culture. In so doing, Salvationists were among the first to mine the interstices of religious tolerance—the rich vein of understanding, emblematic of the American experiment, that allowed Jew and gentile, agnostic and believer to affirm a shared religion of action.

There is a lesson here, too, for the Cassandras of our own age, clustering at opposite ends of the social and political spectrum. Both those alarmed by the encroachment of the secular upon the sacred and those who fear the sacred will overwhelm the secular appear equally shortsighted. Whatever else The Salvation Army's experience suggests, the interplay between religion and society is not an either/or proposition. Each has an impact on the other, and neither looks quite the same afterward. Media professionals and academics alike tend to frame discussions about religion in terms of growth and decline, secularization or fundamentalism, rather than change, shifts, and transformation. And despite this demonstration of the limited explanatory power of dichotomy, I expect that the tendency to dualize will persist in our determinedly Manichaean culture. Still, in describing the rise and transformation of a significant religious institution, I hope I have illustrated Leigh Eric Schmidt's apt observation "that the sacred and the secular have been ceaselessly combined and recombined, that these categories have regularly dissolved in lived experience."[1]

Lived experience is always messier, and therefore more interesting, than written accounts of it. Ideally this chronicle of one movement's transforming and transformative encounter with the urban American culture will rend the neat wrapping in which we package all too many of our messier and more interesting religious phenomena.

NOTES

Introduction

1. AWC, Sept. 23, 1896, 8.
2. AWC, June 15, 1918, 4.
3. David M. Scobey, "Empire City: Politics, Culture, and Urbanism in Gilded-Age New York" (Ph.D. diss., Yale University, 1989), 209. William R. Taylor, *In Pursuit of Gotham: Culture and Commerce in New York* (New York: Oxford University Press, 1992), xvii.
4. David Scobey, "Commercial Culture, Urban Modernism, and the Intellectual *Flaneur,*" *American Quarterly* 47 (June 1995): 330.

1. The Cathedral of the Open Air

1. AWC, Dec. 24, 1892, 2; Apr. 11, 1896, 12; Mar. 9, 1912, 6.
2. *New York Tribune,* Mar. 26, 1906, II: 2. The women in the group were Capt. Emma Westbrook and soldiers Rachel Evans, Clara Price, Mary Ann Coleman, Elizabeth Pearson, Annie Shaw, and Emma Eliza Florence Morris.
3. AWC, Apr. 11, 1896, 12; Mar. 9, 1912, 6. Bernard Watson, *Soldier Saint* (London: Hodder and Stoughton, 1970), 53; Robert Sandall, *The History of The Salvation Army,* vol. II, 1878–1886 (London: Thomas Nelson and Sons, 1950), 233; NYT, Mar. 11, 1980, 5.
4. Watson, *Soldier Saint,* 56; Herbert A. Wisbey Jr., *Soldiers without*

Swords (New York: Macmillan, 1955), 24. *New York Tribune*, Mar. 11, 1880, 8.

5. William Booth, "The Millennium; or, The Ultimate Triumph of Salvation Army Principles," *All the World* 7 (Aug. 1890), 337–343. AWC, Sept. 23, 1896, 8.

6. AWC, Jan. 28, 1893, 1.

7. William Leach, *Land of Desire: Merchants, Power and the Rise of a New American Culture* (New York: Pantheon, 1993), 3.

8. Josiah Strong, *Our Country: Its Possible Future and Its Present Crisis* (New York: Baker and Taylor, 1885), 129. Josiah Strong, *The Challenge of the City* (New York: Missionary and Education Movement of the United States and Canada, 1911), 16.

9. AWC, Mar. 23, 1895, 4. Army statistics from this era are unreliable. Other Salvationist accounts place the number as much as ten times higher.

10. Glenn K. Horridge, *The Salvation Army: Origins and Early Days, 1865–1900* (Godalming, U.K.: Ammonite Books, 1993), 48–49. AWC, May 31, 1890, 8; Feb. 7, 1891, 5; June 4, 1892, 3.

11. AWC, Aug. 20, 1887, 12; June 8, 1888, 8; Sept. 1, 1888, 6; Apr. 13, 1889, 4; Apr. 4, 1891, 1.

12. AWC, Apr. 3, 1886, 1.

13. Norman H. Murdoch, "The Salvation Army's U.S. Arrival," *OAH Newsletter* (1987): 12–13; Herbert A. Wisbey Jr., "A Salvation Army Prelude: The Christian Mission in Cleveland, Ohio," *Ohio Historical Quarterly* 64, no. 1 (1955): 77–81; James Jermy file, SAA; manuscripts by Christine McMillan, Dorothy Hitzka, and anonymous, SAA; AWC, Feb. 9, 1980, 10–11.

14. Edward H. McKinley, *Marching to Glory: The History of The Salvation Army in the United States, 1880–1980* (San Francisco: Harper and Row, 1980), 4–9; Herbert A. Wisbey Jr., "Religion in Action: A History of The Salvation Army in the United States" (Ph.D. diss., Columbia University, 1951), 28–34; Shirley family file, SAA; AWC, July 9, 1881, 1; Sept. 12, 1925, 10; Sept. 19, 1925, 10.

15. On Booth see Harold Begbie, *The Life of General William Booth*, 2 vols. (New York: Macmillan, 1920); Richard Collier, *The General Next to God* (New York: Dutton, 1965); St. John Ervine, *God's Soldier: General William Booth*, 2 vols. (New York: Macmillan, 1934); Thomas F. G. Coates, *The Prophet of the Poor: The Life Story of General Booth* (New York: Dutton, 1906); A. M. Nichol, *General Booth and the Salvation Army* (London: Herbert and Daniel, 1910).

16. On Catherine Booth see Pamela Walker, "Pulling the Devil Down: Gender and Popular Culture in The Salvation Army, 1865–1895" (Ph.D. diss., Rutgers University, 1992), ch. 1; Frederick Booth-Tucker, *The Life of Catherine Booth*, 3rd ed., 2 vols. (London, 1892); Catherine Bramwell-

Booth, *Catherine Booth: The Story of Her Loves* (London: Hodder and Stoughton, 1970).

17. Norman H. Murdoch, *Origins of the Salvation Army* (Knoxville: University of Tennessee Press, 1994), 5–20; Richard Carwardine, *Transatlantic Revivalism: Popular Evangelicalism in Britain and America, 1790–1865* (Westport, Conn.: Greenwood, 1978), 28–45.

18. Carwardine, *Transatlantic Revivalism,* 116; Begbie, *Life of General William Booth,* I: 9–14, 61–62; Murdoch, *Origins,* 7–12; John Kent, *Holding the Fort: Studies in Victorian Revivalism* (London: Epworth, 1978), 77–87.

19. Charles G. Finney, *Lectures on Revivals of Religion* (New York: Leavitt, Lord, 1835); Murdoch, *Origins,* 12–15; Carwardine, *Transatlantic Revivalism,* 4–10.

20. Timothy Smith, *Revivalism and Social Reform: American Protestantism on the Eve of the Civil War* (1957; Baltimore: Johns Hopkins University Press, 1980).

21. Norman H. Murdoch, "Female Ministry in the Thought and Work of Catherine Booth," *Church History* 53 (1984): 348–352. Olive Anderson, "Women Preachers in Mid-Victorian Britain: Some Reflections on Feminism, Popular Culture, and Social Change," *Historical Journal* 12, no. 3 (1969): 469.

22. Arthur Augustus Rees, "Reasons for not Co-operating in the Alleged 'Sunderland Revivals'" (Sunderland: Wm. Henry Hills, 1859). Catherine Booth, "Female Teaching," (London: W. J. Stevenson, 1861), 32. Pamela Walker generously shared her copy of this early edition of Catherine Booth's pamphlet with me.

23. Watson, *Soldier Saint,* 13, 61.

24. Horridge, *Salvation Army,* 222–223; Kent, *Holding the Fort,* 298; Norman Murdoch, "Evangelical Sources of Salvation Army Doctrine," *Evangelical Quarterly* 87, no. 3 (1987): 235–244. Murdoch, *Origins,* 31.

25. William Booth, *In Darkest England and the Way Out* (London: International Headquarters of The Salvation Army, 1890); William Booth, "The Millennium," 337–343. Norman Murdoch and Glenn Horridge argue that Booth's social schemes were an attempt to revive the Army's flagging fortunes.

26. Kent, *Holding the Fort,* 298, 331, 340; Murdoch, *Origins,* 67–68. Murdoch, "Evangelical Sources," 243. The Smiths were Presbyterian laity.

27. Murdoch, *Origins,* 65–66.

28. Booth quoted in McKinley, *Marching to Glory,* (1980), 33. The eleven doctrines are: "(1) We believe that the Scriptures of the Old and New Testaments were given by inspiration of God; and that they constitute the divine rule of Christian faith and practice; (2) We believe there is only one God, who is infinitely perfect—the Creator, Preserver, and Governor of all things—and

who is the only proper object of religious worship; (3) We believe that there are three persons in the Godhead—the Father, the Son, and the Holy Ghost—undivided in essence and co-equal in power and glory; (4) We believe that in the person of Jesus Christ the divine and human natures are united; so that He is truly and properly God, and truly and properly man; (5) We believe that our first parents were created in a state of innocency but, by their disobedience, they lost their purity and happiness; and that in consequence of their fall all men have become sinners, totally depraved, and as such are justly exposed to the wrath of God; (6) We believe that the Lord Jesus Christ by His suffering and death, made an atonement for the whole world, so that whosoever will may be saved; (7) We believe that repentance toward God, faith in our Lord Jesus Christ, and regeneration by the Holy Spirit are necessary to salvation; (8) We believe that we are justified by grace, through faith in our Lord Jesus Christ; and that he that believeth hath that witness in himself; (9)We believe that continuance in a state of salvation depends upon continued obedient faith in Jesus Christ; (10) We believe that it is the privilege of all believers to be 'wholly sanctified,' and that their 'whole spirit and body and soul' may 'be preserved blameless until the coming of our Lord Jesus Christ' (1 Thessalonians 5:23); (11) We believe in the immortality of the soul; in the resurrection of the body; in the general judgment at the end of the world; in the eternal happiness of the righteous; and in the endless punishment of the wicked." Edward H. McKinley, *Marching to Glory: The History of the Salvation Army in the United States, 1880–1992,* 2nd ed. (Grand Rapids, Mich.: William B. Eerdman, 1995), 351–352.

29. *New York Tribune,* Mar. 2, 1903, 7.

30. AWC, Mar. 10, 1888, 4; Sept. 1, 1888, 6.

31. AWC, Apr. 3, 1886, 1; Aug. 13, 1887, 7; Aug. 20, 1887, 12; Jan. 5, 1889, 12. *Brooklyn Eagle,* Apr. 30, 1893, 4. Horridge, *Salvation Army,* 48–49.

32. NYT, Mar. 15, 1880, 8; *Harper's Weekly,* Apr. 3, 1880, 214; Collier, *The General Next to God,* 81–82; Wisbey, *Soldiers without Swords,* 3–5; McKinley, *Marching to Glory,* (1980), 13–14.

33. NYT, Mar. 16, 1880; 8. Watson, *Soldier Saint,* 61; Sallie Chesham, *Born to Battle: The Salvation Army in America* (Chicago: Rand McNally & Co., 1965), 62.

34. Chesham, *Born to Battle,* 59.

35. NYT, Mar. 16, 1880, 8.

36. Ibid.; Paul A. Gilje, *The Road to Mobocracy : Popular Disorder in New York City, 1763–1834* (Chapel Hill: University of North Carolina Press, 1987), 212–214.

37. John W. Wertheimer, "Free Speech Fights: The Roots of Modern Free Expression Litigation in the United States" (Ph.D. diss., Princeton University, 1992), 150. NYT, Mar. 16, 1880, 8.

38. *New York Tribune*, Mar. 17, 1880, 8; Sandall, *History of The Salvation Army*, II, 234. NYT, Mar. 19, 1880, 8.

39. James D. McCabe Jr., *New York By Sunlight and Gaslight* (Philadelphia: Hubbard Brothers, 1882), 563–570; Helen Campbell, *Darkness and Daylight or Lights and Shadows on New York Life* (Hartford: Hartford Publishing, 1897), 55.

40. *New York Tribune*, Nov. 9, 1880, 2.

41. Ibid., Nov. 13, 1880, 4.

42. Aaron Abell, *The Urban Impact of American Protestantism, 1865–1900* (London: Archon, 1962), 28–29, 35–37, 39–40; Ralph E. Luker, "Missions, Institutional Churches, and the Settlement Houses: The Black Experience, 1885–1910," *Journal of Negro History* 69 (1984): 101–113; *New York Tribune*, Nov. 13, 1880, 4.

43. The Army's records from this period are scant. Railton published three issues of *The Salvation News* in July 1880 and the first copy of the American *War Cry* on Jan. 15, 1881, but only fragments of the originals remain. For a profile on Westbrook see AWC, Aug. 6, 1881, 1.

44. AWC, Apr. 8, 1882, 1.

45. Wisbey, *Soldiers without Swords*, 41–42.

46. AWC, Apr. 17, 1884, 1.

47. Wisbey, *Soldiers without Swords*, 42–43. See, e.g., C. A. Stork, "The Salvation Army: Its Methods and Lessons," *Lutheran Quarterly*, Oct. 1882; "The Salvation Army," *New Englander*, July 1883; Agnes Maule Machar, "Red-Cross Knights: A Nineteenth Century Perspective," *Andover Review* II (1884); M. A. Lewis, "The Salvation Army," *MacMillan's Magazine*, 1882; Mrs. Charles Garnett, "With The Salvation Army," *Good Words*, 1883.

48. Karen Halttunen, *Confidence Men and Painted Women* (New Haven: Yale University Press, 1982), 165–167.

49. Stork, "Salvation Army," 557–559, 570. *The Nation*, Aug. 17, 1882, 126–127.

50. NYT, July 16, 1883, 8; Feb. 10, 1885, 4; Mar. 22, 1885, 4. Machar, "Red-Cross Knights," 206–207.

51. E.g., see AWC, June 29, 1946, 5, 14. Norman Murdoch, "The Salvation Army: An Anglo-American Revivalistic Social Mission" (Ph.D. diss., University of Cincinnati, 1985), 367.

52. In England Booth held all of the Army's property in his own name, and he wanted to do the same overseas. This was nearly impossible in the United States because many states did not permit foreigners to own property. Moore, intending to become an American citizen, placed Army holdings in his name as Booth's agent. This was problematic because Moore owned and was liable for all the Army property in the United States. Thus he could be accused of personally benefiting from the Army's growth. Moore's legal responsibilities became intolerable when one New Jersey corps, incorporating

under its own state laws, sought the return of funds already deposited by the New York headquarters. When Moore refused to give back the money, he was arrested by New Jersey authorities.

Booth sent his own team to investigate. These officers reported that Moore was financially incompetent and administratively inept. They doubted whether the Army had sufficient popular support to win favorable incorporation status in New York, and if that failed the Army's assets would be handed over to local trustees. Booth decided the status quo would continue: Moore would retain legal ownership of the Army's American property in the General's name.

Moore initially swore fidelity to Booth, but when the General sent Major Frank Smith to take over the American Army, he renamed his organization the Salvation Army of America and declared himself General. Despite claiming a majority of officers and assets, Moore's Army soon faltered. Unable to attract sufficient funds or converts, Moore's own officers relieved him of command and rejoined Booth's Army. See Wisbey, *Soldiers without Swords*, 45–55; McKinley, *Marching to Glory* (1980), 24–31.

53. On Smith see Murdoch, *Origins*, 152–154; Wisbey, *Soldiers without Swords*, 52–63; Norman Murdoch, "Salvationist-Socialist Frank Smith, M.P.: Father of Salvation Army Social Work," presented at The Salvation Army Historical Conference, New York, Sept. 1978. AWC, Dec. 26, 1885, 8; Apr. 3, 1886, 1.

54. Frank Smith, *The Salvation War in America for 1885* (New York: Headquarters and Trade Dept., 1886), 18; NYT, Mar. 22, 1885, 8.

55. *The Nation*, Aug. 17, 1882, 126.

56. Smith, *Salvation War in America*, 76–77.

57. NYT, Mar. 20, 1885, 2; Mar. 22, 1883, 8; AWC, Dec. 24, 1887, 13.

58. Olive Anderson, "The Growth of Christian Militarism in Mid-Victorian England," *English Historical Review* 86, no.338 (1971).

59. *The Nation*, Aug. 17, 1882, 126; Jan. 25, 1883, 78.

60. Mary Ryan, *Women in Public: Between Banners and Ballots* (Baltimore: Johns Hopkins University Press, 1990), 22–24; Thomas J. Schlereth, *Victorian America* (New York: HarperCollins, 1991), 52–53; William Taylor, ed., *Inventing Times Square: Commerce and Culture at the Crossroads of the World* (New York: Russell Sage, 1991), 71–72.

61. *New York Tribune*, Mar. 20, 1885, 2; NYT, Mar. 20, 1885, 2.

62. *New York Tribune*, Mar. 20, 1885, 2.

63. Smith, *Salvation War in America*, 135; AWC, July 11, 1885,1; Apr. 3, 1886, 1; Aug. 1, 1885, 1; Aug. 8, 1885, 1; Aug. 29, 1885, 3.

64. AWC, July 18, 1885, 1; James E. Beane, "Early Black Salvationists in America," manuscript, 1974, SAA. AWC, Aug. 29, 1885, 4; Sept. 26, 1885, 2; Nov. 7, 1885, 1; Nov. 28, 1885, 1.

65. Norris Magnuson, *Salvation in the Slums: Evangelical Social Work, 1865–1920* (Methuen, N.J.: Scarecrow, 1977), 120; Thomas Lee Philpott, *The Slum and The Ghetto* (Belmont, Calif.: Wadsworth, 1991), 101. AWC, Feb. 14, 1885, 1; May 2, 1885, 2; June 23, 1888, 2; Sept. 18, 1888, 9. E.g., AWC, Jan. 31, 1890, 4; May 2, 1891, 3; May 20, 1899, 10.

66. AWC, July 14, 1894, 8; July 21, 1894, 8; July 28, 1894, 5; June 16, 1894, 4; Dec. 7, 1895, 8; Dec. 28, 1895, 1; Aug. 22, 1896, 1–2; Apr. 7, 1900, 6; June 28, 1913, 8; *New York Tribune*, May 4, 1899, 7; Magnuson, *Salvation in the Slums*, 118–126.

67. *Conqueror*, Oct. 1896, 475. AWC, Feb. 28, 1903, 4.

68. Begbie, *Life of General William Booth*, II: 67, 69.

69. William R. Hutchison, *The Modernist Impulse in American Protestantism* (Durham: Duke University Press, 1992), 8–11.

70. R. Laurence Moore, *Selling God: American Religion in the Marketplace of Culture* (New York: Oxford University Press, 1994).

2. The New Woman

1. According to Victoria Glendinning, the term "new woman" was adopted in the mid-1890s during a debate between two women novelists. Juliet Gardiner, ed., *The New Woman* (London: Collins and Brown, 1993), 6. AWC, Sept. 21, 1895, 5.

2. AWC, Sept. 21, 1895, 5; *New York Tribune*, Sept. 2, 1895, 1; NYT, Sept. 2, 1895, 5; *Conqueror*, Oct. 1895, 464.

3. Wisbey, *Soldiers without Swords*, 85. A contingent of the American Salvation Army would continue until 1910, when the International Salvation Army won a protracted legal battle which enjoined the secessionist group from using the Army's name and identifying hallmarks (the crest, the *War Cry*) in its work.

4. James Grant Wilson, ed., *Memorial History of the City of New York and the Hudson River Valley*, vol. IV (New York: New York History Co., 1892), 608–609.

5. Susan Curtis, *Consuming Faith: The Social Gospel and Modern American Culture* (Baltimore: Johns Hopkins University Press, 1991), xv.

6. In 1885 Charlesworth circulated a small book chronicling his loss of Maud to the Army. The pamphlet, *Sensational Religion: As Resorted to in the System Called the "Salvation Army" In Its Influences Upon the Young and In Its Effects Upon the Duties and Claims of Home Life*, 120-plus pages, criticized the Booths for encouraging young people to renounce their families and their social obligations. NYT, Mar. 11, 1883, 5.

7. Maud Booth, "Memories of Childhood and Girlhood," manuscript, SAA.

8. William and Catherine Booth had eight children: William Bramwell (1856–1929), Ballington (1857–1940), Catherine (1858–1955), Emma Moss (1860–1903), Herbert Howard (1862–1926), Marian (1864–1937), Eveline Cory (1865–1950), Lucy Milward (1867–1953). Except for the sickly Marian, all were Army leaders, although Ballington, Catherine, and Herbert resigned. When they married, the Booth daughters and their husbands used hyphenated names—Booth-Clibborn (Catherine), Booth-Tucker (Emma), and Booth-Heilberg (Lucy). Eveline Booth was called Eva by her family and changed her name to Evangeline when she took command of the American Salvation Army.

9. Maud Ballington Booth, "Salvation Army Work in the Slums," *Scribner's*, Jan.–June 1895, 103.

10. Several of the Booth children had special titles. Ballington was the Marshall, Kate was La Marechale, Herbert was the Commandant, and Emma was the Consul.

11. NYT, Oct. 27, 1894, 8. *New York Tribune*, Sept. 23, 1894, 5.

12. *New York Tribune*, Feb. 27, 1895, 2; Oct. 24, 1894, 4.

13. G. A. Davis, "Under the Blood-Red Banner—II," *Frank Leslie's Weekly*, Nov. 23, 1893, 331.

14. Ibid.

15. Ibid.

16. Eva Wilder McGlasson, "Fourteenth Street at Nightfall," *Harper's Weekly*, Mar. 12, 1894, 250.

17. "The Headquarters of The Salvation Army," *Harper's Weekly*, Mar. 30, 1895, 292–293.

18. NYT, June 4, 1895, 16.

19. McKinley, *Marching to Glory* (1980), 76.

20. Susan Welty, *Look Up and Hope!* (New York: Thomas Nelson and Sons, 1961), 100.

21. On the "Maiden Tribute" campaign see Judith Walkowitz, *City of Dreadful Delight: Narratives of Sexual Danger in Late Victorian London* (Chicago: University of Chicago, 1992), chs. 3–4.

22. Booth, *In Darkest England and the Way Out*, 12. See K. S. Inglis, *The Churches and the Working Classes in Victorian England* (London: Routledge and Kegan Paul, 1963), 199–204; Murdoch, *Origins*, 160–164; Murdoch, "Salvationist-Socialist Frank Smith, M.P."; Norman Murdoch, "European Idea Sources of William Booth's Darkest England Scene of 1890," presented at the International Conference, Utopian Thought and Communal Experience, New Lanark, Scotland, July 1988; Norman Murdoch, "Rose Culture and Social Reform: Edward Bellamy's Looking Backward and William Booth's Darkest England the Way Out," *Utopian Studies* 3 (1992).

23. Campbell, *Darkness and Daylight*, 37–54.

24. AWC, Jan. 16, 1892, 9; Jan. 23. 1892, 3; Feb. 6, 1892, 1, 4–5; Feb. 27, 1892, 11; Mar. 5, 1892, 2; Apr. 9, 1892, 2.

25. Edward H. McKinley, *Somebody's Brother: A History of The Salvation Army's Men's Social Service Department, 1891–1985* (Lewiston, Me.: Edwin Mellon, 1986), 19.

26. AWC, Nov. 3, 1888, 8; Feb. 16, 1889, 8; Mar. 9, 1889, 8, 13; *Brooklyn Eagle*, Mar. 7, 1894, 7; NYT, Feb. 6, 1889, 8.

27. NYT, Feb. 13, 1889, 8; Feb. 15, 1889, 8; Feb. 17, 1889, 8; AWC, Jan. 18, 1890, 13; May 2, 1891, 7; *New York Tribune*, Mar. 1, 1893, 5; NYT, Mar. 9, 1894, 3; *Conqueror*, Jan. 1895, 41–42; Mar. 1896, 135–136.

28. Suzie Swift, "Five Steps: An Auxiliary Story," *Conqueror*, Apr. 1897, 90–92.

29. AWC, Feb. 22, 1890, 1–2; *Conqueror*, Feb. 1895, 61–65; Jan. 1896, 18–20; AWC, Mar. 21, 1903, 3. NYT, Dec. 10, 1892, 8; July 31, 1893, 2.

30. See, e.g., AWC, Jan. 15, 1887, 3; Aug. 8, 1891, 6; G. A. Davis, "Under the Blood-Red Banner—II," "Under the Blood-Red Banner—III," and "Under the Blood-Red Banner—IV," *Frank Leslie's Weekly*, Nov. 23, Nov. 30, and Dec. 21, 1893; Nora Marks, *Facts about The Salvation Army* (Chicago: Rand and McNally, 1889).

31. Marks, *Facts about The Salvation Army*, 5, 8–9.

32. Ibid., 145.

33. Ibid., 221.

34. AWC, July 8, 1894, 4; Oct. 14, 1893, 4.

35. Booth, "Salvation Army Work in the Slums"; *Social News*, July 1911, 3.

36. AWC, Aug. 17, 1889, 4; Apr. 12, 1890, 3; Jan. 31, 1891, 1.

37. "In the Dark Places," *Social News*, July 1911, 3–5; Maud B. Booth, *Beneath Two Flags* (New York: Funk and Wagnalls, 1889), ch. 7; AWC, Dec. 22, 1906, 14–15; Aug. 17, 1889, 4; Aug. 24, 1889, 4; Oct. 19, 1889, 13; Dec. 21, 1889, 6; Feb. 22, 1890, 8; Mar 1, 1890, 1.

38. Booth, "Salvation Army Work in the Slums," 104.

39. *Conqueror*, Jan. 1898, 29.

40. Ballington and Mrs. Ballington Booth, *New York's Inferno Explored* (New York: Salvation Army Headquarters, 1891), 91.

41. On the slum nursery's early years: *Conqueror*, Mar. 1892, 10–12; Nov. 1894, 429–430; May 1895, 220; NYT, Feb. 27, 1896, 10. Bown, "In the Dark Places," 4–5; Davis, "Under the Blood-Red Banner—IV," 420; AWC, June 6, 1890, 14. AWC, Aug. 8, 1891, 6.

42. Booth, "Salvation Army Work in the Slums," 106.

43. AWC, Mar. 1, 1890, 1; Feb. 22, 1890, 8. Davis, "Under the Blood-Red Banner—IV," 420.

44. *The Nation*, July 7, 1892, 4–5; George Ethelbert Walsh, "The Salva-

tion Army as Social Reformer," *Chautauquan,* Apr.–Sept. 1893, 328–333; Harry B. Wilson, "Contrasting Methods of Salvation Army Warfare," *Harper's Weekly,* Dec. 23, 1894; 1219; *Brooklyn Eagle,* Feb. 13, 1893, 5.

45. John Devins, "The Salvation Army as a Rival of the Churches," *Literary Digest,* Apr. 11, 1896, 706.

46. AWC, Apr. 12, 1890, 3. *New York Tribune,* Dec. 29, 1894, 10; Nov. 17, 1894, 4.

47. Murdoch, *Origins,* 131–136; Horridge, *Salvation Army,* 222–228. *Conqueror,* Oct. 1895, 468.

48. AWC, Nov. 30, 1889, 5. Edwin G. Lamb, "The Social Work of The Salvation Army" (Ph.D. diss., Columbia University, 1909), 120.

49. AWC, May 9, 1891, 6; Nov. 9, 1889, 5; Dec. 6, 1890, 15; June 6, 1891, 5; Jan. 2, 1892, 2; Sept. 9, 1893, 8; Feb. 20, 1892, 10.

50. NYT, Feb. 2, 1892, 4.

51. AWC, Dec. 26, 1885, 5; Aug. 15, 1886, 1; Oct. 15, 1892, 9.

52. AWC, Sept. 24, 1887, 8.

53. Letter from Maud Booth to Sarah Snyder, June 8, 1887, SAA; AWC, Dec. 17, 1892, 9; July 22, 1893, 8; Aug. 27, 1892, 9.

54. AWC, July 5, 1890, 3; July 1, 1893, 11.

55. AWC, Aug. 4, 1894, 9; Aug. 19, 1893, 8.

56. AWC, Oct. 14, 1894, 4; July 8, 1893, 4.

57. AWC, Mar. 21, 1903, 3. NYT, Dec. 10, 1892, 8; July 31, 1893, 2; AWC, June 11, 1892, 1, 4.

58. Mrs. F. M. Howard, "The Reevers' New Year," *Conqueror,* Jan. 1896, 18–20; AWC, Mar. 24, 1888, 1,12; Oct. 27, 1888, 1–2. See, e.g., AWC, Mar 26, 1887, 1; May 12, 1888, 4; Feb. 16, 1889,1; Mar. 8, 1889, 1; May 11, 1889, 1; Aug. 24, 1889, 9; July 8, 1893, 4; Aug. 17, 1895, 13; Dec. 12, 1895, 10; Nov. 21, 1903, 3.

59. AWC, Feb. 22, 1890, 1, 2.

60. AWC, Oct. 4, 1890, 10. *Conqueror,* Feb. 1895, 61–65; Brig. Wallace Winchell file, SAA.

61. AWC, Mar. 5, 1887, 1.

62. E.g., see NYT, Dec. 9, 1888, 8; Thomas Dixon Jr., *The Failure of Protestantism in New York and Its Causes* (New York: Strauss and Rehn, 1896), 18.

63. Olive Anderson, "The Growth of Christian Militarism in Mid-Victorian England," *English Historical Review* 86, no. 338 (1971). William E. Winn, "Tom Brown's Schooldays and the Development of 'Muscular Christianity,'" *Church History* 29 (1960). Janet Forsythe Fishburn, *The Fatherhood of God and the Victorian Family: The Social Gospel in America* (Philadelphia: Fortress Press, 1981).

64. AWC, May 29, 1897, 4. Edward Justus Parker, *My 58 Years* (New York: Salvation Army National Headquarters, 1943), 9, 39.

65. AWC, Sept. 22, 1894, 8.

66. AWC, Oct. 13, 1894, 9; Dec. 8, 1894, 8.

67. AWC, Sept. 18, 1886, 1.

68. McKinley, *Marching to Glory* (1980), 40; Elizabeth Ewing, *Women in Uniform throughout the Centuries* (London: B. T. Batsford,1975), 58–59.

69. Elizabeth Wilson, *Adorned in Dreams* (London: Virago 1985), 11; *New York World,* Mar. 11, 1880, 5; *New York Tribune,* Mar. 11, 1880, 4.

70. Sandall, *History of The Salvation Army,* II, 45–46.

71. AWC, July 25, 1885, 1; May 28, 1887, 7; June 9, 1888, 4; Sept. 18, 1886, 1.

72. AWC, Aug. 5, 1893, 10.

73. AWC, Aug. 5, 1893, 10.

74. AWC, Oct. 11, 1890, 15.

75. Wilson, *Adorned in Dreams,* 9.

76. AWC, Sept. 7, 1889, 8.

77. AWC, Aug. 5, 1893, 10.

78. AWC, July 13, 1889, 5; Oct. 10, 1891, 9.

79. AWC, Oct. 10, 1891, 9.

80. AWC, Oct. 10, 1891, 9.

81. AWC, Feb. 6, 1892, 1. Booth, *New York's Inferno Explored,* 41.

82. AWC, Feb. 28, 1891, 3. E.g., AWC, Apr. 5, 1890, 1; June 4, 1892, 1.

83. Jay Mechling, "The Collecting Self and American Youth Movements," in *Consuming Visions: Accumulation and Display of Goods in America, 1880–1920,* ed. Simon J. Bronner (New York: Norton, 1989), 264.

84. NYT, Sept. 20, 1895, 8.

85. Timothy Gilfoyle, *City of Eros: New York, Prostitution and the Commercialization of Sex, 1790—1920* (New York: Norton, 1992), 232. AWC, Mar. 14, 1896, 2.

86. AWC, Aug. 8, 1908, 3.

87. AWC, May 11, 1901, 15.

88. Anna Howard Shaw, "Women in the Ministry," *Chautauquan* 17–18 (1898): 494. Barbara Welter, *Dimity Convictions* (Athens: Ohio University Press, 1976).

3. The Red Crusade

1. AWC, Apr. 28, 1900, 9.

2. Luc Sante, *Low Life: Lures and Snares of Old New York* (New York: Vintage, 1991), 92–93.

3. AWC, Feb. 11, 1899, 4; Feb. 25, 1899, 4.

4. AWC, Feb. 11, 1899, 4.

5. Parker, *My 58 Years,* 144; AWC, Feb. 11, 1899, 4; "Programme of Consul Emma Booth-Tucker's Meeting," SAA, Emma Booth-Tucker file, nd.

6. "Programme of Consul Emma Booth-Tucker's Meetings," SAA, Emma Booth-Tucker file, nd.

7. David Nasaw, *Going Out : The Rise and Fall of Public Amusements* (New York: Basic Books, 1993), 34.

8. AWC, Feb. 24, 1894, 4; Nov. 2, 1895, 12; NYT, Jan. 29, 1895, 7.

9. AWC, Sept. 19, 1896, 9.

10. AWC, Oct. 10, 1896, 1.

11. AWC, Apr. 15, 1904, 9.

12. McKinley, *Somebody's Brother*, 37. Clark C. Spence, *The Salvation Army Farm Colonies* (Tucson: University of Arizona Press, 1985).

13. *Conqueror*, Oct. 1895, 468–472.

14. Robert H. Bremner, *The Discovery of Poverty in the United States* (New York: New York University Press, 1956).

15. Samuel Lane Loomis, *Modern Cities and Their Problems* (New York: Baker and Taylor, 1887), 5.

16. Strong, *Challenge of the City*, 41.

17. Ibid., 119, 121.

18. *Conqueror*, May 1896, 204.

19. AWC, Jan. 9, 1904; Jan. 16, 1904, 16; Apr. 18, 1896, 4.

20. *Conqueror*, May 1896, 203–204; AWC, Apr. 18, 1896, 4; Welty, *Look Up and Hope*, 36, 49, 123.

21. NYT, Mar. 29, 1896, 2; *New York Tribune*, Mar. 29, 1896, 7.

22. Begbie, *Life of General William Booth*, II, 230, 264, 282.

23. *New York Tribune*, Mar. 29, 1896, 7; NYT, Mar. 29, 1896, 2.

24. *Conqueror*, June 1896, 277–278. Emma and Frederick had two children who accompanied them to the United States. The third, baby Tancred, died before he came to America. Emma had six more children, two of whom died in infancy. She also adopted an orphan. When she died there were seven children under the age of thirteen in the family.

25. AWC, Oct. 16, 1896, 6. *New York Tribune*, Nov. 1, 1903, II, 4. *Conqueror*, June 1896, 277–278; *Harbor Lights*, July 1899, 198–202; AWC, Jan. 16, 1904, 16.

26. On Frederick Booth-Tucker see F. A. MacKenzie, *Booth-Tucker: Sadhu-Saint* (London: Hodder and Stoughton, 1930); Watson, *Soldier Saint*; Harry Williams, *Booth-Tucker: William Booth's First Gentleman* (London: Hodder and Stoughton, 1980); Harry Williams, "Booth-Tucker's Contribution to the Development of The Salvation Army in the United States of America," SAA, manuscript, nd.

27. Williams, *Booth-Tucker*, 13.

28. One reporter described Booth-Tucker as "quiet" and "sober." *New York Post*, Apr. 4, 1896, 2.

29. AWC, May 23, 1896, 1–2.

30. *New York Tribune*, Apr. 29, 1896,3; Apr. 30, 1896, 13; NYT, Apr. 29, 1896, 1; AWC, May 23, 1896, 9.

31. *New York Tribune*, Apr. 30, 1896, 13.

32. NYT, Feb. 21, 1897, 8; May 13, 1897, 12; *New York Tribune*, May 13, 1897, 7; Feb. 2, 1897, II, 3. NYT, May 14, 1897, 3; *New York Tribune*, May 14, 1897, 3.

33. AWC, June 5, 1897, 1; June 12, 1897, 9; July 3, 1897, 9.

34. NYT, May 27, 1897, 1; *New York Tribune*, May 27, 1897, 1.

35. Paul *Boyer, Urban Masses and Moral Order in America, 1820–1920* (Cambridge, Mass.: Harvard University Press, 1978), 123–131. Walter Rauschenbusch, *Christianizing the Social Order* (New York: Macmillan, 1912).

36. Commander Booth-Tucker, *Light in Darkness: Being an Account of The Salvation Army in the United States* (New York: Salvation Army Printing and Engraving Dept., 1902), np. AWC, Jan. 13, 1900, 6.

37. Clark Spence, "The Landless Man and the Manless Land," presented at The Salvation Army Territorial Historical Commission Meeting, Asbury Park, N.J., June 8, 1984, 21–23, SAA.

38. See Frederick Booth-Tucker's works *The Salvation Army in the United States* (New York: The Salvation Army, 1899), *The Social Relief Work of The Salvation Army in the United States* (New York: Monographs on American Social Economics, 1900), and *Light in Darkness*.

39. AWC, July 17, 1897, 3; "Information for 'History of The Salvation Army' USA Salvage Work," SAA; McKinley, *Somebody's Brother*, 40–43.

40. See *New York Tribune*, Oct. 9, 1904, II, 6–7; Oct. 5, 1902, II, 8; AWC, Mar. 21, 1903, 3; Jan. 2, 1904, 2.

41. Frederick Booth-Tucker, *Our Future Pauper Policy in America* (New York: Salvation Army Press, 1898), 16. See Booth-Tucker, *The Salvation Army in the United States, The Social Relief Work of the Salvation Army in the United States, Light in Darkness, Farm Colonies of the Salvation Army* (Washington: Bulletin of the Bureau of Labor, 1903), "The Salvation Army as a Temperance Movement," presented at the Chautauqua Assembly, New York, nd; and "Commander Booth-Tucker on the Pauper Problem in America," *Review of Reviews,* Jan.–June 1897, 728; as well as "The Need and the Remedy," *Conqueror,* May 1897, 116–120; "A Permanent Philosophy," *Harbor Lights,* May 1898, 144–147; "Christian Sociology," *Harbor Lights,* June 1899, 186–189; AWC, Feb. 14, 1899, 8.

42. AWC, Feb. 13, 1897, 4.

43. AWC, Feb. 20, 1897, 7.

44. AWC, Feb. 6, 1897, 4; Mar. 6, 1897, 4; July 4, 1896, 4; Feb. 23, 1901, 9.

45. AWC, Sept. 5, 1896, 2; July 11, 1896, 4; Aug. 28, 1897, 5; Sept. 23, 1899, 3; July 19, 1902, 11; Nov. 6, 1897, 9; Nov. 13, 1897, 5.

46. *New York Tribune,* Dec. 12, 1902, 14; AWC, Sept. 24, 1898, 7; May 26, 1900, 8; June 23, 1900, 8; July 14, 1900, 4; July 20, 1901, 9; July 26, 1902, 5; Nov. 15, 1902, 4; Feb. 7, 1903, 4; June 6, 1903, 12; July 18, 1903, 1; July 25, 1903, 1; Aug. 15, 1903, 3.

47. AWC, July 17, 1897, 9.

48. AWC, May 12, 1900, 12; May 19, 1900, 4; May 26, 1900, 4; June 16, 1900, 6; June 23, 1900, 11; July 21, 1900, 12; Apr. 20, 1901, 5; Nov. 1, 1902, 4.

49. AWC, May 26, 1900, 4; May 19, 1900, 4.

50. Dixon later became more famous for his fiction, including *The Leopard's Spots* and *The Clansmen,* which denigrated African-Americans. The latter was made into the film *Birth of a Nation.*

51. Campbell, *Darkness and Daylight,* 46.

52. AWC, Dec. 22, 1900, 3.

53. AWC, Oct. 8, 1887, 9.

54. *Review of Reviews,* Jan.–June 1897, 207–209.

55. NYT, Apr. 28, 1896, 5. AWC, Oct. 24, 1896, 1, 12. NYT, Oct. 7, 1896, 9; *New York Tribune,* Oct. 7, 1896, 12; AWC, Feb. 27, 1897, 6; Aug. 31, 1896, 8. Booth-Tucker either was ignorant of or ignored his predecessors' efforts to set up shelters for men (the Lighthouse) and women (Daybreak).

56. Williams, *Booth-Tucker,* 150.

57. NYT, Feb. 7, 1897, 9.

58. Commander Booth-Tucker, "A Christmas Dinner for 300,000 Guests," *Country Life in America,* Dec. 1903, 114–116.

59. McKinley, *Somebody's Brother,* 21–22. AWC, Jan. 20, 1894, 1; Jan. 19, 1895, 5; Jan. 18, 1896, 5; Jan. 9, 1897, 1.

60. AWC, Feb. 14, 1899, 3. *Social News,* Dec. 1916, 10.

61. NYT, Dec. 16, 1899, 1. AWC, Dec. 2, 1899, 9. *World,* Dec. 26, 1899, 3.

62. NYT, Dec. 26, 1899, 1. *World,* Dec. 26, 1899, 3.

63. Edwin D. Solenberger, "Relief Work of the Salvation Army," in *Proceedings of the National Conference of Charities and Corrections,* ed. Alexander Johnson (Philadelphia: Fred J. Meer, 1906), 349–366.

64. *New York Tribune,* Dec. 26, 1900, 3.

65. AWC, Jan. 9, 1904, 13.

66. Booth-Tucker, "Salvation Army as a Temperance Movement," 8.

67. It is impossible to know where Booth-Tucker found his statistics. Army statistics tend to vary widely and there are no extant records from the period. *New York Tribune,* July 17, 1904, 5; Oct. 9, 1904, II, 7.

68. Evangeline Booth, *The Salvation Army Appraises Prohibition* (New York: National Headquarters, nd).

69. AWC, Dec. 11, 1909, 12; *Social News,* July 1915, 5.

70. *New York Tribune,* Oct. 17, 1902, 4.

71. James Beane, "The Incorporation of The Salvation Army in the United States (1882–1899)," Jan. 1975, SAA; *New York Tribune,* May 13, 1899, 3; NYT, May 13, 1899, 3; AWC, May 20, 1899, 5.

72. *Conqueror,* Aug. 1896, 377–380. *New York Tribune,* Jan. 23, 1898, supp. 1, 14; AWC, Mar. 15, 1902, 15; July 11, 1903, 15.

73. NYT, Apr. 17, 1904, 8.

74. *Conqueror,* Aug. 1896, 377.

75. AWC, May 15, 1897, 16.

76. Booth-Tucker, *Salvation Army in the United States,* np. The Army held property in sixteen states and Hawaii. The only southern state on the list was Virginia. Mortgages on Army property totaled $300,409. *New York Tribune,* Mar. 20, 1900, 3.

77. AWC, Nov. 12, 1904, 11.

78. Solenberger, "Relief Work of The Salvation Army," 350–351. These ventures are not well documented. See AWC, June 20, 1903, 5; June 3, 1905, 13; Reliance Trading Company folder, SAA; McKinley, *Somebody's Brother,* 59–61.

79. McKinley, *Somebody's Brother,* 60–61. NYT, Nov. 25, 1900, 1; *New York Tribune,* Nov. 26, 1900, 2; Nov. 27, 1900, 4.

80. SAA file on Frederick Booth-Tucker; *New York Tribune,* Sept. 9, 1899, 5.

81. AWC, Jan. 9, 1904, 4.

82. *New York Tribune,* Nov. 11, 1903, II: 4.

4. *The Commander in Rags*

1. NYT, May 13, 1906, III, 5; May 14, 1906, 5; Jan. 29, 1906, 9.

2. AWC, Apr. 25, 1908, 13.

3. *Outlook,* July 1, 1911, 476.

4. Charles L. Ponce de Leon, "Idols and Icons: Representations of Celebrity in American Culture, 1850–1940" (Ph.D. diss., Rutgers University, 1992), iii.

5. P. W. Wilson, *General Evangeline Booth of The Salvation Army* (New York: Charles Scribner's Sons, 1948), 26, 43. There are no scholarly biographies on Evangeline Booth, but there are several popular accounts of her life, including P. W. Wilson, *General Evangeline Booth* (New York: Fleming Revell, 1935); Margaret Troutt, *The General Was a Lady: The Story of Evangeline Booth* (Nashville: A. J. Holman, 1980).

6. See, e.g., McKinley, *Marching to Glory* (1980), 94–95; Wisbey, *Soldiers without Swords,* 141: Ervine, *God's Soldier,* II, 893–894.

7. Wilson, *General Evangeline Booth of The Salvation Army,* 46–47.

8. NYT, July 18, 1950, 29. On the relationship with McKie see in Troutt, *General Was a Lady;* Garry Allighan, *Four Bonnets to Golgotha* (London: MacDonald, 1961).

9. Troutt, *General Was a Lady,* 136-137. Dorothy Walworth, "General of an Army," *Reader's Digest,* Aug. 1947, 37.

10. The movie *Klondike Annie* (1936), starring Mae West, borrows this plot line.

11. The Evangeline Booth file at the SAA contains an unmarked piece of paper that identifies the children as Pearl Hamilton, Willie McPhail, Dorothy Jones Graham Lang, and Jai. Pearl Hamilton stayed with Evangeline the longest; she joined the Army and married a Salvationist.

12. Troutt interview with Mrs. Col. Richard Shelton, SAA.

13. Letter from Evangeline Booth to Susie Terrell Forrest Swift, Nov. 22, 1912, Susie Terrell Forrest Swift file, SAA.

14. Troutt interview with Commissioner William Parkins, SAA.

15. Booth, *The Salvation Army Appraises Prohibition,* 5, 10.

16. Evangeline Booth, *Woman* (New York: Fleming H. Revell, 1930), 16.

17. Ibid., 33.

18. Kathy Peiss, *Cheap Amusements: Working Women and Leisure in Turn-of-the-Century New York* (Philadelphia: Temple University Press, 1986), 6.

19. AWC, Oct. 6. 1906, 13. Peiss, *Cheap Amusements,* 34.

20. E.g., *The Salvation Army Lass* (1908), *Salvation Nell* (1915), *The Power of Evil* (1916), *The Whirlpool of Destiny* (1916), *The Terror* (1917).

21. AWC, June 2, 1906, 11. *Secrets of Success in Slumland,* undated pamphlet, SAA; AWC, May 5, 1906, 11; June 2, 1906, 11; Dec. 23, 1911, 6; Dec. 27, 1913, 14, 21; Dec. 20, 1913, 13; *Social News,* Aug. 1912, 6-7. AWC, Dec. 23, 1911, 6; Dec. 27, 1913, 14.

22. AWC, Dec. 23, 1911, 6.

23. AWC, Oct. 2, 1886, 6; Oct. 9, 1886, 1; Oct. 16, 1886, 1; Feb. 5, 1887, 8; Major Fleur Booth, "The Early Years of The Salvation Army Rescue Work in the United States of America," nd, manuscript, SAA. AWC, July 2, 1887, 8; July 30, 1887, 9.

24. E.g., Booth, *Beneath Two Flags,* 84-87; *Conqueror,* Mar. 1898, 82-83; Apr. 1898, 130-132; AWC, Oct. 31, 1896, 7; Oct. 1, 1898, 7; Aug. 8, 1903, 3; Aug. 15, 1903, 3.

25. AWC, Apr. 2, 1887, 8; June 25, 1892, 7.

26. Booth-Tucker, *Light in Darkness.* AWC, Jan. 5, 1901, 12. "Mended Links: The Annual Report of The Salvation Army's Rescue Work in the United States" (1903); Emma Booth-Tucker, *The League of Love of The Salvation Army* (New York: Salvation Army National Headquarters Publishing House, 1896); *Harbor Lights,* Jan. 1898, 7-10.

27. Timothy J. Gilfoyle, *City of Eros: New York City, Prostitution and the Commercialization of Sex, 1790–1920* (New York: Norton, 1992).

28. *Social News,* Mar. 1911, 5, 9; Feb. 1913, 6, 7; Feb. 1914, 13–16; AWC, June 25, 1910, 9; Nov. 22, 1913, 13. NYT, Oct. 8, 1911, V, 6.

29. Regina Kunzel, *Fallen Women, Problem Girls: Unmarried Mothers and the Professionalization of Social Work, 1890–1945* (New Haven: Yale University Press, 1993). As early as 1901 the Army assigned a probationary officer to Jefferson Market Court. The officer tried to convince defendants and judges that the Army's rescue home was a better alternative than jail for prostitutes. AWC, Oct. 28, 1905, 10.

30. AWC, June 11, 1910, 8.

31. AWC, Jan. 24, 1914, 7. There were some African-American residents and Army officers at the New York Rescue Home. The first rescue home for unwed African-American mothers, the Evangeline Home, opened in Cincinnati in Sept. 1917. It had five "colored" doctors on staff and 30 beds. AWC, Oct. 13, 1917, 4, 16; Nov. 17, 1971, 8, 13.

32. NYT, Mar. 12, 1912, 9; Mar. 24, 1912, III, 16; AWC, Nov. 22. 1913, 13; Mar. 21, 1914, 8; Jan. 10, 1914, 10; Jan. 17, 1914, 10.

33. AWC, June 18, 1910, 8, 12; Apr. 17, 1915, 10; Jan. 14, 1914, 10.

34. AWC, Mar. 21, 1913, 10.

35. AWC, July 27, 1907, 9.

36. Ben Primer, *Protestants and American Business Methods* (Ann Arbor: UMI Research Press, 1979).

37. Jackson Lears, *Fables of Abundance: A Cultural History of Advertising in America* (New York: Basic Books, 1994), 53.

38. AWC, Apr. 1, 1905, 15; June 10, 1905, 15.

39. AWC, May 15, 1897, 16; Jan. 8, 1916, 8.

40. Moore, *Selling God,* 42.

41. AWC, Apr. 25, 1908, 13.

42. Stanley Weintraub, "The Salvation Army's General Booth," in *Shaw: The Annual of Bernard Shaw Studies,* ed. Weintraub and Fred D. Crawford, vol. 10, *Bernard Shaw in Darkest England: GBS* (University Park: Pennsylvania State University Press, 1990), 50.

43. Arch R. Wiggins, *The History of The Salvation Army,* vol. V, 1904–1914 (London: Thomas Nelson and Sons, 1968), 251–252.

44. NYT, Dec. 10, 1915, 13; Dec. 19, 1915, IV, 8. *Brooklyn Eagle,* Apr. 30, 1893, 4.

45. Gerald Bordman, *The Oxford Companion to American Theatre* (New York: Oxford University Press, 1984), 69–70. The Broadway version of *Belle* ran 56 performances and starred the popular actress Edna May. NYT, Sept. 29, 1897, 7; Apr. 14, 1898, 9; Jan. 23, 1900, 7; Jan. 24, 1900, 11.

46. Bordman, 595; NYT, Nov. 15, 1908, VI, 1; Nov. 18, 1908, 5; Nov. 22, 1908, VI, 7.

47. *Salvation Nell* (1911), *A Gutter Magdalene* (1916), *The Power of Evil* (1916), *Salvation Joan* (1916), *The Whirlpool of Destiny* (1916), *The Terror* (1917), *America's Answer: Following the Fleet to France* (1918), *How Could You. Jean?* (1918), *Shifting Sands* (1918), *The Belle of New York* (1919), *The Blue Bonnet* (1919), *The Capitol* (1919), *Fires of Faith* (1919), *The Petal on the Current* (1919), *Hell's Oasis* (1920).

48. See Patricia King Hanson, ed., *The American Film Institute Catalog* (Berkeley: University of California Press, 1988).

49. Peiss, *Cheap Amusements*, 155.

50. David Glassberg, *American Historical Pageantry: The Uses of Tradition in the Early Twentieth Century* (Chapel Hill: University of North Carolina Press, 1990).

51. AWC, May 8, 1909, 12.

52. AWC, Nov. 4, 1911, 7; Dec. 2, 1911, 8-9, 12.

53. Glassberg, *American Historical Pageantry*, 285.

54. AWC, May 8, 1909, 8-9.

55. Parker, *My 58 Years*, 107-108.

56. W. T. Stead, "The Magic Lantern Mission," *Review of Reviews*, Dec. 1890, 562.

57. Ina Bertrand, ed., *Cinema in Australia: A Documentary History* (Kensington, N.S.W.: New South Wales University Press, 1989), 21-23; Graham Shirley and Brian Adams, *Australian Cinema: The First Eighty Years* (North Ride, N.S.W.: Angus Robertson, 1983), 10-14.

58. Parker, *My 58 Years*, 126.

59. The cinematograph was first used by British Salvationists in 1903. Wiggins, *History of The Salvation Army*, IV, 394. Parker, *My 58 Years*, 168-170; AWC, Apr. 23, 1910, 1, 6; Dec. 28, 1912, 25.

60. NYT, Mar. 22, 1914, 1.

61. NYT, Mar. 22, 1914, 1. McKinley, *Marching to Glory* (1995), 138-139.

62. AWC, Jan. 4, 1908, 9.

63. McKinley, *Somebody's Brother*, 69-71.

64. Solenberger, "Social Relief Work of the Salvation Army"; John Manson, *The Salvation Army and the Public* (London: Routledge, 1906). S. B. Williams, *The Salvation Army Today* (Lincoln, Neb.: Church Press, 1914); S. B. Williams, *The Salvation Army Today: An Exposure* (Lincoln, Neb.: Church Press, 1915). AWC, Mar. 25, 1911, 11.

65. Wilson, *General Evangeline Booth of The Salvation Army*, 149. AWC, Mar. 3, 1906, 9; Feb. 11, 1911, 9; Apr. 1, 1911, 9; Mar. 25, 1911, 8.

66. Begbie, *Life of General William Booth*, II, 263. NYT, Feb. 7, 1916, 11; Feb. 29, 1916, 12; Apr. 8, 1916; Apr. 9, 1916, I, 12; Apr. 14, 1916, 4.

67. AWC, Oct. 11, 1913, I, 12.

68. AWC, Dec. 27, 1913, 6.

69. AWC, Mar. 6, 1915, 9; Mar. 20, 1915, 11; Mar. 27, 1915, 9. NYT, Feb. 19, 1915, 15.

70. NYT, Feb. 7, 1915, III, 4; Feb. 18, 1915, 6.

71. NYT, Mar. 18, 1916, 6; Mar. 20, 1916, 10.

72. *New York Post,* June 3, 1913, 9.

73. C. C. Carstens, "Shall the Salvation Army Take the Public Into Its Confidence," *Charities and The Commons,* Apr. 27, 1907. Lamb, "Social Work of The Salvation Army." I. L. Nascher, *The Wretches of Povertyville: A Sociological Study of the Bowery* (Chicago: Joseph J. Lanzit, 1909), 252, 257.

74. Unidentified newspaper clipping dated May 11, 1906, SAA.

75. Chesham, *Born to Battle,* 161. Evangeline used the phrase in a *War Cry* advertisement.

76. AWC, Nov. 14, 1914, 8, 9, 12; Nov. 21, 1914, 1, 9; Nov. 28, 1914, 9; Dec. 5, 1914, 9; Dec. 26, 1914, 9; NYT, Nov. 10, 1914, 4; Dec. 16, 1914, IV, 3; Dec. 31, 1914, 3.

77. On World War I see "War Service Report of The Salvation Army, 1917–1919," World War I file, SAA; Evangeline Booth and Grace Livingston Hill, *The War Romance of The Salvation Army* (Philadelphia: Lippincott, 1919); "The Motherly Salvationist," *Literary Digest,* May 11, 1918; "The Salvation Army Pie and Prayers at the Front," *Literary Digest,* Oct. 19, 1918; "Pies and Doughnuts in the Trenches," *Ladies' Home Journal,* Sept. 1918; Evangeline Booth, "Mothering the Boys at the Front," *Forum,* Sept. 1918; Raymond C. Starbard, "Pies and Doughnuts: A New Kind of War Munitions Furnished by The Salvation Army," *Outlook,* June 5, 1918; also most 1917–1918 editions of the *War Cry.*

78. AWC, June 15, 1918, 4.

79. Booth, *War Romance of The Salvation Army,* 79.

80. Margaret Sheldon diary, np, SAA.

81. Ibid.

82. Diaries of Margaret Sheldon, Mary Robinson Young, Ethel Renton, Florence Turkington; Mary Bishop memoirs (1974); Helga Ramsay memoirs, nd; Helen Purviance, oral history, 1980; Myrtle Turkington, oral history, 1978; all in SAA.

83. AWC, May 25, 1918, 2.

84. AWC, Oct. 18, 1918, 12; June 15, 1918, 4, 5. NYT, July 21, 1918, 17; *Ladies' Home Journal,* Sept. 1918, 21; *Outlook,* June 5, 1918, 220–221.

85. Booth, "Mothering the Boys at the Front"; *New York Post,* May 14, 1918, 9; June 29, 1918, 2. Lester S. Levy, *Give Me Yesterday: American History in Song, 1890–1920* (Norman: University of Oklahoma, 1975), 155–156.

86. AWC, July 27, 1907, 9.

87. AWC, Oct. 18, 1918, 12.

88. Hugh McLeod, *Piety and Poverty: Working-Class Religion in Berlin, London and New York, 1870–1914* (New York: Holmes and Meier, 1996).

89. Margaret Sheldon diary, SAA. AWC, July 31, 1907, 2.

5. Fires of Faith

1. *Fires of Faith* press packet, 19, University of Southern California Cinema-Television Library, Doheny Library.

2. Lincoln Center Library for the Performing Arts, microfilm Zan T213, reel 37, unidentified scrapbook.

3. In scrapbooks on *Fires of Faith,* several references say Jesse Lasky went to Evangeline Booth with the idea for a film and "she was quick to grasp the idea." One newspaper clip says the Army went to Lasky. New York Library for the Performing Arts, Zan T213 reel 37, clips undated.

4. Other movies with Salvation Army characters between 1920 and 1929 include: *The Big Punch* (1921), *Salvation Nell* (1921), *Human Wreckage* (1923), *The Spirit of the USA* (1924), *Satan Town* (1926), *For Heaven's Sake* (1926), *Salvation Jane* (1927), *The Angel of Broadway* (1927), *His Last Haul* (1928), *The Good-bye Kiss* (1928), and *The Street of Sin* (1928).

5. New York Library for the Performing Arts, Zan T213 reel 37, "Fires of Faith Worth Seeing," by Louella Parsons (clip without name of paper or date).

6. *Fires of Faith* press packet, 7.

7. Ibid., 18–19.

8. Ibid., 9–10.

9. Ibid., 16.

10. *Literary Digest,* July 19, 1919, 34.

11. AWC, Aug. 8, 1908, 3.

12. McKinley, *Marching to Glory* (1995), 174.

13. *Baltimore Sun,* Oct. 25, 1922; Rheba Crawford file, SAA.

14. Rheba Crawford file, SAA.

15. Crawford's story is based on the following sources: NYT, Oct. 16, 1922, 1; Oct. 17, 1922, 13; Oct. 18, 1922, 18; Oct. 21, 1922, 16; Oct. 23, 1922, 15; Oct. 30, 1922, 4; Oct. 31, 1922, 14; Nov. 4, 1922, 2; Feb. 26, 1923, 13; Jan. 8, 1966, np; *Baltimore Sun,* Oct. 25, 1922, np; *New York Journal,* Feb. 24, 1923, np; *San Francisco Chronicle,* May 18, 1924, 22; Edith L. Blumhofer, *Aimee Semple McPherson: Everybody's Sister* (Grand Rapids, Mich.: William B. Eerdman, 1993) ; and, from the Rheba Crawford file, SAA: "Former Salvationist Lass Intends to Follow in the Footsteps of 'Billy' Sunday"; Rheba Crawford, "My Fight to Save the Soul of Broadway"; "Hitting the Trail with the Prettiest Girl on Broadway"; ; letter from W. M. Himes Sr. to Commander Holland French, Sept. 15, 1963.

16. *Baltimore Sun,* Oct. 25, 1922.

17. *New York Journal,* Feb. 24, 1923.

18. NYT, Feb. 26, 1923, 13.

19. After Crawford left the Army she married three times, served as associate pastor of Aimee Semple McPherson's Angelus Temple, was ordained as a Congregationalist minister in San Francisco, was appointed director of the California State Department of Social Welfare, and in her later years became a coordinator for the Los Angeles County Department of Senior Citizens Affairs. She died in 1966 at age 67.

20. NYT, May 23, 1920, II, 14.

21. AWC, Nov. 5, 1921, 10; Nov. 19, 1921, 10; Jan. 13, 1923, 10; NYT, Sept. 23, 1924, 25.

22. AWC, Jan. 18, 1930, 1; June 18, 1932, 1; Oct. 15, 1932, 1; Oct. 22, 1932, 1; Aug. 5, 1933, 1; Nov. 18, 1933, 1; Oct. 5, 1935, 3; Oct. 24, 1931, 1.

23. *Laughing Sinners* (1931), *Law of the Tong* (1931), *Salvation Nell* (1931), *The Good Woman* (1931), *The Miracle Woman* (1931), *Behind the Tambourine* (1931), *The Birth of a New America* (1931), *She Done Him Wrong* (1933), *Limehouse Blues* (1934).

24. *Harrison's Reports,* July 11, 1931, 110; *New York American,* July 4, 1931; *Variety,* Mar. 25, 1931; and July 7, 1931; *Filmograph,* Mar. 28, 1931, in *Laughing Sinners* clipping file and *Laughing Sinners* pressbook, Lincoln Center Library for the Performing Arts.

25. NYT, Oct. 20, 1919, 26; AWC, July 9, 1921, 9; July 12, 1924, 5; June 7, 1941, 11; Apr. 6, 1929, 36–38.

26. NYT, Sept. 15, 1922, 1, 6; Oct. 5, 1922, 14; Oct. 31, 1922; *Outlook,* Nov. 24, 1926, 392–393.

27. NYT, Mar. 20, 1930, 1, 2; Apr. 27, 1930, 3; June 27, 1932, 13; May 25, 1933, 2; AWC, July 23, 1932, 8, 9. NYT, June 28, 1932, 13, 16; AWC, July 30, 1932, 4.

28. NYT, Sept. 4, 1934, 1, 17; Sept. 5, 1934, 20; Sept. 14, 1934, 4; Sept. 23, 1934, 6, 16; Nov. 2, 1934, 25; *Newsweek,* Nov. 10, 1934, 18; AWC, Sept. 22, 1934, 1, 8,9, 12; Sept. 29, 1934, 9,12; Oct. 6, 1934, 9,12; Oct. 13, 1934, 13; Oct. 20, 1934, 8,15; Nov. 17, 1934, 5–9, 14–15; Nov. 24, 1934, 8,9.

29. New York Library for the Performing Arts, Zan T213 reel 37, unidentified clip.

30. Sally Levitt Steinberg, *The Donut Book* (New York: Knopf, 1987); Molly McGaughey, "Doughnuts: An Informal Summary History," manuscript (Manhattan, Kan: American Institute of Baking, nd).

31. AWC, Aug. 17, 1918, 2.

32. Roland Barthes, "Toward a Psychosociology of Contemporary Food Consumption," in *Food and Drink in History,* ed. Robert Forster and Orest Ranum (Baltimore: Johns Hopkins University Press, 1979).

33. Mrs. Major Arnold, "The Salvation Army Doughnut," AWC, July 13, 1918, 2.

34. AWC, Mar. 8, 1919; NYT, May 18, 1919, IV, 13; Mar. 9, 1930, V, 3, 19.

35. NYT, May 12, 1919, 11.

36. NYT, May 19, 1919, 20.

37. For ads see NYT, May 16, 1919, III, 8; May 19, 1919, 11. AWC, July 5, 1919, 10.

38. NYT, May 18, 1919, II, 2.

39. NYT, May 21, 1919, 10; May 22, 1919, 15; AWC, June 7, 1919, 12–13.

40. Flyer, Salvation Army file, Lincoln Center Library for the Performing Arts.

41. NYT, May 23, 1919, 13; May 25, 1919, 14; May 26, 1919, 8; May 27, 1919, 32; May 28, 1919, 15; May 29, 1919, 9. McKinley, *Marching to Glory* (1995), 173; Chesham, *Born to Battle,* 175.

42. AWC, June 26, 1920, 4.

43. Leo P. Ribuffo, "Jesus Christ as a Business Statesman: Bruce Barton and the Selling of Corporate Capitalism," *American Quarterly,* Summer 1981, 106–232; NYT, Apr. 9, 1922, IX, 4.

44. NYT, Dec. 24, 1922, 3; Dec. 26, 1924, 9; Nov. 21, 1920, II, 13; AWC, Jan. 13, 1923, 9; May 3, 1924, 5.

45. NYT, Aug. 7, 1927, II, 23; AWC, Aug. 1, 1931, 10; Nov. 1, 1936, 1.

46. NYT, Jan. 28, 1923, II, 15.

47. Glassberg, *American Historical Pageantry,* 67.

48. Program of "Historical and Industrial Presentation of Progress," The Salvation Army Eastern Territorial Congress, Nov. 21, 1924, SAA.

49. NYT, Oct. 11, 1924, 14; Wilson, *General Evangeline Booth of The Salvation Army,* 150. NYT, Nov. 8, 1930, 5; Dec. 3, 1930, 52; Dec. 14, 1930, 1; Dec. 24, 1930, 1.

50. NYT, Dec. 19, 1930, 19; Dec. 28, 1930, 24; AWC, Jan. 3, 1931, 2, 9; Jan. 10, 31, 2; Jan. 17, 1931, 4. NYT, May 22, 1931, 26; May 26, 1931, 21; May 27, 1931, 29.

51. NYT, May 8, 1932, II, 3; June 14, 1932, 23.

52. NYT, Mar. 26, 1933, 31; AWC, Apr. 27, 1935, 3.

53. McKinley, *Marching to Glory* (1995), 186–187.

54. NYT, June 24, 1923, VIII, 7; AWC, June 8, 1929, 3. Ann Douglas, *Terrible Honesty: Mongrel Manhattan in the 1920s* (New York: Farrar, Straus and Giroux, 1995).

55. NYT, Jan. 2, 1928, 1; Jan. 9, 1928, 25; AWC, Jan. 28, 1928, 7.

56. NYT, Jan. 16, 1928, 8; Feb. 12, 1928, IX, 2; AWC, Feb. 11, 1928, 2.

57. NYT, Aug. 25, 1933, 6; Apr. 9, 1936, 17; May 15, 1937, 3; June 12, 1937, 4; Dec. 10, 1938, 6; Nov. 3, 1934, 14; Nov. 7, 1937, IV, 8.

58. AWC, Aug. 12, 1933.

59. NYT, Oct. 23, 1932, 31; AWC, Oct. 8, 1932, 2; Oct. 15, 1932, 1; Oct. 22, 1932, 1, 4; Oct. 29, 1932, 2. NYT, June 29, 1935; AWC, July 13, 1935, 12; June 26, 1937, 3; Sept. 23, 1933, 3.

60. AWC, Jan. 19, 1929, 3; Jan. 26, 1929, 8, 9; Feb. 2, 1929, 8; Feb. 9, 1929, 8, 9; Feb. 23, 1929, 1, 9; Mar. 9, 1929, 9; NYT, Dec. 22, 1928, 1, 14; Dec. 23, 1928, 1, 7; Jan. 3, 1929, 3; Jan. 4, 1929, 6; Jan. 7, 1929, 3; Jan. 11, 1929, 1, 3; Jan. 12, 1929, 1, 3; Jan. 17, 1929, 1, 2; Jan. 18, 1929, 2; Jan. 19, 1929, 1; Jan. 28, 1929, 22; Feb. 14, 1929, 1, 9; Feb. 16, 1929, 3; Mar. 7, 1929, 27.

61. AWC, Mar. 29, 1929, 8, 9. *Literary Digest,* Feb. 9, 1929, 24–25; Mar. 9, 1929, 24–25; *Outlook,* Jan. 9, 1929, 60; Mar. 23, 1929, 421.

62. AWC, Apr. 19, 1930, 12; Apr. 26, 1930, 16; June 7, 1930, 8–9; May 31, 1930, 9; NYT, Jan. 14, 1930, 22; Mar. 10, 1930, 20, 27; Mar. 11, 1930, 21; May 19, 1930, 22; *Literary Digest,* Apr. 12, 1930, 24.

63. "The Rise and Progress of The Salvation Army in the United States," program, SAA; NYT, May 11, 1930, II, 2; May 17, 1930, 18; AWC, Apr. 19, 1930; May 31, 1930, 4. AWC, May 17, 1930, 9; May 31, 1930, 4–5, 11–12; NYT, May 21, 1930, 18.

64. AWC, Aug. 4, 1923, 5; Jan. 12. 1924, 2; July 12, 1924, 5; Sept. 22, 1928, 2. NYT, Oct. 18, 1928, 1; Wisbey, *Soldiers without Swords,* 174–175.

65. AWC, Apr. 12, 1930, 2, 11; May 17, 1930, 2; June 28, 1930, 2.

66. AWC, Sept. 13, 1930, 8; Sept. 20, 1930, 4; Oct. 18, 1930, 1; Nov. 8, 1930, 8; Nov. 22, 1930, 9; Nov. 29, 1930, 8, 11; Dec. 6, 1930, 9; Dec. 13, 1930, 9; Dec. 27, 1930, 2; NYT Oct. 24, 1930, 3; Nov. 9, 1930, 2; Nov. 10, 1930, 13. NYT, Dec. 3, 1930; Dec. 24, 1930, 1.

67. NYT, Jan. 11, 1931, 32; Nov. 29, 1930, 16. NYT, Dec. 19, 1930, 19; Dec. 28, 1930, 24; AWC, Jan. 3, 1931, 2, 9; Jan. 10, 1931, 2; Jan. 17, 1931, 4.

68. NYT, Dec. 12, 1931, 15; AWC, June 22, 1935, 8; NYT, May 8, 1932, II, 3; Feb. 28, 1933, 18.

69. AWC, July 15, 1933, 8; NYT, July 27, 1932, 22.

70. NYT, Feb. 20, 1933, 16; Nov. 20, 1931, 21; AWC, Dec. 5, 1931, 8.

71. AWC, Apr. 11, 1931, 8; Oct. 24, 1931, 6–7; Nov. 14, 1931, 8. NYT, Nov. 20, 1931, 43; Mar. 26, 1935, 17; AWC, Dec. 26, 1931, 3; Jan. 23, 1932, 3.

72. AWC, Mar. 11, 1933, 3.

73. NYT, Jan. 18, 1932, 3; June 11, 1932, 11; June 14, 1932, 23; AWC, May 7, 1932, 8, 9, 12; May 28, 1932, 9, 12; June 4, 1932, 4.

74. John Steinbeck, *The Grapes of Wrath* (New York: Viking Penguin, 1986), 406. AWC, Jan. 23, 1932, 6; NYT, Dec. 16, 1935, 2. AWC, Apr. 27, 1935, 3; NYT, Apr. 13, 1934, 22; Feb. 18, 1934, 34; Jan. 5, 1935, 19; Aug. 30, 1935, 10.

75. NYT, Sept. 28, 1940, 3; Apr. 10, 1941, 9; Sept. 12, 1941, 9. AWC, June 22, 1940, 9–10; June 29, 1940, 9; Aug. 17, 1949, 9; Oct. 19, 1940, 1; Jan. 18, 1941, 10; June 7, 1941, 9; Mar. 8, 1941, 11; Mar. 29, 1941, 3; May 3, 1941, 10.

76. AWC, May 10, 1941, 7: May 31, 1941, 1, 3, 5, 7, 9, 11; Nov. 6, 1943, 5.

77. AWC, May 8, 1943, 2; Mar. 24, 1945, 5.

78. NYT, Jan. 25, 1945, 18; Feb. 16, 1945, 26.

79. Lieutenant Commissioner Llewellyn Cowan, interview by Nicki Tanner, Aug. 19, 1986, Salvation Army Oral History Project, 54–57; NYT, Jan. 27, 1947, 22; Apr. 24, 1947, 22; Jan. 9, 1949, 55; Jan. 7, 1948, 4; Jan. 2, 1948, 25; Feb. 2, 1949, 34.

80. AWC, Feb. 15, 1949, 8; Nov. 11, 1949, 9; NYT, Jan. 26, 1949, 27; *Newsweek*, Feb. 7, 1949, 22–23; *Time*, Feb. 7, 1949, 16.

81. *New Yorker*, Apr. 13, 1940, 40–53.

82. *New Yorker*, Sept. 21, 1946, 34–49.

83. *Time*, Jan. 26, 1948, 70, 72; *NYT Magazine*, Feb. 15, 1948, 22–23, 28.

84. *Newsweek*, Dec. 15, 1941, 69–70; *NYT Magazine*, Apr. 29, 1945, 22–23, 27; *Etude*, Jan. 1949; Feb. 1949; *New Yorker*, Apr. 23, 1949, 19–20; *Conqueror*, Jan. 1895, 33–34.

85. *New Yorker*, Apr. 23, 1949, 20.

86. Colonel Anita Robb, interview with Nikki Tanner, Sept. 17, 1986, 11, SAA.

87. NYT, Dec. 21, 1946, 16; Feb. 11, 1945, 34; July 12, 1948, 12; Robb interview.

88. *Ladies' Home Journal*, June 1949, 23, 164–166; NYT, Jan. 24, 1947, 15.

89. AWC, Jan. 28, 1950, 8; NYT, Nov. 7, 1949, 30; Mar. 6, 1950, 23; Mar. 10, 1950, 32.

90. *Time*, July 24, 1950, 76; NYT, July 18, 1950, 29; July 19, 1950, 31; July 21, 1950, 19; July 19, 1950, 30.

91. AWC, Aug. 12, 1950, 3, 7, 9–11.

92. *Time*, Dec. 26, 1949, 41.

Epilogue

1. Leigh Eric Schmidt, *Consumer Rites: The Buying and Selling of American Holidays* (Princeton: Princeton University Press, 1995), 297.

ACKNOWLEDGMENTS

WHEN I LEFT the newsroom to pursue a doctoral degree, I yearned to spend more than two days and 2,000 words on a story. Seven years later I consider myself fortunate to have had the opportunity to do just that. Even more fortunately, I began this new venture without understanding how difficult it would be. Despite one professor's reassurance that my new profession wasn't so different from the old one—except that now all my sources were dead—I discovered that being an historian requires a different kind of engagement with one's subject than does reporting. Learning how to read artifacts and to interpret the world they create has been an exhilarating challenge.

I could not have tackled this project without the grounding in reporting and writing that I received from colleagues at the *Raleigh News and Observer,* the *Dallas Times Herald,* and the *Baltimore Sun.* My editors— as well as my fellow reporters—taught me to get the story and to tell it with style. Their lessons on organization and clarity have served me well. So has their demand to meet deadlines.

I am equally grateful to my teachers at Princeton University. Albert Raboteau, John Wilson, and Robert Wuthnow consistently challenged and encouraged me to do my best work. Jenna Weissman Joselit, Martin Marty, Christine Stansell, James Moorhead, David Carrasco, Christine Leigh Heyrman, Timothy Gilfoyle, Claudia Kidwell, Betty DeBerg, Jane

Shaw, Leora Batnitzky, John Giggie, Bruce Buursma, Sally Jacobs, and Brad Verter all read and offered helpful comments on parts of this book. Edward H. McKinley, Norman Murdoch, and Pamela Walker, historians of The Salvation Army, have been generous with their expertise. Thanks, too, to Peg Fulton and Camille Smith at Harvard University Press for their guidance.

The assistance of archivists and librarians has also been indispensable. Mary George and Mary Ann Jensen at the Princeton University Library patiently answered questions and directed me to excellent sources. Susan Mitchem, Director of the Salvation Army National Archives, and her staff, archivist Connie Hagood and assistant archivist Scott Badio, provided unstinting assistance. Ned Comstock of the USC Cinema-Television Library, Mary Corliss and Terry Geeskin of the Museum of Modern Art, and Madeline F. Matz of the Library of Congress directed me to film collections and resources. Last but hardly least, my thanks to research assistants Brendan Wood and Jim Ford, who provided much-needed respite from the microfilm room.

Research and editorial help notwithstanding, I could not have written this book without financial support. For that support I am grateful to Princeton University, the Center for the Study of American Religion at Princeton University, the Pew Program for Religion and American History at Yale University, and the Material History of American Religion Project funded by the Lilly Endowment. Thanks also to my "material culture" colleagues, Marie Griffith, James Hudnut-Beumler, Colleen McDannell, Robert Orsi, Dan Sack, Leigh Schmidt, David Watt, and Judith Weisenfeld, whose savvy critiques were always delivered graciously. Likewise, sessions at Yale for the Pew program and workshops at the Center for the Study of American Religion introduced me to graduate students, researchers, and professors who prodded my thinking and stretched my work. Special thanks to Anita Kline, the Center's administrator, for her kindness and unfailing good humor.

Faye Ginsburg first visited The Salvation Army with me many years ago when we decided to investigate an odd-looking building on 14th Street. When I returned to scholarly pursuits she cheered me on, and when I cast about for a dissertation topic she lobbied hard for the Army. Faye's fingerprints run through this work, and her own scholarship has been an inspiration.

Throughout this project I have been fortunate to have the love and support of family and friends. Special thanks to Barbara Abrash for early inspiration and to the Monthly Women's Dinner Group for their enthusiasm. Bill and Darlene Winston, Robin and Ernestine Bugbee, and Erin and Sara Walters-Bugbee have cheered me on each step of the way. My parents, Dan and Suzanne Winston, have—as always—demonstrated an unflagging interest in my work and an empathetic sharing of the journey that has been part of it.

Christopher Bugbee has shared this entire intellectual and emotional trek with me, reading every word I've written and editing many of them. He has saved me from computer crises, sharpened my arguments, and sweetened my prose. He is among the best editors I have had and one of the smartest, too.

While doing research on The Salvation Army, I had occasion to meet many soldiers and officers. They displayed the dedication and humanitarianism that distinguishes a calling for love and faithful service. The commitment of today's Salvationists gave me insight into their nineteenth-century comrades, reminding me that institutions are, at bottom, a reflection of their members' passions.

INDEX